Rapture and Resurrection

The Blessed Hope of All Believers

The Glorious Appearing of our Lord and Savior Jesus Christ;

Don T. Phillips

"Rapture and Resurrection, the Blessed Hope of All Believers," by Don T. Phillips. ISBN 978-1-63868-051-2.

Published 2022 by Virtualbookworm.com Publishing Inc., P.O. Box 9949, College Station, TX 77845, US. Copyright ©2022 Don T. Phillips.

PREFACE

When Jesus Christ was about to end His 3.5-year Ministry of Reconciliation through His sacrificial death, He met with His disciples on the Mt. of Olives and announced that He must die on the Cross of Calvary to redeem all mankind to God…living and dead.

As Jesus Christ ascended into heaven at the completion of His mortal ministry, two angels declared to His Apostles: *This same Jesus, which is taken up from you into heaven, shall so come in like manner as ye have seen him go into heaven*" (Acts 1:11). Since that time, believers have looked forward to the Second Coming of Jesus Christ.

It is known from the Holy Scriptures that Jesus Christ would return again to end the Church Age and initiate the 1000 Year Millennial Kingdom. This will be *preceded* by an event which we call the *Rapture*, at which the ecclesia or the saints would be gathered to Jesus Christ to be with Him forever.

For many who study prophecy and expectantly await the return of Jesus Christ there is some confusion regarding His 2nd advent. The end of this current Age of Grace or what we call the Church Age will actually involve two distinct and separate events: (1) The Resurrection and Rapture of the saints (2) The 2nd coming or 2nd advent of Christ.

What we call the Rapture often includes the resurrection of the righteous dead but this is not correct. In order to be *raptured*, one must be alive. In order to be *resurrected* one must be dead. The apostle Paul wrote:

[15] *For this we say unto you by the word of the Lord, that we which are alive and remain unto the coming of the Lord shall not prevent them which are asleep.*
[16] *For the Lord himself shall descend from heaven with a shout, with the voice of the archangel, and with the trump of God: and the dead in Christ shall rise first:*
[17] *Then we which are alive and remain shall be caught up together with them in the clouds, to meet the Lord in the air: and so shall we ever be with the Lord.*
[18] *Wherefore comfort one another with these words*   I Thessalonians 4: 15-18

The Lord will descend from heaven with a shout and with the audible voice of an archangel and with the sound of a trumpet. The dead in Christ shall rise 1st, followed by those who are alive and remain. They will both meet Christ in the air. When this happens, Christ will not physically return to earth.

The Apostle John wrote:

[11] *And I saw heaven opened, and behold a white horse; and he that sat upon him was called Faithful and True, and in righteousness he doth judge and make war.*
[12] *His eyes were as a flame of fire, and on his head were many crowns; and he had a name written, that no man knew, but he himself.*

i

[13] And he was clothed with a vesture dipped in blood: and his name is called The Word of God.

[14] And the armies which were in heaven followed him upon white horses, clothed in fine linen, white and clean.

[15] And out of his mouth goeth a sharp sword, that with it he should smite the nations: and he shall rule them with a rod of iron: and he treads the winepress of the fierceness and wrath of Almighty God   Revelation 19: 11-15

For almost 2000 years biblical scholars and ordinary Christians have investigated, studied and probed the scriptures to characterize and explain this great event. It is recognized and acknowledged that the Rapture of all living saints and resurrection of the righteous dead is closely associated with a period of time called the *Great Tribulation*. The controversy and mystery of the Rapture is not *if* it will take place but **when**. There are four logical positions that are taught today: (1) A Pre-Tribulation Rapture (2) A Post-Tribulation Rapture (3) A Mid-Tribulation Rapture and (4) A Pre-Wrath Rapture. These will be discussed later in some detail in Chapters 2 and 7. A second and related issue is the *duration* of the Great Tribulation: Either 7 years or 3.5 years. It will be seen in Chapters 2 and 3 that the duration of the Great Tribulation will depend upon an Old Testament prophecy given to Daniel, when the prophecy began and how prophetic years are measured.

This book will investigate, biblically support and logically argue a new *Pre-Wrath Rapture* Theory that will meet all scriptural requirements and eliminate doctrinal conflicts. There are five key issues which must be carefully studied and harmonized. The *1st* is the interpretation and meaning of the 70-Week Daniel prophecy (Chapter 3). The *2nd* is to harmonize and analyze what Jesus Christ said to His disciples (and us) in the Olivet Discourse (Matthew 24-25). The *3rd* is how the 7 seals in the Book of Revelation fit into the Chronological structure of the Great Tribulation (Chapters 4 and 5) The *4th* is the prophetic meaning of the 7 Feasts of Israel, and how they teach of the first and second advent of Jesus Christ. The *5th* is to show that based upon both Christian and Jewish beliefs, there is strong evidence that the Rapture will take place as the 7th Trumpet sounds (Chapter 7). The *6th* is an examination of the times that are mentioned in the Book of Daniel (Old Testament) and the Book of Revelation (New Testament). This investigation will show that the duration of the Great Tribulation is 1267 days and not 1260 days as is commonly taught.

The Rapture will take place between the *Wrath of Satan* and the *Wrath of God*. This is by definition a Pre-Wrath Rapture which will follow the Wrath of Satan (the 7 Trumpet Judgments) and precede the Wrath of God (the 7 Bowl Judgments). Not one Christian is destined to go through the Wrath of God (Revelation 15:1, Revelation 16:1, Romans 5:9, Ephesians 5:6, I Thessalonians 1:10, I Thessalonians 5:9).

This book is devoted to a deeper understanding of the end-times period of Tribulation based upon scriptural verification, and not wild, unsustainable theories. Does this book propose to be 100% correct or infallible in interpreting the Book of Revelation?......Absolutely not. However, it does promise to offer clear and simple explanations of difficult passages. Each conclusion and explanation are supported by scripture from both the Old and New Testaments. I am confident that the reader with an open mind will find concepts and explanations both convincing and logical. Unfortunately, this does not guarantee inerrancy. Hopefully, this book will present concepts and conclusions that will be challenged by other others and in doing so, eventually: *Ye shall know the truth, and the truth shall make you free* (John 8:32).

Why would this author be confident that this book is correct while so many fine books written by other scholars of prophecy have preceded it...each claiming scriptural truth? In the Book of Daniel, the prophet was told by a mighty angel: *But thou, O Daniel, shut up the words, and seal the book, even to the time of the end: many shall run to and fro, and knowledge shall be increased* (Daniel 12:4). We are now living in an unprecedented time during which information is increasing at an incredible rate. According to recent studies (2020):

Over 2.5 quintillion bytes of data are created every single day, and it's only going to grow from there. By 2020, it's estimated that 1.7MB of data will be created every second for every person on earth. Social mediatoday.com

Over the last two years alone 90 percent of the data in the world was generated
Forbes\com, 2020

The evolution and power of the digital computer has enabled and sustained this growth in knowledge, and powerful search engines (Google, Microsoft) have allowed each person to access volumes of papers, books, articles and websites devoted to biblical topics; some are very good, some are not scriptural, and some are simply fantasy and conjecture. All contain useful information, and the inquiring and discerning mind must be able to distinguish truth and *rightly divide the word of God* (II Timothy 2:15). In addition to extensive access to biblical research and opinions, the digital computer and powerful computer programming languages have been used to construct algorithms to accurately predict days, months and years and historical dates in Jewish cultural evolution thousands of years into the past. These things have all been done in the past 50 years...a mere spec in the timeline of creation and eternity.

But: *Who am I to challenge biblical beliefs, some of which have persisted for over 1500 years?* I am nothing but a student of prophecy who is dependent upon the Holy Scriptures and the Holy Spirit for wisdom and understanding. It is amazing, that over the last 40 years I have read the Book of Revelation probably over 500 times and taught the entire Book of Revelation over 20 times; and every time I read it, I learn new and amazing things. Again, I do not claim to have all of the truth, but only portions of foundational truth. I have learned many things in just writing this book. I am asking all students and teachers of the Book of Revelation to carefully study and analyze the conclusions which have been presented.

This book will use the Authorized King James Bible. In studying both the Daniel 70-Week prophecy and the Book of Revelation, it will be necessary to determine There are several places where it will be required to determine the month and day when events took place. There are three calendars which have been commonly used to reference ancient events: The Hebrew Calendar... The Julian Calendar which was in use in the 1st Century AD, and the modern Gregorian calendar which is predominately in use today. These calendars are all different and have frequently been used by modern biblical scholars to date 1st century AD dates; particularly the Death of Jesus Christ. We will propose that Jesus Christ was crucified on the Feast of Passover Nisan 14, in 30 AD. We will show that this was on a Wednesday. This has been validated by many students of prophecy.

Except for when Christ was crucified, it is not necessary in this study to determine the day of the week when any event (past or future) will occur. We will present evidence that the current Hebrew Calendar in use today by the Jews is the same calendar that was in use when Jesus Christ was crucified. Strong arguments will be made that the Hebrew Calendar in use today was given to Moses after the Exodus... continued to be used during the 70-year Babylonian exile... and is still in use today.

Since the ancient Hebrew Calendar was being used by both Israel and the Babylonian Empire when the Daniel Prophecy went forth... and it has been in use since at least from the 5th century BC, why would one want to use any other calendar to determine ancient dates? The Hebrew Calendar is very accurate over thousands of years, but that is of little interest. It makes no difference what any other calendar day and date might be...only the Hebrew calendar day. There are many accurate software programs which have been constructed by NASA and brilliant computer programs which will produce Hebrew dates thousands of days in the past. Chapters 3 and 6 will explain Calendar assumptions and calendar dates.

A New Pre-Wrath Rapture Theory

Chapter 2 and Chapter 3 will use biblical facts, archeological evidence and other scholarly investigations to show that the 70-Week prophecy of Daniel was initiated by Nebuchadnezzar in 458 BC-457 BC in the 70th year of his reign. It will also be shown that after 486.5 years the Daniel 490-year prophecy was interrupted by the Church Age. After some unknown period of time, the last 3.5 years of the Daniel Prophecy

Chapter 4 and Chapter 5 will show that the 7 Seals in the Book of Revelation are not time-delay events which must precede the 7 trumpet Judgments (Wrath of Satan) and the 7 Bowl Judgments (Wrath of God), but only predict conditions and events which will take place over the 3.5-year *Great Tribulation*.

Chapter 6 will address the different periods of time which are used in the Book of Revelation (1260 days, 42 months and Times, Time and Half-a-time) and will show beyond reasonable doubt that thewy are not all equal to 1260 days.

Chapter 7 will present and justify a new Rapture theory which is a *Pre-Wrath Rapture*. We will show that the rapture and resurrection of the saints will take place as the 7th Trumpet sounds. This conclusion is based upon scriptural clues, previous results and Jewish Messianic Expectations and beliefs.

This book is not a "casual read" but will require slow and dedicated time. May the Holy Sprit lead you as you study.

All scripture is given by inspiration of God, and is profitable for doctrine, for reproof, for correction, for instruction in righteousness   II Timothy 3:16

Don T. Phillips

February, 2022

Table of Contents

Chapter 1

Prophets and Prophecy

The Holy Bible is a book which was written by prophets of God who were chosen to reveal the history of mankind as it evolves from the creation record in Genesis to the end of this world as we know it as described in the Book of Revelation.

The first complete English translation of the Bible was that of John Wycliffe in 1382, but the Authorized King James Version of 1611 is often considered to be the best English translation from the original Greek and Hebrew manuscripts. William Tyndale was martyred in 1536 for his early Protestant translation, but his work and that of Tyndale became a major source of information for the King James Version which was published in 1611 AD. The Authorized King James Bible (AKJ) was produced by a committee of fifty scholars working in six teams between 1604 and 1611. The AKJV contains 39 books in the Old Testament and 27 books in the New Testament.

OLD TESTAMENT		
Genesis	Ezra	Joel
Exodus	Nehemiah	Amos
Leviticus	Esther	Obadiah
Numbers	Job	Jonah
Deuteronomy	Psalms	Micah
Joshua	Proverbs	Nahum
Judges	Ecclesiastes	Habakkuk
Ruth	Song of Solomon	Zephaniah
1 Samuel	Isaiah	Haggai
2 Samuel	Jeremiah	Zechariah
1 Kings	Lamentations	Malachi
2 Kings	Ezekiel	
1 Chronicles	Daniel	
2 Chronicles	Hosea	

NEW TESTAMENT		
Matthew	Philippians	1 Peter
Mark	Colossians	2 Peter
Luke	1 Thessalonians	1 John
John	2 Thessalonians	2 John
Acts	1 Timothy	3 John
Romans	2 Timothy	Jude
1 Corinthians	Titus	Revelation
2 Corinthians	Philemon	
Galatians	Hebrews	
Ephesians	James	

The *Catholic Church* produced their own version which contains 46 books in the Old Testament and 27 books in the New Testament for a total of 73 books. An early version called the *Clementine Vulgate* was issued by Pope Clement VIII in 1592, and it became the authoritative biblical text of the Roman Catholic Church. In March of 2011 the Catholic Church released its first Catholic Bible in 40 years… The *New American Bible*.

Judaism generally recognizes a set of 24 canonical books known as the *Tanakh* or *Hebrew Bible*, which also defines the *Old Testament* of the Christian bible. These books were primarily written in Hebrew with small portions in Aramaic between about the 9th Century and 4th Century BCE by prophets of God. Every book in the Bible contains prophetic scripture: The Old Testament Prophets all spoke of a *messiah* who would come to redeem all of Israel from sin… over 300 prophecies were fulfilled in the 1st coming of Jesus Christ. There are far more dedicated to the 2nd coming of Christ, including what is called the *Minor Prophets* of Hosea, Joel, Amos, Obadiah, Jonah, Micah, Nahum, Habakkuk, Zephaniah, Haggai, Zechariah and Malachi. The Books of Isaiah, Jeremiah, Ezekiel and Daniel are called the *Major Prophets*. The term Major refers to length and content, and not significance.

MINOR PROPHETS - 12
HOSEA
JOEL
AMOS
OBADIAH
JONAH
MICAH
NAHUM
HABAKKUK
ZEPHANIAH
HAGGAI
ZECHARIAH
MALACHI

MAJOR PROPHETS - 5
ISAIAH
JEREMIAH
LAMENTATIONS
EZEKIEL
DANIEL

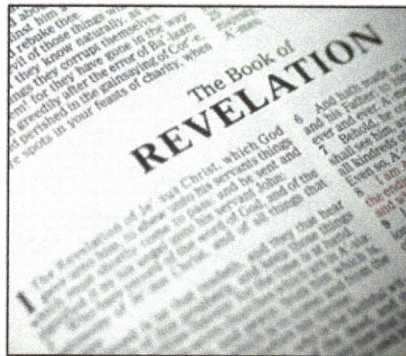

There are two books of the Holy Bible that are particularly significant to prophecy; these are the *Book of Daniel* and the *Book of Revelation*. Together, they are considered to form the *bookends of prophecy*. The Book of Daniel is concerned with both the first and second advent of Christ and the Book of Revelation with the second advent of Christ. The linkage between these two events represents the primary focus of this book. Of particular interest is when the rapture of the *Ecclesia* will take place.

The Daniel 70-Week Prophecy

The key to unlocking the Rapture issue is to understand the Book of Daniel. Perhaps the most important and mysterious prophecy in the entire Old and New Testaments is the Seventy Week Prophecy in Daniel 9.

[24] *Seventy weeks are determined upon thy people and upon thy holy city, to finish the transgression, and to make an end of sins, and to make reconciliation for iniquity, and to bring in everlasting righteousness, and to seal up the vision and prophecy, and to anoint the most Holy.*
[25] *Know therefore and understand, that from the going forth of the commandment to restore and to build Jerusalem unto the Messiah the Prince shall be seven weeks, and threescore and two weeks: the street shall be built again, and the wall, even in troublous times.*

[26] *And after threescore and two weeks shall Messiah be cut off, but not for himself: and the people of the prince that shall come shall destroy the city and the sanctuary; and the end thereof shall be with a flood, and unto the end of the war desolations are determined.*

[27] *And he shall confirm the covenant with many for one week: and in the midst of the week he shall cause the sacrifice and the oblation to cease, and for the overspreading of abominations he shall make it desolate, even until the consummation, and that determined shall be poured upon the desolate*   Daniel 9: 24-27

Daniel 9: 24-27 is called the Daniel 70-Week prophecy or the Daniel 490-Year Prophecy. All scholars agree that the 70 weeks equate to 490 days, and based upon the day-for-a year principle (Ezekiel 4: 5-6, Numbers 14:34) the 70-weeks represent 490 years (70*7=490). It is generally considered to be the backbone of all Old Testament prophetic passages, and was given to Daniel to reveal what would happen to the nation of Israel and to the Jews after the Babylonian Captivity. The Nation of Israel and the Holy Temple was destroyed by Nebuchadnezzar and the Babylonian army in the 5th century BC. God caused Israel to be conquered and taken into Babylonian exile for 70 years because they failed to observe a *Sabbatical Year* 70 times. The Sabbatical year was ordained by God to occur in the 7th year of every 7-year cycle. Its purpose was to let the land *rest* or remain *fallow* so that it could renew itself (Leviticus 25: 1-5). Daniel realizes from reading *books* (Daniel 9:2) that the 70-year exile in Babylon was nearing an end. He fasted and petitioned God to explain to him what was going to happen to Israel and the Jews after the exile had run its course.

The concept of what constituted a year in the prophecies off Daniel will prove to be critical in determining the scope and meaning of the Daniel 70-Week prophecy. Many scholars have assumed that a year was only 360 days long consisting of 12 months… each of 30 days. In context, it should be recognized that Daniel and the Nation of Israel were in Babylonian captivity for 70 years because they had failed to honor and obey God's command to let the land rest 1 year out of 7. There were obviously 490 years involved in ignoring 70 Sabbatical years. These were 70 years of 365.25 years which occurred over 490 years. There is not the slightest hint that these 490 years consisted of 360 days, or the 70 years in Babylonian captivity were only 360 days per year. It is the opinion of this author that the Daniel 70-week prophecy must refer to 490 normal Jewish Calendar years and not 360- day years. This is not a trivial observation but is crucial to determining the scope and meaning of the Daniel end-time prophecy. This will be discussed later in great detail.

The Daniel Prophecy: *Overview*

Seventy weeks are determined upon thy people and upon thy holy city, to finish the transgression, and to make an end of sins, and to make reconciliation for iniquity, and to bring in everlasting righteousness, and to seal up the vision and prophecy, and to anoint the most Holy   Daniel 9:24

Daniel 9:24 reveals that there are 490 years which are *determined* upon *thy people* (Israel and the Jews) and upon the *Holy City* (Jerusalem). The Hebrew word for *determined* means to *finish, complete*. It carries the meaning to be *cut-off* or *separated* to accomplish a specific purpose. There are 6 things that must be accomplished by the Jews and Israel. The first three are concerned with *sin*, and the last three with the *end of the age*.

(1) Finish the transgression

This is concerned with cessation of an activity which is contrary to the will and commands of God. The Jews have continually turned to idols and sinful behavior ever since God set them apart as His chosen people. Even after God had miraculously saved them from the Pharoah and his army at the dead sea, they began to worship idols when Moses went to talk to God at Mt. Sinai. Even Aaron joined their sinful behavior. The Jews have continued their unbelief and rebellion against God from then to the present time. However, God is not through with His chosen people and one day soon He will once again be their protector. The corporate transgression and rebellion against God, and their continuing rejection of Jesus Christ as their redeemer will come to an end before the age of Grace closes.

(2) Make an end to sins

The Hebrew word for sins (plural) means to *miss the mark* or *to be mistaken*. The idea of ending their corporate sins is to cease disobedience and remove it. This word translated sin occurs in only one other place in the Book of Daniel, and that is in Daniel 9:20: *And while I was speaking, and praying, and confessing my sin and the sin of my people Israel...*Since *sins* is plural, it seems to refer to the entire nation of Israel and not just a single group (Romans 11:26).

(3) Make reconciliation for iniquity

Iniquity again refers to *sin* or sinful behavior. It is the act of being unrighteous or disobedient. *Reconciliation* involves *a permanent atonement for sins*. It is in reference to the Sacrificial System in the Old Testament in which a blood offering was offered to God upon the Altar of Sacrifice as a *temporary* atonement covering for sin(s). In the sacrificial death of Jesus Christ upon the Cross of Calvary, Christ offered Himself as the final offering for sin... Jews and Gentiles alike.

> The first three of the six goals in Daniel 9:24 have to do with the sins of Daniel's people, Israel. Although the sin issue was settled by Jesus Christ at Calvary, the sacrificial death and atoning sacrifice of Jesus Christ was rejected by the Jews. The application of this wonderful provision for sin will not be realized for Daniel's people until the end of the 70 weeks. This will be fulfilled by the second coming of Messiah at the end of the tribulation period, which is yet future. Only then will Israel as a nation turn to Christ as their long-awaited Messiah (Jeremiah 31:33, 34, Ezekiel. 37:23, Zechariah 13:1, Romans. 11:25-27).
>
> Based upon comments by Thomas Ice and Leon Wood

This interpretation of Daniel 9:24 is extremely important because it demands that the 70 weeks of the Daniel prophecy have not yet been fulfilled, and is yet future to the 2nd advent of Christ.

(4) Bring in everlasting righteousness

Righteousness us not a natural human characteristic. Because of the sin nature which has been passed on from Adam to everyone who is born of a natural man, every man and woman has the propensity to sin. The body is weak and the sin nature is strong. When one is born again and receives the Holy Spirit, sinful man becomes a new creature in Christ to which righteousness is imputed. The sin nature is still there, but it can be overcome with the help of spiritual power.

As it is written: There is none righteous, no, not one   Romans 3:10

For therein is the righteousness of God revealed from faith to faith: as it is written: The just shall live by faith   Romans 1:17

Whatever righteousness man might possess is imputed to him by Jesus Christ. A new creature in Jesus Christ will live by faith and seek to obey the commands of God. That new man will die to the world and live again in Him. Righteousness can never be fully obtained until we are united with Jesus Christ in the life hereafter.

For now, we see through a glass, darkly; but then face to face: now I know in part; but then shall I know even as also I am   I Corinthians 13:12

Everlasting and complete righteousness will never be achieved by Israel until they accept Jesus Christ as their lord and Savior and are joined to Him for all eternity.
At that time, the Lord will award everlasting righteousness to not only a redeemed Israel but to all who call upon the name of the Lord.

(5) Seal up vision and prophecy

The Holy Bible is full of prophecies concerning the 1st and 2nd advent of Jesus Christ. In the Old Testament, prophets wrote of how a Jewish Messiah would arise who would redeem Israel from sin and set up a Kingdom on this earth that would never end. This was accomplished by Jesus Christ when He was crucified on the Cross of Calvary. He was both the offer and the offering that would satisfy all Old Testament Prophecies concerning His 1st advent. The New Testament confirmed His ministry of reconciliation and forgiveness of sins as a suffering servant, and then prophesied that He would return again as a conquering King, and set up an earthly Kingdom which would last for 1000 years. After that period of time, God would set up an eternal kingdom of peace and righteousness that would never end. The current Holy Bible was written by prophets of God to describe how this would be accomplished. Everything that concerns how one can be saved and be awarded eternal life has been recorded and explained in God's word. Prophecies and prophets in the New Testament spoke of how this current Age of Grace would one day come to an end. The Book of Daniel spoke of what would happen to the Jews after the Babylonian exile, and spanned time from the end of the Babylonian exile until the 2nd advent of Christ.

After Jesus Christ came and satisfied every Old Testament Messianic prophecy concerning His birth, death and resurrection in His 1st advent, the apostle John was told to write the Book of Revelation to describe what would happen as the Church Age comes to and end. The Book of Revelation also reveals a 1000- year Millennial Kingdom in which the Jews would finally inherit the Land of Promise to complete all Jewish Old Testament promises. The prophecies and end-time events described in the Book of Revelation will come to pass, and after the 1000-year Millennial Kingdom has ended… new heavens and a new earth would emerge which would never end. When all of this comes to pass, there will be no need of prophets or prophecy. The phrase *seal up visions and prophecy* bring the force of completion. All visions and prophecy will be fulfilled after the 2nd advent of Christ. *All of Israel will be saved*, and the scales of disbelief will be removed from their eyes. ALL prophecy concerning the 1st and 2nd advent of Jesus Christ will be fulfilled will be fulfilled when He arrives as a Conquering King.

5

(6) Anoint the most holy

This phrase has been the subject of much debate concerning Messianic expectations. There are two dominate views concerning its meaning. (1) The first is that it concerns the anointing of Jesus Christ when He assumes His rightful place as King of Kings and ruler over the entire world from His throne in Jerusalem as the Millennial Kingdom begins. This could well be true, but this requires no anointing or dedication of Jesus Christ as King of Kings. Every born-again Christian believes that Jesus Christ will rule forever over all who would believe upon His Holy name. God has already anointed His Son to fulfill His eternal plan for mankind.

The Spirit of the Lord is upon me, because he hath anointed me to preach the gospel to the poor; he hath sent me to heal the brokenhearted, to preach deliverance to the captives, and recovering of sight to the blind, to set at liberty them that are bruised   Luke 4:18

(2) The *Most Holy* which will be anointed will be the Temple and Throne of God in Jerusalem.

> The German commentator C. F. Keil notes that the same phrase most holy is used in Ezekiel 45:3 of a future temple and concludes that "the reference is to the anointing of a new sanctuary, temple, or *most holy* place

> The phrase *most holy* and "most holy of holies" occurs thirty-nine times in the Old Testament, always in reference to the Tabernacle or Temple or to the holy articles used in them. In view of this phrase, it is highly likely that it refers to the Temple, which, in view of the context, must be a future Temple; and, hence the phrase used here must be in reference to the Millennial Temple.
>
>   Thomas Ice quoting both Theil and Wood

Daniel 9:24 listed six things that were to be accomplished by Israel and the Jews, and by the Holy city of Jerusalem. The Jews would never be abandoned by God for they are His chosen people… His bride. God made an unconditional, covenant promise to Abraham that blessed all of his offspring: *And if you are Christ's then you are Abraham's seed, and heirs according to the promise* (Galatians 3:29). We Christians are also blessed as heirs to the promise by our faith in Jesus, and this makes us spiritual descendants of Abraham and co-heirs of the promised blessings.

> *Know therefore and understand, that from the going forth of the commandment to restore and to build Jerusalem unto the Messiah the Prince shall be seven weeks, and threescore and two weeks: the street shall be built again, and the wall, even in troublous times*   Daniel 9:25

In 586 BC the City of Jerusalem was invaded by Nebuchadnezzar and his Babylonian army. The City of Jerusalem fell, the Holy Temple was burned and destroyed, the Holy Vessels in the Temple were seized and taken to Babylon. All of the inhabitants of Jerusalem except for the very young and the very old were captured and taken to Babylon for 70 years. The 70 years of exile were punishment for not observing the *Sabbatical Year* 70 times over a 490- year period of time. A Sabbatical year was to occur every 7th year in a 7-year sabbatical cycle to let the land rest and lie fallow after 6 years of planting and reaping crops. This was patterned after God's creative process when He created the heavens and earth in 6 days and then rested for one day. It can also be seen as representing the 7-day cycle each week when man was to rest on the 7th day. It was an antitype of the manna during the 40 years when Moses led the Israelite's through the Wilderness. Six days in each week God provided manna to the people for food. The food would spoil after 24 hours, but on the 6th day the people could pick enough manna to last 2 days without spoiling.

Daniel fasted and prayed, asking God to tell him what was to become of both his people and the temple. God answered the prayers of Daniel in Daniel 9:25. First, God told Daniel that a commandment (decree) would be issued to allow both Jerusalem and the Holy Temple to be rebuilt. Although not explicitly stated, it is understood that a believing remnant of the Jews would be allowed to return to accomplish this goal and that they would live in houses that would be built in the city of Jerusalem. This commandment/decree is perhaps the most important, far-reaching and revealing prophecy found in the Old Testament. It was composed of two distinct parts: (1) The Temple and the City would be restored over a 7-week period of time (49 years). The streets of the city and walls would be rebuilt, but it will be during troublous times (severe opposition). After another time period of 62-weeks (434 years), Messiah the Prince would appear. These two time periods result in a total elapsed time of 483 years. Who is this *Messiah the Prince*? All agree that this is the long- awaited Jewish Messiah who would be sent by God to redeem Israel and atone for their sins. We now know that this was Jesus Christ the Son of God. He began his 3.5 ministry of reconciliation when He came to the River Jordan and was baptized by John. Daniel evidently understood what he had been told (Daniel 9:22), but he did not know *who* would issue this decree, *when* this decree would be issued, or the name of this anointed redeemer. When, who and to whom this proclamation was issued will be determined in Chapter 3. The astute reader will immediately recognize that there are still 7 years left in the 490 -year prophecy. The remarkable prophecy continues.

And after threescore and two weeks shall Messiah be cut off, but not for himself   Daniel 9: 25a

After a period of 483 years have elapsed, the Messiah will be *cut off*. This is a Hebrew idiom that means *to be killed*. After being anointed for his ministry by the baptism of John in the River Jordan, Jesus Christ began His 3.5-year ministry. As prophesied, Jesus Christ was *cut off* or crucified on the Cross of Calvary on the Feast of Passover, Nisan 14. The duration of his earthly ministry was not revealed to Daniel, only that Messiah the Prince would be killed *after* a period of 483 years had elapsed. By studying the New Testament gospel of John, it can be determined that Christ was crucified about 486.5 years after the 70-week Daniel prophecy had been initiated. He was crucified not for himself but for the sins of the world… not for Himself but for the sins of Jews and gentiles alike. The next part of Daniel 9:26 must have greatly troubled Daniel.

and the people of the prince that shall come shall destroy the city and the sanctuary; and the end thereof shall be with a flood, and unto the end of the war desolations are determined
Daniel 9:26

Daniel had just been told that the City of Jerusalem and the Temple would be rebuilt, now he is told that it would be destroyed again. *When will it be destroyed and by who?* We now know that Titus and his Roman legions destroyed the City of Jerusalem and Herod's Temple in 70 AD. The Temple was burned to the ground and nothing remained but the foundation, which today is called the *wailing wall*. This act of destruction and devastation against the Jews and Jerusalem was not the 1ˢᵗ and it would not be the last. The Jews have been conquered, killed and persecuted for millennia and yet they have survived… They are god's chosen people. The Herod's Temple was burned, desecrated and defiled… The Muslim Dome of the Rock now stands upon the Temple mount, but the Holy Temple of God will be rebuilt and used by the Jews before the Tribulation begins. One of the first acts of the Antichrist will be to invade Jerusalem once again and then sit in the Temple declaring himself to be God. These Holy Wars will not cease until the 2ⁿᵈ advent of Christ at the Battle of Armageddon: *Desolations are determined* until the war with Satan ends.

And he shall confirm the covenant with many for one week: and in the midst of the week, he shall cause the sacrifice and the oblation to cease, and for the overspreading of abominations he shall make it desolate, even until the consummation, and that determined shall be poured upon the desolate   Daniel 9:27

This is perhaps the most highly debated and controversial verse in the bible.
he shall confirm the covenant…

The controversy swirls around who the personal pronoun *he* represents. There are only two real choices that have been considered: (1) *he* is the end-time antichrist or (2) *he* is Jesus Christ. This a hotly debated topic, and will require careful investigation. Most of Chapter 3 will be to resolve this question. For those who require an immediate answer the bulk of scriptural evidence seems to favor Jesus Christ.

- *He* will confirm a covenant. When Jesus Christ began his 3.5 years of earthly ministry: He was confirming a covenant made to Abraham and Moses.

*And this I say, that the **covenant**, that was confirmed before of God in Christ, the law, which was four hundred and thirty years after, cannot disannul, that it should make the promise of none effect*   Galatians 3:17

[31] *Behold, the days come, saith the LORD, that I will make a new covenant with the house of Israel, and with the house of Judah:*
[32] *Not according to the **covenant** that I made with their fathers in the day that I took them by the hand to bring them out of the land of Egypt; which my covenant they brake, although I was a husband unto them, saith the LORD:*
[33] *But this shall be the covenant that I will make with the house of Israel; After those days, saith the LORD, I will put my law in their inward parts, and write it in their hearts; and will be their God, and they shall be my people*   Jeremiah 31: 31-33

If *he* was Satan in the Antichrist, there is not the slightest hint that Satan ever confirmed any covenant. Satan is the father of lies, and never confirmed a covenant with anyone.

…with many for one week

Christ came to Israel to offer salvation and permanent atonement for sin, but the Jewish spiritual leaders and the people rejected His offer of salvation by faith and grace. If Israel and the Jews had accepted him as their long-awaited Messiah and redeemer… the 70-week prophecy would have ended and there would be no need for the entire period of great tribulation. But, when

Israel, the Jews and their spiritual leader rejected Christ and crucified Him, the 490-year prophecy given to Daniel was suspended after approximately 486.5 years. God and His Son then set aside the Jews and turned to the Gentiles to offer salvation to both Jews and Gentiles alike. This *new man... the body of Christ...* would be formed under a *New Covenant* based upon faith and grace which would carry on the good news and finally (yet future) save all of Israel. The last week (7-years) of the Daniel prophecy would be interrupted or a *gap* would take place in the Daniel Prophecy which is called the *Church Age*. This age or dispensation will continue until God will once again turn to the Jews and offer salvation through His Son... Jesus Christ. The last 3.5 years of Daniel's 70-week prophecy would be the *Time of Jacob's Trouble* or the *Great Tribulation.*

*... in the **midst of the week** he shall cause the sacrifice and the oblation to cease.*

When Jesus Christ was crucified after a 3.5 ministry to the Jews, He caused the Old Testament sacrificial system to cease forever. The Old Testament economy or dispensation of salvation by works of the law was replaced by one in which salvation would come by faith and grace. The Old Testament sacrificial system and oblation (something offered to God for atonement of sin) was replaced by a new and better covenant. The ritualistic and sacrificial system for which the Temple stood was annulled and changed. When Christ died, the veil which separated the holy Place from the Holy-of Holies was rent in two from top to bottom. The way to God was open to all by faith through our Lord Jesus Christ. Sacrifice and oblations ceased... Christ was the final sacrifice and perfect Lamb of God who had paid the final price for the permanent atonement of sin.

for the overspreading of abominations, he shall make it desolate, even until the consummation, and that determined shall be poured upon the desolate   Daniel 9:27

The sacrificial system of the Old Covenant had been replaced by a *new and better covenant.* Christ said before He died:

*Behold, your house is left unto you **desolate**: and verily I say unto you, Ye shall not see me, until the time come* (the consummation) *when ye shall say: Blessed is he that cometh in the name of the Lord*   Luke 13:35

The temple was an artifact of salvation by works, and it was made spiritually desolate by the sacrificial death of Christ. The Jews were given another 40 years to turn to Christ but they would not (the number 40 generally symbolizes a period of testing, trial or probation). In 70 AD Herod's Temple was ransacked and burned to the ground by the Roman General Titus and his Centurions. History records that the Muslim Dome of the Rock was built on the southern side of the temple grounds in the 8th century AD. Both the Jewish Temple and the Jewish Temple Mount had become *desolate.* The Temple will be rebuilt just before the tribulation begins. The great European World leader who will be slain and resurrected as the Satanically indwelled Antichrist will initiate or *cut a covenant* with Israel and somehow manage to have a new temple built on the Temple Mount in Jerusalem (Compare this to Daniel 9:27) where *he* will *confirm a covenant.* There is a great deal of difference in *confirming* a covenant (Jesus Christ) and establishing or initiating a covenant (Antichrist). The covenant which Jesus Christ confirmed concerned the *spiritual redemption* of the Jews... The covenant which was established by the Antichrist after the last 3.5 years of Daniels 70th week will begin will be the *spiritual destruction* of all Jews who turn to the antichrist, take his mark, and worship him as God. The temple of Jewish sacrifice and worship will remain desolate until the *consummation* (end of the Church Age) and *that determined* will be *poured out.* The 7th bowl of God's Wrath will be poured out which will launch the Battle of Armageddon. The *desolate* is the Antichrist, the False Prophet and all who have denied Jesus Christ as their Lord and Savior.

This Chapter has provided a short overview of the 70-Week prophecy given to the prophet Daniel by Gabriel; sent by God to reveal the fate of Israel and the Jews to Daniel. The 70-week Prophecy of Daniel will be discussed and examined in more detail in Chapters 3. *When* this prophecy began and *who* issued the decree which launched the 490-year prophecy is the subject of Chapter 2. This prophecy will be used to reveal the ultimate purpose of God and His eternal plan to redeem His beloved Jews, and to offer salvation to the Jews and Gentiles alike through faith in his only begotten Son... Jesus Christ.

Chapter 2

The Decree That Initiated Daniels Prophecy

The Commandment to Restore the Temple and Rebuild Jerusalem

It is crucial that we determine exactly when the commandment to *restore and rebuild the City of Jerusalem went forth*. There are two basic things to consider. The *First* is that we are able to look back in time and determine the most likely time and place that this commandment occurred. *Second*, the decree which will initiate the 70-week prophecy of Daniel must lead to the *beginning* of the ministry of Christ when he came to the River Jordan to be baptized by John the Baptizer 483 years later. Every Biblical scholar agrees that Christ was crucified between 30 AD - 34 AD. It can be shown that Christ was born in 5 BC (Phillips, *The Birth and Death of Christ*) and that Christ was crucified in 30 AD (Phillips, *The Birth and Death of Christ; A Forensic Analysis*). We will now show that these two dates can be confirmed by the Daniel prophecy. There are four possible decrees that must be considered.

The Decree of Cyrus

In 539 BC, the Persian King Darius conquered Babylon and installed Cyrus to act as king. This happened after the prophet Daniel had almost completed his 70 years of exile, which had previously been prophesied by Jeremiah (Jeremiah 29:10). In Ezra 1:1 we read: *Now in the first year of Cyrus king of Persia, that the word of the Lord by the mouth of Jeremiah might be fulfilled, the Lord stirred up the spirit of Cyrus, king of Persia, that he made a royal proclamation.* This proclamation or decree authorized the return of Israel to Jerusalem to *build (rebuild) the house (temple) of the Lord.* From 539 BC, a span of 483 years *unto the Messiah the Prince* (Jesus Christ), would take us to 56 BC. This is way too early, so we must look elsewhere.

The Decree of Darius

The rebuilding of the temple authorized by Cyrus did not go well. The *people of the land* (Ezra 4:4) resisted the project, and it is recorded in Ezra 4:24 that the work *ceased until the second year of the reign of Darius, king of Persia.* Darius succeeded Cyrus as King of Babylon in 518 BC. The work of restoring the Temple in Jerusalem resumed in 520 BC under Haggai and Zechariah. The governor of the province surrounding Jerusalem came to the temple site and inquired: *Who hath commanded you to build this house?* (Ezra 5:3). They replied that *King Cyrus* had authorized the project. The governor then sent a letter to Darius asking him to produce such a decree, if indeed one existed. A search was made and the original decree was found. Darius then reinforced this decree with one of his own. *Let the governor of the Jews and the elders of the Jews build this house of God in His place.* So, Darius simply reissued and augmented the decree of Cyrus authorizing that the Temple of God be rebuilt. Based upon Ezra 4:24 and biblical/ archeological research, this event likely occurred in 520 BC. Again, moving forward 483 years, we find an ending date of 37 BC. This was about when King Herod began to reign in Jerusalem, and is again much too early. We must search further.

The First Decree of Artaxerxes

In Ezra 7:1-10, we read that Ezra the scribe, who was a descendent of Aaron, approached King Artaxerxes I and petitioned the king to allow him and a band of Israelites to return to Jerusalem. Biblical scholars are in almost universal agreement that this occurred in either 458 BC or 457 BC. Ezra wanted to *set magistrates and judges* in place, *teach the laws of God,* and *let judgment be executed speedily*, upon all who would not obey the laws of God (Ezra 7). The petition was granted, and Ezra left *on the first day of the first month of Artaxerxes Seventh year*, and arrived in Jerusalem *on the first day of the Fifth month* (Ezra 7:9). We will later show that the decree went forth on *Tishri 15, 458 BC* (Sept/Oct). Ezra departed from the city of Babylon on Nisan 1 (Mach/April) in 457 BC (Ezra 7:9). Ezra could not have possibly received permission to go on Nisan 1 and then left Babylon the same day. It must have taken some time to prepare for his departure. The year 458 BC was a Jewish Sabbatical Year. If the decree to Ezra was issued in 458 BC, then the total elapsed years from 458 BC must be 483 years. This would bring us to 26 AD. Please note that to arrive at 26 AD; we must subtract one year from a total of 484 years because when one crosses from BC to AD, there is no year zero. 26 AD is considered by many to be a strong candidate for the year in which Jesus Christ came to the River Jordan and started his ministry of 3.5 years. This would suggest that Christ was crucified in 30 AD. This is a strong candidate, but we will consider the final possible decree.

The Second Decree of Artaxerxes

In the 20th year of King Artaxerxes (Nehemiah 1:1) word came to Nehemiah that things were not going so well in Jerusalem: *The remnant that are left of the captivity there in the province are in great affliction and reproach. The wall of Jerusalem also is broken down, and the gates thereof are burned with fire* (Nehemiah 1: 1-3). Nehemiah… who was the King's personal cupbearer (Nehemiah 1:11; 2:1) … wept, mourned, fasted and petitioned God to move the heart of Artaxerxes to let him go to Jerusalem. God did move Artaxerxes' heart, and he gave Nehemiah permission to return. He also sent a letter to a merchant called *Asaph* informing him to supply timber to rebuild the gates, the walls and the temple (Nehemiah 2:6-8). Since the 7th year of Artaxerxes was September 1, 448 BC - Elul 29, 447 BC, the 20th regnal year of Artaxerxes would be Tishri 1, 445 BC – Elul 29, 444 BC. Adding 483 years to 445 BC would bring us to 39 AD which is much too late.

In 1882 Sir Robert Anderson published a book called *The Coming Prince.* Anderson knew from Nehemiah 2:1 that King Artaxerxes had issued a decree on Nisan in the 20th year of Artaxerxes reign which permitted Nehemiah to go to Jerusalem. He decided that the decree must have been issued on *Nisan 1 in 445 BC*. If we move forward 483 years of 365.2422 days per year from this date Using these assumptions, we would arrive in 39 AD for the arrival of Jesus Christ to begin His 3.5-year ministry at the River Jordan. He would be crucified 3.5 years later on the Feast of Passover (Nisan 14). This is much too late for the death of Christ. At this point, Anderson made a unique assumption. Using the flood account in the Book of Genesis, he declared based upon Genesis 7:11, 7:24 and 8:4 that a *prophetic month* was only 30 days long, and a 12-month *prophetic year* was 360 days long. He supported this theory by referring to the Book of Revelation, which equates 1260 days to 42 months (Revelation 11:2-3). We will deal with this assumption in Chapter 6. Assuming that the Daniel prophecy was using a 360-day prophetic year, he multiplied 360 days times 483 years. He then converted this number of prophetic days into a *Gregorian* calendar year, even though the Gregorian calendar had not even been implemented in Daniel's time. After adjusting for leap years,

Anderson arrived at Nisan 10, *Palm Sunday* in 32 BC. The subsequent date for the crucifixion of Christ would then be on Thursday, Nisan 14, in 32 AD. The 7 years remaining in Daniel's 490-year prophecy were then given to the tribulation period in the Book Revelation. His results have been widely accepted since they were published, but it has been shown that many of his assumptions were flawed. If all of this seems strange and implausible…it is. Thomas Ice has published a series of papers which uncover many illogical and wrong assumptions (http://www.pickle-publishing.com/papers/sir-robert-anderson.htm). His approach was clever, but contained several fatal errors.

Dr. Harold Hoehner of the Dallas Theological Seminary in his 1978 book, *Chronological Aspects of the Life of Christ*, published an improvement on Anderson's dates. Hoehner re-examined the work of Anderson and set out to correct his mistakes. After careful investigation, he determined that the 20th year of Artaxerxes reign was actually Tishri 1 (Sept/Oct) of 445 BC to Tishri 1 (Sept/Oct) of 444 BC, and that the decree was not issued in 445 BC but on Nisan 1 in 444 BC. Following Anderson, he then adopted the supposition that Gabriel was using prophetic years of 360 days duration, and using 173,380 days He calculated that this period of 483 prophetic years would start on Nisan 1, March 5 in 444 BC end on March 30, Friday in 33 AD. March 30 in 33 AD was Nisan 14 (Feast of Passover). This would still leave 7 years to complete the Daniel prophecy. Ice has also examined the work of Hoehner, and could find nothing to challenge. To date, no one has successfully rejected his work.

Be completely aware that this book does not reject the brilliant work of Hoehner, but it does reject the basis of his conclusions. *This book* assumes that: (1) The 70-week prophecy of Daniel is based upon God defined years of 360.2422 days …Genesis 1:14 (2) The Daniel prophecy is Jewish through and through, and it is based upon the Jewish calendar which is exactly the same today as it was then (3) The starting point for the Daniel prophecy was in the 7th year of Artaxerxes reign (Tishri 1, 448 BC-Elul 29, 457 BC. (4) The first 483 years of the 490- year Daniel prophecy would end in 26 BC at the River Jordan when Christ came to John and be Baptized into His 3.5 year ministry of reconciliation.

We can only applaud Sir Robert Anderson and Harold Hoehner for using such a clever approach to arrive at either 32 AD (Newton) or 33 AD (Hoehner) as the year of the crucifixion. Both dates have been widely acclaimed as correct by two large and different groups of followers. However, the basic assumptions and methods used by Anderson have been critically assailed and claimed in error by Ice and Jones among others. ***First***, the flood account in Genesis *does* state that over a period of 150 days, five months elapsed, but this does not guarantee that *every month* of the *year* was 30 days in duration or that *a year was 360 days long*. In fact, if anyone wants to carefully study the narrative in Genesis 7 & 8 they will find that from when Noah entered the ark until he left the ark was 365 days, and it could have been exactly one solar year of 365.2422 days which would imply a normal year. (Phillips, Noahs Ark: *Historical and Prophetic Truths*). ***Second***, the book of Revelation would not be written for about another 620 years, so Daniel would have no knowledge of that text. ***Third***, Daniel was nearing the end of the 70-year period of Babylonian exile when he received the prophecy. He was not experiencing 360-day prophetic years during his exile, but full solar years. He was also well aware that the 70 years of exile were almost over when he petitioned God in prayer and fasting. There would be no confusion whatsoever in associating full solar years with the 70-week prophecy given to Daniel (Daniel 9:24). ***Fourth***, if Daniel *understood* (Daniel 9:23) that the 490-year prophecy was *not* based upon the Babylonian calendar year or the Jewish calendar year… which is on the average very close to a modern solar year, there was certainly no indication of that in his response to Gabriel nor in the Biblical record. There is no proof or any hint of divine revelation whatsoever to Daniel that a 360-day *prophetic year* ever existed in the Holy Scriptures. In fact, to keep the Passover every year in the correct month at the correct time of year, a 360 year *could not* be in use. Of course, the 360-day year claim that a 360-day year applies from Genesis to Revelation. They simply state with a great deal of confidence that the *360-day prophetic year* was a *mystery* hidden until Sir Isaac Newton discovered it! Ah ha! They say, Daniel was told this by Gabriel and he knew it all along. After all, Gabriel told Daniel that he would *understand.* This is *high conjecture* at best. In this author's opinion, the assumption of a 360-day *prophetic year* is simply unwarranted. The conclusion of the matter is that the only decree which makes logical sense, and fits all the requirements of a normal 490-solar year prophecy, is the one issued by Artaxerxes in either 457 BC or 458 BC. We will now show that 458 BC is indeed the correct year.

> **Authors Comment:** It is proposed without unassailable scriptural verification, that it is entirely possible that a 12-month year of 30 days was in existence at the Flood. Until God chose Israel and his beloved Jews as His holy people and His bride, there were no Holy Days, New Moon Festivals or the 7 Feasts of Israel in existence. It was not until after the children of Israel left Egypt and God spoke the Law that He commanded strict observance of these celebrations. He went further and told the people that they were to be *perpetually celebrated every year at their appointed times.* This required that a Lunar calendar exist to predict every new moon and a solar calendar exist to track the seasons simultaneously. To enable His commands, it is proposed that he gave to Moses and the priesthood a unique Lunar/Solar calendar so that they could obey His commands. This Hebrew calendar has not changed since that point in time.

After examining the available options, the commandment to restore and to rebuild Jerusalem (Daniel 9:25), which initiated the 70-week prophecy of Daniel is the decree from Artaxerxes to Ezra. We will show in Chapter 3 that the decree to Rebuild Jerusalem and the Temple was by Artaxerxes, and was likely issued on Tishri 15 in 458 BC. We know for certain that Ezra *left Babylon on the first day of the first month* (Ezra 7: 1-9). After gathering the people together and assembling a group of Levites to conduct temple services, he *departed from the River of A-Haya on the 12th day of the first month* (Ezra 8:31). A-hava was a River North and West of Babylon where he gathered the Levitical priests. He arrived in Jerusalem on the *first day of the 5ᵗʰ month.* Hence, the actual journey took about 3.5 months. Ezra left Babylon on the 1ˢᵗ day of first month and arrived on the 1ˢᵗ day of the fifth month in Artaxerxes 7ᵗʰ year of reign. There are three key questions yet to be answered: *When was Artaxerxes 7ᵗʰ year? What month was the 1ˢᵗ month? What date did the decree go forth?* To determine the seventh regnal year of Artaxerxes, we need to discuss two fundamental issues. Artaxerxes was a Persian king: (1) *In what month of the year did Persian kings begin to count their regnal years?* (2) *How did Persian kings transition from the death of one king to the next?*

The Beginning of Regnal Years

We will briefly review calendar systems used to mark time. Each ancient kingdom had their own calendar system which was used to determine the beginning of a king's reign. Each ancient kingdom employed a slightly different calendar, but most had learned when each season changed, and that the length of a solar year was determined by the sun; which we now know is exactly 365.2422 days. A calendar year was composed of 12 months and a week of seven, 24-hour days. All ancient societies used a basic 12-month year, but the number of days in each month varied from calendar to calendar, as did the actual number of total days in each year. The length of a month in ancient times was usually set at either 29 or 30 days. This is because the actual length of a lunar month is determined by the rotation of the moon around the earth, and is 29.53059 days. Calendars are designed to mark time by the passage of months, with the number and initiation of each month designed so that a series of months would coincide with the solar year. However, there is no combination of 30 and 29 day months that can equate to a solar year on a yearly basis. There were two common solutions to the problem: the first was to add days at the end of each year; the second is to periodically add an extra (13th) month to the normal 12-month year. For example, the Egyptians used a simple 12-month calendar consisting of 12 months of 30 days per year. This would total to 360 days per year. They then added 5 days at the end of the 12th month, so that their year was 365 days. This was close to the actual solar year, but fell short about 0.25 days per year. Hence, the calendar *drifted backward* about one day every four years. It would continue to drift back through the solar year, so that after about 1460 years, the Egyptian year would move back in sync with a true solar year. For example, if today was Christmas using the ancient Egyptian 365 days per year calendar, in about 730 years Christmas would be in July!

The calendar used by the Jews was a *Lunar-Solar* calendar. The *basic calendar* consists of 12 alternating 30- and 29-day months. Simple math shows that the *basic Hebrew year* was only 354 days, which is about 11.25 days short of a solar year. About every three years, the calendar would drift back approximately 33.75 days. To keep the lunar-based 12-month year in sync with the solar year, it was discovered that by adding seven extra months over a 19-year period of time and periodically adding or subtracting a day from selected Fall months… 19 Jewish calendar years of 12 or 13 months would almost exactly equal a solar-based calendar over the same period of time. This 19-year period of time with seven inter-calculated months is called a *Metonic cycle*. This extra month was called Adar II, added at the end of the year; and that year was called a *Leap Year*. The same Jewish calendar that Daniel used in the Babylonian Exile has been used for over 2,500 years and is still in use today. It must again be stressed that since the *Seven Feasts of Israel* were ordained by God, and were to be observed every year following agricultural cycles, the Hebrews after the exodus *had* to keep their 12-month lunar calendar in sync with the solar year. After the 70-year Babylonian exile, the Hebrews adopted the Babylonian calendar names with only slight variations. Mechanics of the Jewish calendar were revealed by Hillel II in 358 AD. The calendar we use today is called the *Gregorian Calendar*. It was derived from the *Julian Calendar* which preceded the Gregorian Calendar. It was in use in the 1st century AD and it was 365.25 days long. By 1582 AD, the calendar was out of sync with the true solar

	Julian	Gregorian	Hebrew	(Civil)	Babylonian	
Month	Name	Name	Name	Months	Name	Months
1	Januarius	Jan	Tishri	Sept/Oct	Nisanu	Mar/Apr
2	Februarius	Feb	Heshvan	Oct/Nov	Aiaru	Apr/May
3	Martius	Mar	Chislev	Non/Dec	Simanu	May/Jun
4	Aprilus	April	Tebeth	Dec/Jan	Duzu	Jun/July
5	Maius	May	Shevat	Jan/Feb	Abu	July/Aug
6	Junius	June	Adar	Feb/Mar	Ululu	Aug/Sept
7	Julius	July	Nisan	Mar/Apr	Tashritu	Sept/Oct
8	Augustus	Aug	Iyyar	Apr/May	Arahsamnu	Oct/Nov
9	Septembris	Sept	Sivan	May/Jun	Kislimu	Non/Dec
10	Octobris	Oct	Tammuz	Jun/July	Tebetu	Dec/Jan
11	Novembris	Nov	Ab/Av	July/Aug	Shabatu	Jan/Feb
12	Decembris	Dec	Elul	Aug/Sept	Addaru	Feb/Mar

year that Pope Gregory XIII introduced the modern Gregorian Calendar to reduce the average length of the year from 365.25 days to 365.2422 days and thus corrected the Julian calendar's drift against the solar year. The Gregorian calendar is very accurate. The previous table is a summary of the Julian, Gregorian, Babylonian and Hebrew calendars.

Before the Exodus from Egypt, *Tishri 1* (September/October) began every Hebrew calendar year. After the Exodus, God ordained that every year would begin on *Nisan 1* (March/April) to commemorate their being freed from Egyptian slavery. Hence, all references in the bible to Month 1 *before* the Exodus referred to Tishri 1, and *after* the Exodus it was Nisan 1. Computer programs have been written for digital computers which can convert any Hebrew calendar date back thousands of years into the corresponding Gregorian or Julian calendar date. Those dates prior to when the Gregorian Calendar was introduced in 582 AD and the Julian Calendar before 46 BC are called *ante* or *proleptic* dates. A date conversion program called *Abdicate* is very accurate and very powerful (https://abdicate.net/cal.aspx). It is used to calculate all dates used in this book and verified by *Hebcal* (https://www.hebcal.com).

After the Medo-Persia empire overthrew the Babylonian empire in 539 BC, the Persian Empire also adopted the Babylonian calendar for their own use. The Babylonians, Hebrews and Persians all used a common method for determining when a king began a yearly reign. The Babylonians, Persians and Hebrews all used *Tishri 1* (September/October). The Egyptians used a month called *Thoth* 1 (December). This was proved and published by Horn and Wood based upon earlier work by Thiele and is now widely accepted. Babylonian and Hebrew *yearly calendar years* start on Nisan 1.

How Was the Reign of Ancient Kings Determined?

Before we proceed, it is necessary to review how ancient kings counted their years of reign. Every civilized nation had a calendar that was used to keep track of time and started at a particular time of year. It is believed by this author that the Hebrew calendar came into existence when it was given to Moses by God at the time of the Exodus. This was because God commanded Israel to observe the New Moons and His 7 holy feasts at exactly the same time each year. It is conjectured that the Assyrians and Babylonians adopted the basic Jewish Calendar, and by the 5th century BC they were almost identical. Both started each month on a New Moon and tracked the seasons with a 19-year average very close to 365.2422 days. The Babylonian calendar began each civil year on Nisan 1 (March/April). Rather than completely abandon their old Tishri 1 New Year's Day after the Exodus, the Jews declared that there would be a *Spiritual year* which would start on Nisan 1 (March/April) and that there would be a *Civil year* that would start on Tishri 1 (September/ October).

Every nation had a King, and the reign of kings would be recorded as *actual years* or *regnal years* (credited years of reign). Fortunately, both Israel and Babylonian Kings had the same coronation day from which credited or regnal years of reign were determined...That was on Tishri 1 (September/October). There were two systems in use to determine how many credited years of reign that a king could claim from when he ascended to the throne. ...an *accession year* system and a *non-accession* year system. Suppose that King Don was a king who started his 5th year of reign on Tishri 1, September 15 in 500 BC, and he was killed in battle on Adar 10, March 2, 499 BC. King John succeeded King Don and assumed the throne on Adar 11, March 3. In an *accession year* system, all of the months between Tishri 1 in 500 BC and Tishri 1, 499 BC would be counted as the reign of King Don and not King John. The 5th and last year of King Don would be Tishri 1, 500 BC to Tishri 1, 499 BC. The 1st regnal year of King John would not begin until Tishri 1 (September/October), 499 BC even though he assumed the throne on March 3, 499 BC. Using an accession year system, one might think of the actual reign of King John between March 2, 499 BC and Tishri 1 (September/Oct), 499 BC as Year 0. In a *non-accession* year system, King Don would still be credited with a full 5 year reign (Tishri 1, 500 BC-Tishri 1, 499 BC) , but King John's 1st year of reign would be counted as a full year between March 3, 500 BC and Tishri 1, 499 BC. The non-accession year system could and usually did create havoc when recording historical events. For example, if King John won a major battle on March 30, 499 BC would it be recorded in the 5th year of King Don or in the 1st year of King John or both if a non-accession year system was in use. When a king died during his reign, the Persians and Babylonians credited the entire year as his last year of reign, even if he died at the beginning of that year and his successor ruled for 11 months. In that case, the first 11 months of reign for the new Assyrian or Babylonian king would be called his *accession year* and credited to the old king. The credited reign of the new king would not start until the 1st day of the following regnal year. This is an *accession year* system or a *post-dating* system. If a *non-accession year system* was in use, both the old king and the new king would be credited with an overlapping full 11 months of reign. This seems to be insane record keeping, but it was used because every ancient king wanted to be remembered as reigning over the maximum number of years possible.

The great biblical scholars Thiele, Horn and Wood proved that both the Persian and Babylonian Kings used the *accession* year system and so did the Hebrews after the fall of the Northern Kingdom of Israel in 723 BC. He also proved that both the Hebrews and the Persians/Babylonians used a *Tishri 1 (Sept/Oct) inauguration day for each year of a King's reign.* Both the Hebrews and the Babylonians used essentially the same method to begin and end a king's reign.

Hebrews in 5th Century BC	Persians/ Babylonians in 5th Century BC
* Started calendar Civil Year on Tishri 1	* Started Calendar Year on Nisan 1
* Started Religious calendar Year on Tishri 1	* Started official yearly reign of Kings on Tishri 1
* Started official yearly reign of Kings on Tishri 1	* Used an Accession Year system
* Used an Acession Year System	

From Ezra 7:9a, we know that Ezra left Babylon in the seventh year of Artaxerxes I reign, on the 1st day of the 1st month, but the Biblical record is silent in recording any *calendar year* or the *name* of the *first month.*

> *...in the reign of Artaxerxes, King of Persia, the King granted him all his requests... This Ezra went up from Babylon.... for upon the first day of the first month began he to go up from Babylon... In the 7th year of Artaxerxes, the King*   Ezra 7: 6-9

Ezra was a Hebrew, and he would know that there were two New Year days recognized by Israel. One was on *Tishri* 1 (Civil Year) and the other on *Nisan* 1 (Religious Year). The Babylonians only had one New Year's Day and it was Nisan 1. If Ezra was writing for the Jews (and He certainly was), then what did he use for the 1st day of the 1st month?

Depending upon which reference point was being used by Ezra, the seventh year of Artaxerxes could be off by one year. Hence, imminent scholars are divided upon exactly when Ezra left Babylon in the 7th year of Artaxerxes reign. Some defend a 458 BC date and some dogmatically defend a 457 BC date. *So, which is to be believed?*

There is a valuable clue in the Book of Ezra. In Ezra 7:8, he writes that *he arrived in the 5th month of the Kings 7th year of reign.* If we could accurately determine the 1st official year of Artaxerxes reign, we could easily determine the 7th year of his reign. We will shortly show beyond any doubt that the king who issued the decree was indeed Artaxerxes I and that his 7th year of reign was Tishri 1, 458 BC – Tishri 1, 457 BC.

The Reign of Artaxerxes I

The critical issue is: *How can the 7th year of Artaxerxes reign be determined?* Nebuchadnezzar was king of Babylon...He was actually a Persian appointed king...and to restate known facts he was living under a calendar which started each calendar year on Nisan 1 (March/April) and the reign of each king on Tishri 1 (September/October). The Babylon Kings used an *accession* system to determine how one king transitioned to the next... his *actual reign* could start any time after the death of a previous king, but his *credited years* always started on the first Tishri 1 after the death of the previous King.

The 70-week prophecy of Daniel (490 years) revealed that the Messiah would appear after 483 years had passed from when Ezra was given a decree from the king to return to Jerusalem. Every biblical scholar has Christ beginning His ministry in the month of September /October in the month of Tishri. This is because he was crucified in the month of Nisan about 3.5 years later. As previously discussed, if 483 solar years were to fully pass until He arrived at the River Jordan in 26 AD, it is obvious that the decree *must* have been issued in September/October in 458 BC.... (458+26-1) = 483 years. We have already shown that the king who issued this decree must have been Artaxerxes I.

[6] *This Ezra went up from Babylon; and he was a ready scribe in the law of Moses, which the LORD God of Israel had given: and the king granted him all his request, according to the hand of the LORD his God upon him.*
[7] *And there went up some of the children of Israel, and of the priests, and the Levites, and the singers, and the porters, and the Nethinims, unto Jerusalem, in the seventh year of Artaxerxes the king.*
[8] *And he came to Jerusalem in the fifth month,* **which was in the seventh year of the king**.
[9] *For* **upon the first day of the first month began he to go up from Babylon**, *and on the* **first day of the fifth month came he to Jerusalem**, *according to the good hand of his God upon him* Ezra 6: 6-9

We now need to prove that *if* the 7th year of Artaxerxes reign was September 1, 458 BC – September 1, 457 BC... his 1st year of reign must have been September 1, 464 BC – September 1, 463 BC. Sound exegesis must prove...or at least present sound evidence... that this is true.

The most acceptable solution is to carefully examine all biblical, historical and archeological records to determine when Artaxerxes began his 1st year of reign, and when he issued the decree to Ezra in the seventh year of his reign. We are quite certain that a Persian King named *Xerxes* preceded Artaxerxes. Xerxes was the biological father of Artaxerxes. All historical records record that Xerxes is known to be the Babylonian King for 21 years, between 486 BC and 465 BC. It is also known that the Persian King Xerxes was assassinated in 465 BC. He was resigning in Babylon during the ministry of both Ezra and Nehemiah. The main source for what actually took place is attributed to an extensive study by a Historical Research Committee of 11 biblical scholars in 1945, led by S. H. Horn and L. H. Wood. They studied over 100 ancient documents 1953, and then published a book called: *The Chronology of Ezra 7*. Much of the following material was derived from their work.

It is certain that King Xerxes was assassinated in 465 BC. There are two different accounts of his murder from ancient documents. The controversy surrounds not *if* but *when* the assassination took place. Regardless of when the assassination took place, Xerxes was murdered by a powerful courtier of his court called *Artabanus* who wanted to usurp the king. He then had the oldest brother of Artaxerxes (Darius) assassinated, and also planned to assassinate Artaxerxes; but his plan was discovered and Artabanus was executed. No record has ever been found that credits Artabanus as a reigning king of Persia, but a second-century historian called Mantheo wrote that a power struggle did indeed take place between Artabanus and Artaxerxes. However, Mantheo wrote his comments more than 500 years after the fact.

There have been two different scenarios which have been set forth. The *first* is that Artabanus assassinated Xerxes in early August of 465 BC. Xerxes had two sons who were heir-apparent. The oldest and crown prince was *Darius*. Artabanus went to Artaxerxes and told him that Darius had murdered his father so that he could ascend to the throne. To avenge his father, Artaxerxes arranged to have Darius killed. Artabanus now only had one man standing between him and the throne.... Artaxerxes. Artabanus then made plans to assassinate Artaxerxes, but a friend came to Artaxerxes and told him of the evil plot. Artaxerxes then killed Artabanus with a knife. Now consider the timeline. if Xerxes was murdered in early August, then *Darius* would immediately ascend to the throne as crown prince. If Darius was killed by Artaxerxes *before Tishri 1*, he (Artaxerxes) would officially begin his rule as king Tishri 1, 465 BC. The short time between the death of Darius and the ascension of Artaxerxes would be called the "accession year" of Artaxerxes. If Darius was not murdered until *after Tishri 1*, he (Darius) would be credited with one year of reign even if he reigned just one day! At that point, using the *accession year* system, Artaxerxes would become the *defacto* king and his accession year would be over 11 months long. His 1st credited year of reign would begin on Tishri 1, 464 BC and end on Elul

	Tishri 1 Start Date
Year	
1	Tishri 1, 465 BC - Elul 29, 464 BC
2	Tishri 1, 464 BC - Elul 29, 463 BC
3	Tishri 1, 463 BC - Elul 29, 462 BC
4	Tishri 1, 462 BC - Elul 29, 461 BC
5	Tishri 1, 461 BC - Elul 29, 460 BC
6	Tishri 1, 460 BC - Elul 29, 459 BC
7	Tishri 1, 459 BC - Elul 29, 458 BC
8	Tishri 1, 458 BC - Elul 29, 457 BC
	Tishri 1 (Sept/Oct)

29, 463 BC. This scenario would make Tishri 1, 458 BC – Tishri 1, 457 BC his 7th year of reign.

There are no known records or documents which credit Darius as ever reigning as king. Artabanus would never be credited with any reign because he did not ever ascend to the throne. As far as I can tell, no one has ever discussed this dilemma in any detail.

The 2nd scenario that has been proposed is that Xerxes was *not* assassinated in August of 365 BC but was murdered in early December several months later. Note almost all chronologists list 465 BC as Xerxes last year...which would be true in either case. Why would one choose to believe this second scenario? *Is there any evidence that Xerxes survived until he was assassinated in December of 365 BC and received credit for the last year of Tishri 1, 465 BC - Tishri 1, 464 BC?* The possibility that Xerxes' death did not occur earlier than December 1, 465 BC rests upon a famous double-dated document written in Egypt on January 1/2, 464 BC called *AP 6*. This document bears the following date line: "on the 18th of Kislev, in the Egyptian month of Thoth, in year 21 (Reign of Xerxes) King Artaxerxes *began to sit* upon the throne. Thoth was the 1st month of the Egyptian calendar and it is equated with the Babylonian date of Kislev 18 which was December 7 in 465 BC. This document also contains information that clearly establishes that it was written in the *accession year* of Artaxerxes I. Unfortunately, the day number of the month Thoth is broken. The digits of that number could be restored to 7, 14, or 17 on paleographic grounds, but only the 17th of Thoth harmonizes with the 18th of Kislev and the proposed death of Xerxes. The 17th of Thoth fell on January 2/3, 464 BC, sunrise to sunrise. It is thus clear that by January 2, 464 BC, the news of Artaxerxes' accession had reached Egypt. It appears that the scribe of AP 6, having been in the habit of dating documents in the 21st year of Xerxes for several months, started out to do this and then finished the date line by adding the year of Artaxerxes' accession (Horn and Wood). Although the exact death date of Xerxes will probably never be known, it is virtually certain that his death occurred near the end of the year in the month of December, 465 BC. By January 1/2, 464 BC the news of his son's accession had reached Egypt.

Horn and Wood provide other supporting evidence that the 2nd scenario concerning the death of Xerxes is correct. The December date of Xerxes' death comes from a cuneiform tablet found in an excavation of Ur in the Chaldees in 1930-1931, The tablet, which was uncovered in an archeological evacuation, was an agreement among four brothers who were dividing one section of land into four pieces. The agreement is dated in the 13th year of Artaxerxes I, but states that the original land division was signed in the Babylonian month of Kislimu (November/December) in the 21st year of Xerxes. In that year Kislimu began, (according to the Parker-Dubberstein tables), on December 17. This document, along with the double - dated papyrus from the Jewish settlement of Elephantine in Egypt, can be used to confidently state that:

- Xerxes was not assassinated until sometime in December, 465 BC

- His death was rapidly followed by that of Darius, so that Darius did not even have time to claim his right to rule as crown prince.

- The usurper Artabanus was murdered by Artaxerxes within days after his brother Darius was accused of murdering Xerxes.

- The news of Xerxes death had not reached Egypt until late, 465 BC in December (Horn and Wood), and a scribe in Elephantine wrote that Artaxerxes was in his accession year on January 1/2 in 464 BC.

- The last credited year of reign for Xerxes would be Tishri 1, 465 BC to Elul 29, 464 BC by the accession system. The accession "year" of Artaxerxes would be from the death of Xerxes in December of 465 BC to Tishri 1 in 464 BC.

- On Tishri 1, 464 BC Artaxerxes began his 1st day of official reign.

- The 7th year of Artaxerxes would begin on Tishri 1, August 28, 458 BC (Prolyptic date on Gregorian Calendar). The decree that authorized Ezra to return to Jerusalem would be *after* His 7th year had started. We will show in Chapter 3 that the decree to Ezra was **likely issued to Ezra** on Tishri 19, September 15, 458 BC.

Regnal Years of Artaxexes I	
Year	
1	Tishri 1, 464 BC - Elul 29, 463 BC
2	Tishri 1, 463 BC - Elul 29, 462 BC
3	Tishri 1, 462 BC - Elul 29, 461 BC
4	Tishri 1, 461 BC - Elul 29, 460 BC
5	Tishri 1, 460 BC - Elul 29, 459 BC
6	Tishri 1, 459 BC - Elul 29, 458 BC
7	Tishri 1, 458 BC - Elul 29, 457 BC
8	Tishri 1, 457 BC - Elul 29, 456 BC
9	Tishri 1, 456 BC - Elul 29, 455 BC
10	Tishri 1, 455 BC - Elul 29, 454 BC
11	Tishri 1, 454 BC - Elul 29, 453 BC
12	Tishri 1, 453 BC - Elul 29, 452 BC
13	Tishri 1, 452 BC - Elul 29, 451 BC
20	Tishri 1, 445 BC - Elul 29, 444 BC

- Ezra would be leaving Babylon forever, and it would likely take him sometime to assemble his personal belongings, gather Jews from other tribes and persuade the Levitical priesthood to return to Jerusalem (Ezra 8-9).

- Ezra **left Babylon** on the 1st day of the 1st month and **arrived** in Jerusalem on the 1st day of the 5th month....in the 7th year of Artaxerxes. This departure could not be on Tishri 1, 458 BC because a decree issued prior to Tishri 1 would not be in year 7. This leaves only one possible alternative: Ezra must have left on Nisan 1, March 21 (Gregorian) in 457 BC and arrived in Jerusalem on Av 1, July 17, four months later. Note that all of these things were in the 7th year of Artaxerxes reign as required

Logical and Practical Evidence

The astute reader might have noticed something unusual. The 1st month in the *Babylonian* calendar year is *Nisan*, and the 1st month of the *Jewish* religious year is also *Nisan 1*. Therefore, the departure date from Babylon and the arrival date in Jerusalem synchronizes with both the Babylonian and the Hebrew calendar. Everything fits like a glove. We now have determined that:

- The last year of Xerxes reign was Tishri 1, 465 - Elul 29, 464 BC.

- The first year of Artaxerxes reign was Tishri 1, 464 BC - Elul 29, 463 BC. The 7th year of Artaxerxes reign was 458 BC - 457 BC. | 7 | **Tishri 1, 458 BC - Elul 29, 457 BC** |

- Xerxes was murdered in December, 465 BC and not in August of 465 BC. September 1, 465 BC - Elul 29, 464 BC was his 21st year of credited reign.

- By December 17, 465 BC, Darius and Xerxes had both been murdered:

- Artabanus was killed by Artaxerxes; certainly before January, 464 BC.

- The double-dated Egyptian Elephantine document AP 6 and the Tablet recovered from Ur both testify that by January 1/2, 464 BC Artaxerxes was in his accession year.

- Artaxerxes 1st year of official reign began on Tishri 1, 464 BC and ended on Elul 29, 463 BC. The 7th year of his reign began on Tishri 1, 458 BC and ended on Elul 29 in 457 BC.

- We will show that Ezra received permission to return to Jerusalem on Tishri 19 in 458 BC, 19 days after Artaxerxes 7th year of reign began on Tishri 1 458 BC.

- Ezra left Jerusalem on Nisan 1, March 21 in 457 BC and arrived in Jerusalem on Av 1, July 17 (Gregorian proleptic date) in 457 BC. Both dates fall in the 7th regnal year of Artaxerxes as required

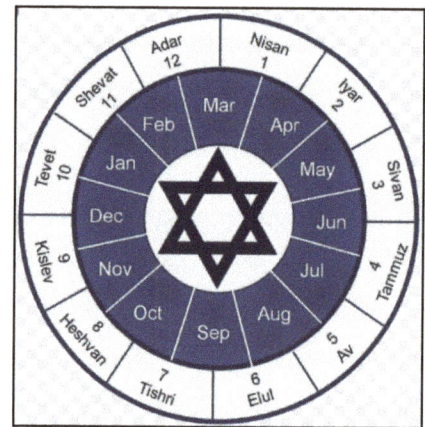

The Arrival of Messiah 483 Years After the Decree of Artaxerxes

It is obvious that if the 490-year prophecy of Daniel began in September of 458 BC when Artaxerxes issued a decree to Ezra allowing him to return to Jerusalem, then Christ started his ministry in September of 26 AD, and 483 Hebrew calendar years would elapse between these two points in time. Note again that one year must be subtracted from the calculated time span because there is no year zero and one year must be subtracted when crossing from BC to AD. It is certain that Ezra arrived in Jerusalem on the 1st day of the 5th month in the 7th regnal year of Artaxerxes reign (Ezra 7:9). Ezra left Babylon in the fall of 458 BC and arrived in Jerusalem 5 months later, *both* in the 7th year of Artaxerxes official reign. This is *impossible* if the 7th year of Artaxerxes was 459 BC to 458 BC. In fact, it can be seen that the 7th regnal year of Artaxerxes *must be* Tishri 1, 458 BC - Elul 29, 457 BC to satisfy all scriptural requirements. As previously shown, Ezra would have left Babylon on Nisan 1, 457 BC and

Regnal Years of Artaxexes I	
Year	
1	Tishri 1, 464 BC - Elul 29, 463 BC
2	Tishri 1, 463 BC - Elul 29, 462 BC
3	Tishri 1, 462 BC - Elul 29, 461 BC
4	Tishri 1, 461 BC - Elul 29, 460 BC
5	Tishri 1, 460 BC - Elul 29, 459 BC
6	Tishri 1, 459 BC - Elul 29, 458 BC
7	Tishri 1, 458 BC - Elul 29, 457 BC
8	Tishri 1, 457 BC - Elul 29, 456 BC
9	Tishri 1, 456 BC - Elul 29, 455 BC
10	Tishri 1, 455 BC - Elul 29, 454 BC
11	Tishri 1, 454 BC - Elul 29, 453 BC
12	Tishri 1, 453 BC - Elul 29, 452 BC
13	Tishri 1, 452 BC - Elul 29, 451 BC
20	Tishri 1, 445 BC - Elul 29, 444 BC

arrived in Babylon about 3.5 months later on Av 1, 457 BC. The decree had to have been issued before he left and no earlier than Tishri 1, 458 BC by Artaxerxes. These inescapable facts show that the 1ˢᵗ official year of Artaxerxes was not Tishri 1, 465 BC to Elul 29, 464 BC, but must be Tishri 1, 464 BC to Elul 29, 463 BC. In fact, this is the only year that will work using the Hebrew calendar or the Babylonian Calendar. Phillips has written two books which show beyond a reasonable doubt that Christ began his earthly ministry on *Tishri 15* which was the 1ˢᵗ day of the *Feast of Tabernacles*. This has also been show to be true by Fred R. Coulter, *The Appointed Times of Jesus the Messiah* and *The Day That Jesus Christ Died.* (See also Richard S. Thompson, http://www.hfbcbiblestudy.org/; Major Dan, https://www.historyandheadlines.com/april-7-30-ad-crucifixion-death-jesus-christ-think/ C. D. Franklin, and many others).

The Birth of Christ and the Daniel Prophecy

Phillips and others have proposed and presented convincing evidence to support a Nisan 14 (Wednesday, April 6) *30 AD crucifixion date* for Jesus Christ. The year 30 AD falls in the middle of Daniel's 70ᵗʰ week, which is approximately 486.5 years since the 490-year prophecy started (Danial 9: 26-27). Clearly, this leaves 3.5 years to finish the prophecy. Many modern prophecy teachers allow the 70-7's to expire on Tishri 1 (Sept/Oct) of 33 AD. The event designated to end the prophecy is proposed to be the stoning of Stephen in Acts 6, but there is actually no real evidence to support this conjecture. Proponents of this theory (rightly so) identify this event as the final act of rejection of Jesus Christ as the promised Messiah by the Corporate Nation of Israel. From this point on, the message of salvation under the New Covenant passed to the Gentiles. We totally reject the logic which ends Daniel's 70ᵗʰ week in 33 AD based upon two platforms. *First*, we have already discussed in some detail the things which must be completed before Daniel's 70 weeks of years expires, and several things can only be accomplished at the second advent of Jesus Christ. This reason is enough to reject the *Steven hypothesis*. A *second* and more compelling reason is the stoning of Steven. In Acts 1-2 we are told how the Holy Spirit fell on the Feast of Pentecost, 50 days after the resurrection. Chapter 3 records a post-Pentecost miracle, the healing of a lame man, followed by Peter's sermon. Chapters 4:1 - 6:7 are concerned with the beginning of persecutions and the preparation for spreading the gospel. Acts 6: 8 records how Steven *full of faith and power* did *great wonders and miracles.* The Jewish leaders turned against him, fearing that he would *destroy this place, and change the customs.* At this point Stephen delivered perhaps the most powerful sermon that was possibly ever preached (Acts 7: 1-53). When he finished his discourse, the Jews cast him out of the city and stoned him. So, Steven became the first Christian to be martyred, and it likely happened shortly after the day of Pentecost. *Third*: The conversion of Paul (Saul) is recorded in Acts 9. This must have been within a year after Christ was crucified. Saul had witnessed the crucifixion of Christ, and the stoning of Steven. He then received a letter from Rome to further persecute and kill any Jew who would follow after Christ. It is unlikely that the stoning of Steven took place 3.5 years after the crucifixion. The last and most important reason is that when Christ was crucified on Passover, Nisan 14 in 30 AD He cried out that: *It is finished.* The agony, torture and persecution on the Cross of Calvary was finished......The sin issue was finished....and the Old Covenant was finished. Less than 24 hours earlier at the Lord's Last Supper, He arose and passed a Cup of Wine around to all of His apostles. He clearly said: *This is my blood of the New Testament, which is shed for many for the remission of sins* Matthew 26:28 In the original Greek language this should read:

28	τοῦτο	γάρ	ἐστιν	τὸ	αἷμά	μου	,	τῆς	διαθήκης	,	τὸ		περὶ	πολλῶν
	This	for	is	the	blood	of Me		of the	covenant		-		for	many

ἐκχυννόμενον	εἰς	ἄφεσιν	ἁμαρτιῶν .
being poured out	for	forgiveness	of sins

When Jesus Christ died on the Cross of Calvary He died for the forgiveness of all sins, and his sacrificial death initiated (by His own words) the **New Covenant**. The Dispensation of the Law and the Old Covenant was finished and the New Covenant had begun. Note that up until this point in time that Jesus had gone to the Jews first, but now He would turn to the Gentiles. This and the Age of Grace was completely hidden and unknown to the Jews....It was a mystery revealed by the Apostle Paul. Salvation would now be by faith and grace, to both Jew and Gentiles alike. Please do not miss the implication of this truth. God had been dealing with the Jews ever since the Daniel prophecy began in 458 BC. He continued to deal with the Jews...not the Gentiles...until Christ was crucified on the Cross of Calvary.

These twelve Jesus sent forth, and commanded them, saying: **Go not into the way of the Gentiles**, *and into any city of the Samaritans* **enter ye not**   Matthew 10:12

Daniel 9:24-27 is a Jewish prophecy, and when God turned away from the Jews and offered salvation to the Gentiles, the 70th week of Daniel would be interrupted before it would resume again. This suspension or interruption of Daniel's 70th Week is called the *gap theory* in the sequential fulfillment of the 490-year prophecy.

The entire church age is a *gap in time* which was not known before Paul revealed its mystery. *When will God once more begin dealing with the corporate Jews*? Most prophecy scholars agree that the 70th week of Daniel will be resumed when the *Great Tribulation* begins.

We have already thoroughly discussed the things that were to be accomplished by the end of Daniel's 70th week, and not all of those things will not be *fully accomplished* until the end of the age of grace, or the church age. Daniels last week (7 years) of the 70-week prophecy is not interrupted with 7 years remaining when He came to be baptized by John, but it would continue for another 3.5 years as Christ preached to the Jews...not to the Gentiles. This left 3.5 years yet to pass which will begin when God resumes his dealing with the nation of Israel. This will be the great tribulation period which will begin when Satan is cast down from heaven (Revelation 12:9), the Antichrist and false prophet arise (Revelation 13: 1-14), and the peace covenant is terminated with Israel (Isaiah 28: 15-18). This is when God will resume His efforts to heal and redeem Israel. As the tribulation period unfolds, it will last only 3.5 years; which is the last half of Daniel's 70th week of years (Revelation 12:14).

Why has this been so hard to believe? the earthly ministry of Christ as recorded in Matthew, Mark, Luke and John was to the JEWS...not the Gentiles. Once this is understood, it is inconceivable that these 3.5 years would not be contiguously contained within the initial part of Daniels 70-Week prophecy to the Jews, and that the last 7 years of the Daniel prophecy must be interrupted as God turns to the gentiles. *Does this fit with the duration of the Great Tribulation?* Not only does it fit, but it makes perfect sense. The Wrath of Satan and the Wrath of God does not take place until after Satan is cast down to earth in Revelation 12. The Antichrist will not arise until Revelation 13. Satan is allowed to persecute all Jews and Gentiles for approximately 3.5 years.

Conclusions

It has always intrigued this author that the earthly ministry of Jesus Christ lasted 3.5 years, and that the period of time that Satan will attack and kill as many Christians as he can in the Great Tribulation is also 3.5 years in duration. This now makes perfect sense once it is realized that the 70-week prophecy of Daniel is dealing with a prophecy to the *Jews*, and no one else, *and* that the earthly ministry of Christ began 483 years after Nebuchadnezzar issued a decree to Ezra the scribe in 458 BC. Christ will be dealing with the Jews for another 3.5 years until He is crucified. There will then be a "gap in time" as God turns to the Gentiles and the Church Age begins to come to an end. The last 3.5 years of Daniels prophecy is when Satan begins His 3.5-year reign of terror against all Jews and Christians. Before these last 3.5 years of the Daniel prophecy begin, there will be tribulation as prophesied by Christ in Matthew 24. Christ Himself said that we are to be aware that this persecution is *not the end*.

[7] *For nation shall rise against nation, and kingdom against kingdom: and there shall be famines, and pestilences, and earthquakes, in divers places.*
[8] *All these are the **beginning of sorrows***   Matthew 24: 7-8

*Study to shew thyself approved unto God, a workman that need not to be ashamed, **rightly** dividing the word of truth*   II Timothy 2:16

The last half of Daniels 70th week will now be examined in great detail.

Chapter 3

The Daniel Prophecy and The Great Tribulation

In about 90 AD the Apostle John was called to heaven where He was shown how the church age or the Age of Grace would come to an end. He recorded what he had seen in the Book of Revelation. Those things which he *saw* and wrote down will not be completely discussed in this book. They are covered in great detail in other publications (Phillips, The Book of Revelation; *Mysteries Revealed*). We will discuss the role of the 7 seals, the 7 trumpets and the 7 bowls in Chapter 4.

Daniel, Shadrach and Meshack were among the 1st Jewish men taken into captivity. After many years, Daniel knew by reading *books* that God had allowed Babylon to conquer the Southern Kingdom of Judah and decreed that they would remain in captivity for 70 years because they had failed to observe 70 Sabbatical years of rest for the land over a 490-year period of time. Daniel knew from reading *books* that the 70 years of Babylonian captivity was nearing an end, and he was concerned about the fate of his brethren the Israelites and the Jews. Daniel prayed and asked God to reveal their fate. *Was He through with His chosen people?* Gabriel assured Daniel that although they had rebelled against God and refused to follow His laws and commands, that He had not cast them aside. Daniel was given a prophecy concerning the Jews which reached from that point in time to the end of what we now know is the Great Tribulation. This was the *Daniel 70-Week Prophecy*, sometimes called the *Daniel 490-year Prophecy*. The Daniel 70-year prophecy would reach far into the future and include both the 1st and 2nd coming of Christ. He would appear the 1st time to offer forgiveness of sins and salvation to all who would believe in faith that He was the Son of God. He would preach a ministry of reconciliation for 3.5 years to the Jews. After those 3.5 years, He would be rejected by the Jews and be crucified on the Cross of Calvary for the not only the sins of the Jews but the whole world… Jews and Gentiles alike. When He was rejected by the people and the Jewish spiritual leaders, He would turn to the Gentiles to preach the good news to Jews and Gentiles alike. Salvation would no longer be by works under the Law but would come by faith and grace. When Christ was crucified, this act of rebellion would launch what we call the *Church Age*. At this point in time, God turned away from the Jews and turned to the Gentiles. What Jesus Christ offered was called the *New Covenant*, and when it began it would interrupt or suspend the 70-week or 490-year Daniel prophecy. This created a *gap* in the 490 years that had been allocated to the Jews and the City of Jerusalem to fulfill their destiny and return to a covenant relationship with Jehovah God. God then turned His face from the Jews until the Great Tribulation begins. The period of Tribulation which was prophesied by Jesus Christ in his Olivet Discourse will begin when Satan and all of His fallen angels are cast down to earth by Michael and his Holy Angels (Revelation 12). Satan will be defeated in a great celestial conflict, confined to this earth, and in great wrath he will war against both Christians and Jews in an attempt to destroy both. This period of warfare will be a time, times and a half-a-time or 3.5 years in duration.

The 490-year prophecy given to Daniel will begin with a decree to Ezra in 458 BC to return to Jerusalem from Babylonian Captivity, establish the judiciary and rebuild the Temple and the city which had been destroyed. (1) From when this decree to return is issued, it would take 7 weeks of years (49 years) to rebuild Jerusalem and the Temple… in perilous times. (2) After those 49 years had been completed, another 62 weeks (434) years would elapse until Messiah the Prince (Jesus Christ) would appear at the River Jordan to be Baptized and begin His 3.5 years Ministry of Reconciliation (3) Jesus would preach salvation to the Jews over this 3.5-year period of time, but He would be rejected. He would be Crucified on the Cross of Calvary and initiate the New Covenant. The total number of years that would elapse from when the decree was issued by Artaxerxes until the sacrificial death of Jesus Christ would be period of (49+434+3.5) = 486.5 years. God had been dealing with Israel for 486.5 years, but after the Crucifixion of His Son He turned to the Gentiles. When God turned to the Gentiles the Daniel 490-year prophecy was interrupted for an unknown period of time (almost 2000 years now) for the Body of Christ to preach the Good News and offer Salvation to Jews and Gentiles alike. God had been dealing with Israel for 486.5 years, but after the Crucifixion of His Son He turned to the Gentiles. The Daniel 490-year prophecy was interrupted for an unknown time (almost 2000 years now) for the Body of Christ…His church…to preach the Good News and offer Salvation to Jews and Gentiles alike. (3) The time which remained in the Daniel 490-year prophecy is 3.5 years. This final period of time will commence at an unknown time yet future. These 3.5 years are what is called the *Great Tribulation.*

After 3.5 years of persecution, tribulation and wrath, God will send His Son Jesus Christ to defeat Satan and his unholy forces at the Battle of Armageddon. It is at this time that: *all Israel will turn back to God and be saved.* This gap in time which began when Christ suffered and died on the Cross of Calvary will end with 3.5 years left in the Age of Grace, and God will again begin dealing with His beloved Jews. *When did all of this begin?*

We have shown in Chapter 2 that the 490 prophecy to Daniel was issued by Nebuchadnezzar, King of Babylon, in his 7th year of reign which was September 1, 458 BC - September 1, 457 BC. We will now show *when* this decree was issued and how the duration of the Great Tribulation will be affected. What we know from Chapter 2 is summarized in the following diagram.

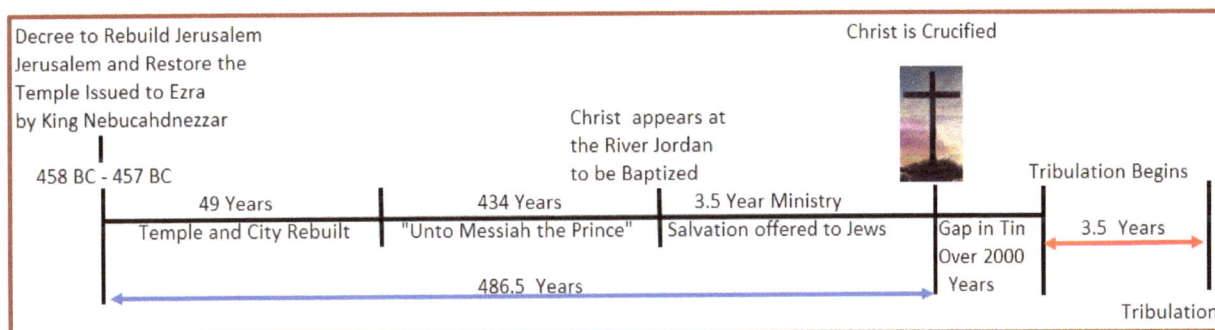

A crucifixion date of Jesus Christ is well known to be on Nisan 14 which is the Day of Passover. The year which Christ was born has been investigated and using biblical clues, Jewish historical writings and astronomical records and has been found to be in 5 BC on Tishri 15, which was on the 1st day of the Feast of Tabernacles (Phillips, The Birth of Christ: *A Forensic Analysis*, Phillips, *The Birth and Death of Jesus Christ*). It is well known and accepted that Christ died on the Feast of Passover: what is disputed is the year in which Christ was crucified. If Jesus Christ was born in 5 BC, then He would have died in 30 AD. Other biblical scholars have investigated the birth and death of Christ and reached the same conclusion (Coulter, F.R., *The Day Jesus the Christ Died*: Bond H., *Dating the Death of Jesus*, Edinburgh University, England; D. G. Waddington, *Dating the Crucifixion* and others… Meir J. P.: Dunn J. D.: and C. G. Humphreys, to name a few. In a recent publication, Oral Roberts University claim that over 60 % of all Biblical scholars support a 30 AD crucifixion. The central issue is whether or not Jesus Christ spent 3 full days and 3 full nights in the grave as He said he would. Based upon widespread belief and two previous books by the author, Nisan 14 in 30 AD is accepted as the day that Jesus Christ was crucified.

> **Authors Comment:** If Christ was born on the Feast of Tabernacles (September/October) on Tishri 15 in 5 BC, then Mary would have conceived about 270 days earlier on or around December 25. December 25 was not the birth date of Christ. Although Jesus Christ was born of a virgin with supernatural insemination, the miracle was not the birth of Christ. Christ was born of Mary just like every other Child was born. The real miracle was the insemination of the virgin Mary without physical intercourse.

The Day and Date of The Crucifixion

The same Hebrew Calendar which is in use today was being used in the first century AD. It is believed to be the same calendar used since the Exodus from Egypt, but that is not important to the following calculations.

It is known with certainty that Christ died on the Feast of Passover, Nisan 14. The day of the

Week and the month can be determined by modern computer programs. Using the Abdicate program introduced in Chapter 2, the date of Nisan 14 in 30 AD is easily determined:

Note that Nisan 14 in 30 AD was Wednesday, April 5 on the Roman calendar which was in use by Rome at that time. The modern Gregorian Calendar was not in use at that time, but if it was, the Gregorian date would be April 3, 30 AD. there are two other displayed pieces of information which are very important to Biblical

Gregorian:	**April 3, 30 (ante** [1]**)**
Julian:	**April 5, 30**
Jewish:	**Nisan 14, 3790**
	י"ד בניסן ג'תשצ"
SDN:	**1732110.5** [2]
Weekday:	**Wednesday**

researchers. Every Jewish calendar year is sequentially numbered; 30 AD is identified as # 3790. Every Jewish day is also numbered and in 30 AD, Nisan 14 was day # 1732110.5 (Hebrew days start at 6:00 PM). For example: *When would Nisan 14* (Feast of Passover) *occur in 33 AD?*

Gregorian:	**April 1, 33 (ante** [1]**)**
Julian:	**April 3, 33**
Jewish:	**Nisan 14, 3793**
	י"ד בניסן ג'תשצ"ג
SDN:	**1733204.5** [2]
Weekday:	**Friday**

Nisan 14 would on April 1 (proleptic Gregorian date) or April 3 (Julian date). 33 AD is Jewish/Hebrew year #3793 and the Jewish calendar day of Nisan 14 in 33 AD is #1733204.5 The number of days between Nisan 14 in 30 AD and Nisan 14 in 33 AD is (1733204.5-1732110.5) = 1094 days. The weekday of Nisan 14 in 30 AD was Wednesday, and the weekday of Nisan 14 in 33 AD was

Friday. Incidentally, this was the day and date that Hoehner calculated was the crucifixion of Jesus Christ. This is also the day and date that the Roman Catholic church dogmatically claims is the crucifixion of Christ. There is no doubt that Christ was crucified at 3:00 PM and was placed in the tomb before 6:00 on Nisan 14. The month of Nisan in 33 AD is shown below.

Nisan

S	M	T	W	T	F	S
						1
2	3	4	5	6	7	8
9	10	11	12	13	14	15
16	17	18	19	20	21	22
23	24	25	26	27	28	29
30						

Christ would have spent Friday Night (6:00 PM-6:00 AM) … Saturday Day (6:00 AM-6:00 PM) … Saturday Night (6:00 AM-6:00 PM) and would be resurrected by God on the morning of Sunday, Nisan 16. Christ said:

*For as Jonah was **three** days and **three** nights in the whale's belly: so shall the Son of man be **three** days and **three** nights in the heart of the earth* Matthew 12:40

Christ banked his entire ministry upon this verse and He said that this was the *sign* He was the Son of God.

[38] *Then certain of the scribes and of the Pharisees answered, saying, Master, we would see a **sign** from thee.*
[39] *But he answered and said unto them, An evil and adulterous generation seeks after a **sign**; and there shall no **sign** be given to it, but the **sign** of the prophet Jonas*:   Mathew 12: 38-39

How did Hoehner get 3 days and 3 nights out of 2 nights and 1 actual day? Those who believe in a 33 AD, Friday crucifixion say *easy*. Christ was *dead* for about 3 hours before he was placed in the tomb, and since any part of a Jewish day counts as a whole day… These 3 hours were counted as a full 24-hour day… the 1st day and the 1st night. Saturday, Nisan 15 was the 2nd day and night… Sunday night was the 3rd night and it is widely believed that Jesus Christ rose early at sunrise on Sunday, Nisan 16. The period of time that Christ was actually in the tomb was only 36 hours…and not 72 hours as Christ prophesied that He would be. By the *partial day is a full day theory* any part of a 24-hour Jewish day (sunset to sunrise) counts as a full day, Sunday between 6:00 PM and 6:00 AM would count as the 3rd day. If this seems hard to believe…It Is. I reject this logic. Was Christ a liar, or did He just fail to reveal how His 3 days and 3 nights in the grave were to be determined; not just to the Jews and the Pharisees but to all Christians today.

Authors Comment; It should be noted that the 3 days and 3 nights was to begin when Christ was placed in the grave and end when He arose

*For as Jonas was three days and three nights in the whale's belly; so shall the Son of man be three days and three nights **in the heart of the earth*** Matthew 12:40

Hence, only 36 hours were counted as 72 hours by Hoehner and the partial day theorists. Yet, Jesus Christ did not mention any of this when He spoke to the Pharisees. This is difficult to believe. Remember…Christ used this as the only sign he would give to prove that He was the Son of God.

It should be noted that only a 30 AD crucifixion will result in a literal fulfilment of Jesus words. Jesus Christ died on a Wednesday afternoon…He was hastily placed in the grave just before Nisan 15 began at 6:00 PM. He was in the tomb Wednesday-Thursday-Friday night, and the day of Wednesday-Thursday and Friday. See for yourself and believe what you will (Remember, a Hebrew day is 6:00 PM-6:00 AM).

Gregorian: **April 3, 30** (ante [1])
Julian: **April 5, 30**
Jewish: **Nisan 14, 3790**
י"ד בניסן ג'תשצ"
SDN: **1732110.5** [2]
Weekday: **Wednesday**

Nisan						
S	M	T	W	T	F	S
					1	2	3
4	5	6	7	8	9	10
11	12	13	14	15	16	17
18	19	20	21	22	23	24
25	26	27	28	29	30	

The Ministry of Christ

We have hopefully firmly established that Christ was crucified on Wednesday, Nisan 14 on the Feast of Passover in 30 AD. *How does this correlate to the Daniel 490-year prophecy?* We have shown in Chapter 2 that the decree which initiated this prophecy was in the 7th regnal year of Artaxerxes; which was Tishri 1, 458 BC – Tishri 1, 457 BC. However, we were not told the exact day when the decree was issued. Now for some detective work. It has also been established that when Christ was crucified on Nisan 14 in 30 AD, the 490 year prophecy given to Daniel by the angel Gabriel was interrupted or suspended. This is the well-known *Gap Theory*. This gap began on the day of Nisan 15. the *Feast of Passover* on Nisan 14 was *approximately* 486.5 years after the decree was issued (Daniel 9:27). It follows that the rest of Daniel's 70th week would not resume until some point in the distant future. This would be when God once more begins dealing with the Jews and the Great Tribulation will commence. It is a logical conclusion that whenever the suspended Daniel Prophecy begins again; it will resume on Nisan 15 (the 1st day of the Feast of Unleavened Bread). We will examine these conclusions in Chapter 6.

If the 490-year prophecy would have continued uninterrupted: *When would it end?* It would be on the Feast of Yom Kippur (Feast of Atonement) in 34 AD, because this is the same day when the Great Tribulation…the defeat of Satan… and the time, times and half a time … and the end of this age will come to an end. This is the day that Jesus Christ will fight the Battle of Armageddon and the purpose of the Great Tribulation will be fulfilled: *All Israel will be saved.* The Church age will end and the 1000-year Millennial Kingdom is about to begin.

Recall that the last week (7 years) of the Daniel prophecy would begin when Jesus Christ came to be baptized at the River Jordan. But… this date and day is not revealed in the scriptures. However, we do know that if 490 years will start and end on the same *Hebrew* day: Nisan 10. *If* the prophecy was

Gregorian: **September 21, 33** (ante [1])
Julian: **September 23, 33**
Jewish: **Tishrei 10, 3794**
י" בתשרי ג'תשצ"ד
SDN: **1733377.5** [2]
Weekday: **Wednesday**

consecutive… which it is not… it would terminate on a proleptic Gregorian date of September 21, 33 AD (or a Julian calendar date of September 23, 33 AD). The duration of the last 3.5 years of the Tribulation is identical to the number of Jewish Calendar Days between Nisan 14 in 30 AD and the Feast of Yom Kippur in 33 AD. This is: (1733377.5-1732110.5) = 1267 days. For now, note that this scenario would completely and accurately satisfy the 490-year prophecy. It would also demand that the degree from Artaxerxes to Ezra was issued on Tishri 10, in 458 BC exactly 490 Jewish calendar years earlier. It has been shown by Horn and Wood in their landmark that when the Battle of Armageddon does take place on the last Nisan 10, we cannot say what month (September/October) or what day of the week it might take place. Jesus said:

But of that day and hour knoweth no man, no, not the angels of heaven, but my Father only Matthew 24:36

We can assume that the Great Tribulation will start on some future Nisan 15, which is the 1st day of the Feast of Unleavened Bread; and it will end on Tishri 10, which is the Day of Atonement (Battle of Armageddon). In the eternal eyes of God… there is no gap in time. The entire 490 years of the Daniel prophecy will end on Tishri 10 when Satan is defeated at the Battle of Armageddon. Using only the Hebrew calendar, if the Great Tribulation ends on Tishri 10 it will begin on Tishri 10 in 458 BC.

Gregorian:	**September 6, 458 B.C.** (ante [1])
Julian:	**September 11, 458 B.C.** (ante [1])
Jewish:	**Tishrei 10, 3304**
	י׳ בתשרי ג׳ש״ד
SDN:	**1554392.5** [2]
Weekday:	**Monday**

We are certain (Horn and Wood, Theil) that the regnal years of Artaxerxes all started on Tishri 1, and we have shown that the 7th year of Artaxerxes reign was Tishri 1, 458 BC – 457 BC. We are dealing with consecutive Hebrew years and the same Hebrew calendar which was in use in the 1st century AD. The actual day of the week on which Tishri 10 occurred in 458 BC is relatively unimportant. The most important thing is that The Feast of Atonement would initiate the Daniel prophecy and end the Daniel prophecy. Hence, on Tishri 10 in 458 BC, the King issued a decree to Ezra authorizing his return to Jerusalem. This decree initiated the Daniel 70-Week prophecy of 490 years. What a perfect day for Ezra to receive permission to return to Jerusalem. Artaxerxes was celebrating his 7th year of reign and Tishri 10 was the holiest day of the year to the Jews. The important result is that the Tribulation period will last 1267 days. We will now show that his result will have a profound impact on the events which will take place in the Great Tribulation.

Chapter 4

Seals, Bowls and Trumpets

In the Book of Revelation, there are a lot of *sevens*; 7 churches (Revelation 2-3), 7 angels (Revelation 8:2), 7 seals (Revelation 6: 1-7, 8: 1-5), 7 trumpets (Revelation 8: 6-13, 9:1-21, 11: 15-19) and 7 bowls (Revelation 16: 1-21). In this chapter we will examine the definition of the seven seals, trumpets and bowls. After these are defined and discussed, we will then show how they are chronologically linked to each other in Chapter 5.

The Seven Sealed Scroll

In Revelation Chapter 5 John saw a book (scroll) that is sealed with 7 royal seals. In Revelation 5:1 we are introduced to a *strong angel* who asks: *Who is worthy to open the book and to loosen the seals*

> And *I saw in the right hand of Him that sat on the throne a book written within* and on the **backside**, *sealed with 7 seals*
> Revelation 5:1

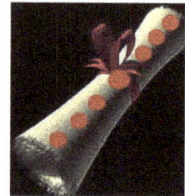

thereof? (Revelation 5:2). An angel proclaimed that *no man in heaven, nor in earth, neither under the earth, was able to open the book, neither to look thereupon* (Revelation 5: 3). The apostle John *wept much because no man was found worthy to open and read the book, neither to look thereon* (Revelation 5:4). *What is in this scroll*? It contains the words of God which describe the events of the Tribulation period. But John and the strong angel were looking for a redeemed man or an angel to open the scroll. One of the 24 elders which surround the throne of God (Revelation 4:5) steps forward and proclaims: ***Weep not: behold, the Lion of the Tribe of Judah, the root of David, hath prevailed to open the book*** (Revelation 5:5). Oh saints, the Lamb is worthy! He is the Son of God who sits in the heavenlies constantly interceding for us and being our advocate. *And he came and took the book out of the right hand of him that sat upon the throne* (Revelation 5:7). One of the interesting things which will be noted at this point is that we will see that the 7 trumpet judgments and the 7 bowl judgments are executed by 7 angels who *stand before God.* (Revelation 8:2; 16:1). According to the apocryphal book of Tobit, there are 7 mighty angels called the *angels of His presence* led by *Raphael.* The seals can only be broken by Jesus Christ. They are successively opened in Revelation 6:1; 6:3; 6:5; 6:7; 6:9; 6:12 and 8:1.

We will now describe what happens when each seal is broken. Seals 1-4 describe general conditions which will characterize the Tribulation period. Seals 5-6 describe several specific events which will take place late in the tribulation period and Seal 7 opens the scroll.

Breaking and Removing The 7 Seals

The 7 Seals which seal the scroll held by God are called *the 7 seal judgments*. This term has created some confusion, since the 7 seals are not actually judgments, but reflect general conditions that will characterize the entire tribulation period. Understanding this is the key to unlocking the correct sequence and order of all events that are described by the Apostle John. God hands the scroll to Jesus Christ who will now break (remove) each one. As Christ removes each seal, John is shown a vision of what is about to take place when the Tribulation begins. The 1st seal is now removed (Revelation 6: 1-2).

Seal 1 *White Horse appears. Satan is the rider. Satan will deceive the nations with lies and deceptions. He will work through both the Antichrist & the False Prophet.* Mat 24:24, Rev 13, Dan11:36-38, I John 2:18, I Thess 5:3	*And I saw, and behold a white horse crown was given to him; and he went forth conquering and to conquer.* Revelation 6:1

The identification of this horse and rider has confused many teachers of prophecy. The rider is often identified as Christ, and the vision a picture of Christ's second coming on a white horse (Revelation 19:11). However, if the rider is Christ, then He rides with Death and Hell (4th seal) and has martyred the saints (5th seal). This is not Christ but Satan. He rides forth looking like he is the long-awaited Jewish Messiah, but he is Satan. He will attack the world for 3.5 years in the form of a person called the *Antichrist*. The second seal brings war and destruction (Revelation 6: 3-4).

Seal 2 *A Fiery Red Horse appears. The rider is the Antichrist. The rider is given a great sword, and he makes war and causes nations to fight nations.* Rev 13:4,7 ; Dan11:36-43	*And there went out another horse that was red: and power was given to him that sat thereon to take peace from the earth, and that they should kill one another: and there was given unto him a great sword* Revelation 6:4

The rider is **the Beast that arises out of the Sea** in Revelation 13:1. This beast is none other than a great world leader who was **wounded to death** (Revelation 13:3), and **his deadly wound was healed: and all the world wondered after this beast**. Satan will completely take over his body and mind, re-creating the death and resurrection of Jesus Christ. As the Antichrist, Satan will conduct a 3.5-year war against all Jews and Christians. This is the Great Tribulation which will end at the Battle of Armageddon.

And they worshipped the dragon (Satan, Revelation 12:9) **which gave power unto the beast** (Revelation 13:1)**, saying who is like unto the beast? Who is able to make war with him?** (Revelation 13:5). This beast is given his power by Satan. **And the dragon gave him his power, and his seat** (in the rebuilt temple... II Thessalonians 2:4), **and great authority** (Revelation 13:2-b). This authority lasts for 1260 days, time-times and half-a-time or 42 months (Revelation 12:9, 12:14 & 13:5; Daniel 12:7). We should point out that during this 1260-day period the 1st 1250 days are known as the **Wrath of Satan** (Revelation 12:12). The Wrath of Satan is the 7 trumpet judgments. The arise of the *Antichrist* and his reign of terror will be described in Chapter 3. He will be Satanically controlled and rule over all the earth, and he will be involved in a blasphemous triangle which is created to mimic God, Jesus Christ and the Holy Spirit. This triumvirate is Satan (the dragon, Revelation 12:9); the antichrist (the beast out of the sea, Revelation 13: 1-2); and the false prophet (the beast out of the earth, Revelation 13:11). They will all meet their destiny at the Battle of Armageddon (Revelation 19:20). Satan will be bound in chains for 1000 years in the *bottomless pit* (Revelation 20:1-2). The antichrist and the false prophet will both be cast into the *Lake of Burning Fire* (Revelation 19:20). Satan will be bound with chains and cast into the *Bottomless Pit* for 1000 years (Revelation 20:2). The last enemies to be destroyed will be **death and hell**, which are both also cast into the Lake of Fire (Revelation 20:14). This is clearly figurative language. **Death**, the last enemy, will be destroyed (I Corinthians 15:26) along with **Hell**, who is identified as Death's escort (Revelation 6:8). The 3rd Seal is now removed (Revelation 6: 5-6).

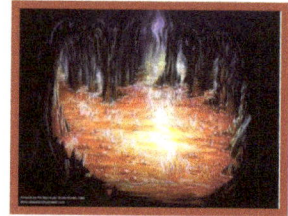

Seal 3	*A black horse appears. The black horse has a rider with a pair of scales in his hand. This horse and rider brings famine and pestilence.* Rev 8:7,10 ; Rev 13:16,17

And I beheld, and lo a black horse, and he that sat upon him had a pair of balances in his hand. And I heard a voice in the midst of the 4 beasts say, A measure of wheat for a penny, and three measures of wheat for a penny; and see that thou hurt not the oil and the wine
Revelation 6: 5-6

As the third seal opens, a black horse appears and a rider Is shown with a scale in his hand. The scale is a symbol that there will be a scarcity of food, and it will be rationed out. This is a direct consequence of two things. *First*, we will see that when the 7th trumpet sounds 1/3 of all the trees are burned up and *all* of the green grass. While it is not directly stated, this indicates that most if not all of the food crops will be burned up also (Revelation 8:7). *Second*, what little food is available cannot be purchased unless one has **the mark of the beast** upon him or her (Revelation 13:17). Be cautioned that if anyone takes the mark of the beast that this will seal his or her fate forever. The punishment will be that anyone who takes the mark of the beast on either their forehead or hand will be thrown into the **Burning Lake of Fire** (Revelation 19:20). The purchase price of a **measure of wheat for a penny** should be translated **measure of wheat for a denarius**, the average daily wage of a Roman worker which was about 16 cents. The 4th Seal is now removed (Revelation 6: 7-8).

Seal 4	*A pale horse appears. It was ridden by "Death" and is followed by Hades. One-fourth of the people on the earth are killed with sword, hunger and the beasts of the earth.* Rev 9:1-12 ; Rev 9:18 ; Rev12:7 ; Rev 13:15 ; Rev 6:10

And I looked and behold a pale horse: and his name that sat upon him was Death, and Hell followed with him. And power was given unto them over the 4th part of the earth, to kill with sword, and hunger, and with death and with the beasts of the earth
Revelation 6: 7-8

As the fourth seal is broken, a **pale horse** appears. The Greek word for **pale** literally means **a sickly green** or a yellowish-green color which seldom appears in nature together. This color is most-often seen in cases of gangrene. Gangrene is a by-product of poor medical care, famine and pestilence. As previously noted, Death and Hell follow the horse and rider. When the 6th seal is removed, it is revealed that ¼ of all the people on earth will be killed. This is a staggering prophecy, over 1.1 billion people in 2020. There are two deaths mentioned in the Bible. The **first death** is a natural death in which the spirit departs from the body and the body lies in the grave. The **second death** is Eternal Separation from God. The Christian has no fear of natural death; it is just a gateway to eternity with our Lord and Savior Jesus Christ. The **second death** is the fate of all who refuse to accept Jesus Christ as their personal savior and reject His free gift of salvation by grace. They will be cast into the **Lake of Burning Fire** where they will be tormented forever (Revelation 19:20). The **second death** will be the fate of all unbelievers, which is to be cast into the **Lake of Fire and Brimstone** (Revelation 20:14).

He that overcometh shall inherit all things, and I will be His God, and he shall be my son. But the fearful and unbelieving, and the abominable, and murderers, and whoremongers, and sorcerers, and idolaters, and all liars, shall have their part in the lake which burns with fire and brimstone: which is the second death. Revelation 21: 7-8

This should forever settle the debate as to whether there is a place of everlasting torment for unbelievers. This does not mean that if you have ever lied, murdered, committed adultery, etc. that you are doomed to the second death: *for we have all sinned and fallen short of the glory of God* (Romans 3:23). What condemns anyone is not believing that Jesus Christ is the son of the Living God, and that He died on the cross for **our sins.** We are delivered from eternal torment to eternal bliss by **faith** and by **grace**.

Note that **Death and Hell** follow closely behind. **Hell** is not well understood by most Christians. In the Bible, the place where departed souls reside is an Old Testament Hebrew word called **sheol.** In the New Testament it is consistently mistranslated as **hell.** This is totally incorrect. Sheol is composed of two distinct compartments where the souls of all dead people temporarily reside: One compartment is called a *place of torments* and the other is called *paradise*. The body goes to the grave at physical death, but the soul lives on in *Sheol*. The soul of all *unbelievers* goes to the *place of torments* and the soul of all *true believers* goes to *paradise*. All *believers* will be Judged at the *Bema Seat Judgment before* the Millennial kingdom begins. All *unbelievers* will be judged at the *Great White Throne judgment after* the 1000-year *Millennial Kingdom*. (These things are discussed and scripturally verified in Phillips: *Life after Death*). The truth of this theology is in the very words of Jesus Christ himself when He hung on the cross of Calvary. Recall that one of the two criminals who hung beside Him asked Jesus to forgive his sins and save him.

And he said unto Jesus, Lord, remember me when thou come into thy kingdom.
        Luke 23:42
Jesus replied:

*Verily I say unto thee. Today thou shalt be with Me in **Paradise*** Luke 23:43

After His physical death on the Cross of Calvary, the body of Jesus Christ was placed in the grave where it remained for 3 days and 3 nights. When Christ died on the cross His mortal soul immediately went to Paradise. There He offered forgiveness of sins and eternal life to all the departed souls who had died in the faith of Abraham who were waiting there.

[8] *Wherefore he saith, when he ascended up on high, he led captivity captive, and gave gifts unto men.*
[9] *(Now that he ascended, what is it but that he also descended first into the lower parts of the earth?*
[10] ***He that descended is the same also that ascended*** *up far above all heavens, that he might fulfill all things.)*   Ephesians 4: 8-10

Those who were already in Paradise when Christ was crucified were born and died under the law, the *Old Covenant*, but like Abraham they were looking forward to a coming Messiah and believed in the promises (Isaiah 9: 6-7, Isaiah 53, Luke 24: 25-26, II Samuel 7: 12-15, Psalms 22).

For he (Abraham) *looked for a city which hath foundations whose builder and maker is God.*
     Hebrews 11:10

Not by the law, but by ***faith,*** was Abraham, Moses, Jacob and all of the Old Testament patriarchs saved. (Read the great Chapter of Faith, Hebrews 11). When Christ died, He *descended* into **Paradise**. For three days and three nights He presented the gospel message to those who were being held captive, and when His body was resurrected His soul rejoined His resurrected body and He *ascended* to **Heaven** as the *First* of the *Firstfruits* (I Corinthians 15:20). After the resurrection of Christ and after He was accepted by God as the perfect Passover Lamb which was offered for all sin (I Peter 2:24), He took ***captives with Him and gave gifts to men*** (Ephesians 4:8). Paradise is now the place where all who have believed in Jesus Christ await what we call the *rapture* at the end of this current age. Before Christ established the New Covenant, the souls of all who died in faith that a Messiah (Jesus Christ) would arise who would permanently forgive their sins *descended* into Sheol to a compartment called Paradise to await His 2nd coming. After His resurrection from the dead, Christ evidently moved Paradise from Sheol to the 3rd heaven where God dwells (Deduced from II Corinthians 12: 2-4). All who die having accepted Jesus Christ as their Lord and Savior now *ascend* to Paradise and rest in the presence of God (II Corinthians 1:4). They will receive their incorruptible resurrection bodies and their rewards at the rapture. As another example of the teachings of Jesus on this subject, consider the following passage in the Book of Luke.

[19] *There was a certain rich man, which was clothed in purple and fine linen, and fared sumptuously every day:*
[20] *And there was a certain beggar named Lazarus, which was laid at his gate, full of sores,*
[21] *And desiring to be fed with the crumbs which fell from the rich man's table: moreover the dogs came and licked his sores.*
[22] *And it came to pass, that the beggar died, and was carried by the angels into Abraham's*

bosom: the rich man also died, and was buried;
[23] *And in hell he lift up his eyes, being in torments, and he saw Abraham afar off, and Lazarus in his bosom.*
[24] *And he cried and said, Father Abraham, have mercy on me, and send Lazarus, that he may dip the tip of his finger in water, and cool my tongue; for I am tormented in this flame*
Luke 16: 19-24

Abraham's bosom was a common Jewish term which is used as a synonym for Paradise ...Luke 23:43, II Corinthians 12: 2-4). The Rabbi's teach that *Paradise* is the place or state of existence where the souls of good men remain from death to the resurrection. The two compartments of Sheol (Abraham's Bosom or *Paradise* and the *Place of Torments* can evidently be seen, one from the other, but there exists a *great gulf* between Paradise and the Place of Torments which cannot be crossed (Luke 16:26). Sheol is always mistranslated as *hell* in the New Testament. The rich man could not only see Lazarus, but he could also see Abraham in Paradise. He called out to Abraham to have mercy on him and send just a small amount of water to sooth his tongue. The response from Abraham was stunning and final.

But Abraham said, son, remember that thou in thy lifetime received thy good things, and likewise Lazarus evil things. But now he is comforted and thou art tormented.
Luke 16:25

Do not misunderstand. The torture of the rich man was not for having worldly possessions or being rich. The reward of Lazarus was not for being poor and being persecuted. The rich man obviously loved his riches and wealth more than he loved Jesus Christ. Lazarus put his faith into the free gift of eternal life, and was awarded the salvation freely offered to all by our Lord Jesus Christ. The message is to Love Christ and not the riches of this world. This passage in God's word also reveals a great truth about the state of death. Both men had sight, hearing and feelings. Both men knew where they were and how they got there. After physical death, there is no such thing as *soul sleep*. The soul lives on in a conscious state of feeling and possesses the ability to think. Luke 16:25 also teaches us that if one dies without accepting Jesus Christ as their Lord and Savior, the soul of that person (which never dies) is cast into the *Place of Torments* where all who reside there await the final judgment

Lay not up for yourselves treasures upon earth, where moth and rust doth corrupt, and where thieves break through and steal: But lay up for yourselves treasures in heaven where neither moth nor rust doth corrupt, and where thieves do not break through nor steal
Matthew 6: 19-20.

A question which begs to be asked is: *Why is the man in torments being tortured at death without first standing before God at the Great White Throne Judgment?* The soul of all unbelievers resides in a place called *torments* where they await final judgment at the Great White Throne Judgment after the 1000-year Millennial Kingdom. All who have accepted Christ as their Lord and savior (true believers) now await their final judgment for rewards at the Bema

Seat Judgment before the Millennial Kingdom begins. The Apostle John further answers this question for us.

He that believeth on him is not condemned: but he that believeth not is condemned already, because he hath not believed in the name of the only begotten Son of God   John 3:18

Christ does not condemn anyone to an eternity of torment…. If anyone rejects the free gift of eternal life by faith and grace, he will be tormented forever after physical death (Revelation 14: 10-11, Matthew 25:46, Revelation 20:10). This is not determined by God…it is a conscious, personal act by anyone during their life upon this earth. If one dies in disbelief, they are condemned already. There is no second chance.

The Four Horsemen of the Apocalypse

Art used by permission by Pat Marvenko Smith, copyright 1992.

The first four seals bring forth four horses with four different riders. These four riders are generally referred to as *the four horsemen of the apocalypse*.

The Olivet Discourse and the First Four Seals

Shortly before Christ would be crucified, he was teaching and healing in the Temple. As He and His disciples were leaving Herod's Temple, Jesus turned to them and revealed that Herod's Temple would be completely destroyed.

[1] *And Jesus went out, and departed from the temple: and his disciples came to him for to shew him the buildings of the temple.*
[2] *And Jesus said unto them, See ye not all these things? verily I say unto you, There shall not be left here one stone upon another, that shall not be thrown down.*   Matthew 24: 1-2

This must have stunned all of the disciples and as they walked across the Kidron Valley, they all pondered His prophetic words. Clearly, they associated the destruction of Herod's Temple with the second coming of their Lord and Savior. As they stopped and rested on the Mount of Olives the following questions were asked by Hs disciples.

And as he sat upon the mount of Olives, the disciples came unto him privately, saying: ***Tell us, when shall these things be? and what shall be the sign of thy coming, and of the end of the world?***   Matthew 24:3

In Matthew 24 and 25 Jesus answered part of their questions. He did not explain *when* the Temple would be destroyed (70 AD), but He addressed the last two. The answer which Christ gave is called the *Olivet Discourse* and is the most complete explanation of what we now call the *Great Tribulation* to be found in the New Testament excluding the Book of Revelation. In Matthew 24: 4-13 He speaks of conditions which exactly parallel those revealed as the first 4 seals are broken, and in the same order.

Seal	Revelation 6	Rider on....	Matthew 24	Condition
1	1 ,2	White Horse	5, 11	Deception
2	3, 4	Red Horse	6, 7	War
3	5, 6	Black Horse	7	Famine
4	8, 9	Pale Horse	7	Pestilence

Christ then spoke the following prophetic words.

[21] *For **then shall be great tribulation**, such as was not since the beginning of the world to this time, no, nor ever shall be.*
[22] *And except those days should be shortened, there should no flesh be saved: but for the elect's sake those days shall be shortened*   Matthew 24: 21-22

We will show in Chapter 3 that regardless of whether a 7-year tribulation or a 3.5-year tribulation is taught, the first 3.5 years of the last 7 years of the Church Age will be relatively peaceful. Severe tribulation will not begin until Satan is cast down to the earth and wages war against all Jews and Christians (Revelation 12:17). We will shortly show that the *Wrath of Satan* (The 7 trumpet Judgments) will fall upon all Jews and Christians for 1250 days. This will be followed by the Rapture of the Church, and God's reclamation of His earth will begin as The *Wrath of God* (The 7 Bowl/Vial Judgments) is released upon all unbelievers over a 10-day period of time. Note carefully that Jesus Christ in Matthew 24: 1-21 said that when the *Abomination that Causes Desolation* will appear in the rebuilt Jewish Temple takes place (Matthew 24:15): **then** *shall be **great** tribulation, such as was not since the beginning of the world to this time, no, nor ever shall be.* We must be careful to note exactly what Christ is showing His disciples in Matthew 24-25 and what John is being shown in Revelation 6: 1-8. The conditions described when the 1st four seals are broken/removed ...wars ...famine... pestilence ... death... have clearly taken place off and on over the last 2000 years, but there will be a future tribulation which is worse than anything that has previously taken place. Now the critical question: *What period of time is Christ referring to?* All agree that the 7 Trumpet judgments precede the 7 Bowl judgments, Hence, this period of great tribulation... which is worse than anything previously experienced by mankind.... must be the last half of Daniel's 70-week prophecy or 3.5 years in duration. Jesus Christ is warning the Jews that these times will be particularly severe before the 2nd advent of Christ. This will be discussed further in Chapters 3-5. The 4th seal has been removed: Christ now removes the 5th seal which reveals a remarkable scene (Revelation 6: 9-11).

> Seal 5
> *As the 5th seal opens, John sees the souls of those who have been martered for Jesus Christ. They plead for justice and revenge. God gives each a white robe. There are more to be slain.*
> *Rev 13:11-15, Rev 17:6*

[9] *And when he had opened the fifth seal, I saw under the altar the souls of them that were slain for the word of God, and for the testimony which they held:*
[10] *And they cried with a loud voice, saying, How long, O Lord, holy and true, dost thou not judge and avenge our blood on them that dwell on the earth?*
[11] *And white robes were given unto every one of them; and it was said unto them, that they*

39

should rest yet for a little season, until their fellow servants and their brethren should be killed as they were killed   Revelation 6: 5-11

As the *fifth seal* is broken and removed, the imagery suddenly changes. This is a remarkable passage. It indicates that a special place **under the altar of God** has been reserved for those who have been martyred for Jesus Christ. They are in His very presence awaiting their resurrection bodies and their rewards. They cry with a loud voice:

How long, oh Lord, holy and true, doest thou not judge and avenge our blood on them that dwell on the earth?   Revelation 6:10

The scene is poignant and revealing. Here are martyrs from all ages who have perished in the service of Christ. They are crying out for justice. This reminds us that after Christ commissioned 70 followers to prepare the way for him during his earthly ministry, He said: *Go your ways; behold I send you forth as lambs among wolves* (Luke 10:3). The response to this outcry is swift and revealing. There will be many more that will be killed for believing upon Jesus Christ.

And white robes were given unto every one of them; and it was said unto them, that they should rest yet for a little season, until their fellow servants also and their brethren that should be killed as they were, should be fulfilled   Revelation 6:1

This passage clearly states that during the tribulation period there would be martyrs who will lose their life for their belief in Jesus Christ. The 6th seal is now broken and removed.

Seal 6

As the 6th seal opens, the earth is torn apart by physical disturbances. Earthquakes, meteorites and volcanoic eruptions. Earth dwellers hide in the rocks & caves. The Wrath of God has come. The end is near
Is 34:4 ; Joel 2:30-31 ; Mat 24:39 ; Rev 8:10-11 ; Rev 16:18-21

1.0 There is a great Earthquake
2.0 The Sun turns black as sackcloth
3.0 The moon becomes the color of blood
4.0 The stars (meteorites) fall onto the earth
5.0 The heavens roll up like a scroll
6.0 Every mountain is moved out of its place

[12] *And I beheld when he had opened the sixth seal, and, lo, there was a great earthquake; and the sun became black as sackcloth of hair, and the moon became as blood;*
[13] *And the stars of heaven fell unto the earth, even as a fig tree casts her untimely figs, when she is shaken of a mighty wind.*
[14] *And the heaven departed as a scroll when it is rolled together; and every mountain and island were moved out of their places.*
[15] *And the kings of the earth, and the great men, and the rich men, and the chief captains, and the mighty men, and every bondman, and every free man, hid themselves in the dens and in the rocks of the mountains;*
[16] *And said to the mountains and rocks, Fall on us, and hide us from the face of him that sits*

on the throne, and from the wrath of the Lamb:
[**17**] *For the great day of his wrath is come; and who shall be able to stand?*
Revelation 6: 12-17

When the **6ᵗʰ seal** is broken, the entire earth reels and is torn apart. There are great physical disruptions that occur all over the earth and in the heavenlies. The opening of the sixth seal is not describing what will happen before Satan is cast out of heaven and begins his reign of terror, but describing what will happen as the *Great Tribulation* nears an end and the *Wrath of God* is about to fall upon the entire world. These things will take place very late in the 3.5-year reign of Satan and will immediately precede the 7 Bowl Judgments which are the *Wrath of God* upon all unbelievers. The Ecclesia.... those who have believed in Jesus Christ as their Lord and Savior… will be Raptured out as the 7ᵗʰ trumpet sounds (II Corinthians 15: 51-52, Chapter 3, Chapter 10).

The earth has experienced great earthquakes and volcanic eruptions before, but nothing can compare to what is being described as the 6ᵗʰ seal is broken. The heavens are ripped apart and the earth will be completely disrupted. Imagine *every* island and mountain being moved out of its place. The devastation will be unparalleled in the history of the world. Surely the events described when the sixth seal is broken indicate that the end is near. As this seal is broken, not only will the heavens and earth be disrupted, but the empires and kingdoms of men will collapse and be useless. Gold, silver and currency will not be enough to save mankind from the Wrath of Almighty God.

[**15**] *And the kings of the earth, and the great men, and the rich men, and the chief captains, and the mighty men, and every bondman, and every free man, hid themselves in the dens and in the rocks of the mountains;*
[**16**] *And said to the mountains and rocks, Fall on us, and hide us from the face of him that sits on the throne, and from the wrath of the Lamb:*
[**17**] *For the **great day of his wrath is come**; and who shall be able to stand?*
　　　　Revelation 6: 15-17

We will come back to the sixth seal in the next chapter when we discuss timing and chronology, but for now it is worth mentioning the context of the 6ᵗʰ seal. The sun is being darkened, every island is being moved out of its place and every mountain moved; the entire world is being thrown into unprecedented catastrophic events. The end of the dispensation of grace must be at the very door. However, common prophetic teaching has the seals taking place over an extended period of time that take place before the Wrath of Satan or the Wrath of God falls upon the earth. This is totally inconsistent and defies common logic. *Can we determine when this devastation will actually occur? Yes,* we can. When the 7ᵗʰ and final Bowl is poured out upon the earth four incredible events will take place: (1) A great earthquake will split the City of Jerusalem into three parts …Revelation 16:19a (2) All cities in every nation will be destroyed…Revelation 16:19b (3) The city of Babylon will be destroyed….Revelation 16:19c and (4) Every island and mountain will be destroyed … Revelation 16:20. But, when the 6ᵗʰ seal is broken and removed Revelation 6:14 says that *every mountain and island will be moved out of its place.* Are we to believe that this catastrophic event will occur twice in a 3.5-year period? All conflict and difficulties are resolved once we recognize that the opening of Seal 6 only predicts that this event

41

will happen later (as the 7th Bowl is poured out). Note that the Battle of Armageddon is fought immediately after the 7th bowl is poured out.

Note also that Revelation 6:17 specifically states that the *Day of God's Wrath has come.* Many (correctly) teach that those who have been saved by faith are not destined to go through the Wrath of God.

*For the **Wrath of God** is revealed from heaven against all ungodliness and unrighteousness of men, who hold the truth in unrighteousness*   Romans 1:18

*Much more then, being now justified by his blood, we shall be saved from **wrath** through him*   Romans 5:9

This scriptural and prophetic truth is the basis of all positional rapture theology. All *Pre-Tribulation* rapture teachers who advocate a 7-year tribulation assume that the seals, trumpets and bowls are sequential in nature. It is true that if all true believers (those alive) are raptured out before any of the seals, trumpets or bowls take place, then all who have accepted Jesus Christ as their savior will certainly not experience the Wrath of God. However, anyone who would then turn to Jesus Christ and believe in faith would have to go through both the Wrath of Satan and the Wrath of God. Another issue is when would any new Christian who would die after the Pre-Tribulation rapture be resurrected and judged. No resolution to this dilemma can be found anywhere in the Holy Scriptures... not a hint. All *Pre-tribulation* and *Mid-Tribulation* advocates (correctly) recognize that neither the Wrath of Satan or the Wrath of God will take place until Satan is cast out of heaven (Revelation 12) and will last only 3.5 years. A more recent theology which attempts to harmonize scripture is called the *Pre-Wrath* rapture theory. It was originally proposed by Van Kampen in a book called *The Sign* and later popularized by Rosenthal in a book called *The Pre-Wrath Rapture*. Both believe that the seals, trumpets and bowls are sequential. When the 6th seal is broken John writes that: *the great day of his wrath is come* (Revelation 6:17). Since all true believers are not destined to go through the Wrath of God (Romans 1:18, Romans 5:9), the rapture must occur as the 6th seal is removed by Jesus Christ from the 7-sealed scroll. This seems to be fundamentally correct. However, both Van Kampen and Rosenthal fail to recognize three important scriptural truths: (1) The 7 seals are *not* in sequential, chronological order with the Trumpets and Bowls. (2) There is a difference in God's Wrath (the 7 trumpets) and Satan's Wrath (the 7 bowls). God's wrath is clearly and without a doubt the 7 Bowl Judgments (Revelation 15:1, Revelation 15:7, Revelation 16:1) (3) If *all* Christians (alive) are to be spared from the Wrath of God, then the rapture must occur as the 7th trumpet sounds. This is exactly what Revelation 11: 15-19 implies and Paul confirms in I Corinthians 15: 51-52 and I Thessalonians 4:15. These observations compel this author to adopt a Pre-Wrath rapture position as the 7th trumpet sounds. We will fully explore, justify and scripturally defend these observations in the Chapter 5 when we discuss the chronological relationship between the seals, bowls and trumpets.

> ***Authors Comment:*** The Wrath of God in the Tribulation Period is His holy justice against Satan and all who follow after him. Not one person who has accepted the Lord Jesus Christ prior to the sounding of the 7th trumpet will experience His Wrath. Conversely, the fate of all who have rejected Christ and have taken the Mark of the Beast is eternal

punishment in the Lake of Burning Fire (Revelation 19:20). This is not the Wrath of God: It is a choice that anyone who does not accept Jesus Christ as their Lord and Savior consciously makes in this life. God does not condemn anyone to eternal punishment…That fate is already determined by the free will of those who reject Christ. Those who refuse the free gift of salvation and eternal life by believing on Jesus Christ are condemned already. There is no second chance.

Jesus Christ now removes the 7th and final seal (Revelation 8: 1-5).

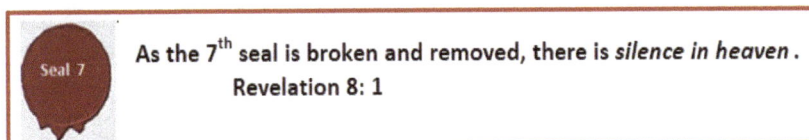

Seal 7	As the 7th seal is broken and removed, there is *silence in heaven* . Revelation 8: 1

When the **7th seal** is broken, the very prospect of these terrible things happening causes an unprecedented event in human history.

And when he had opened the seventh seal, there was silence in heaven about the space of half an hour.   Revelation 8:1

There is: ***silence in heaven, about the space of half an hour***. We do not know how long *half an hour* implies, and it is foolish to speculate. When the 7th seal is broken, the entire contents of the scroll which are ***written within and on the backside*** (Revelation 5:1) can now be revealed. It is time for John to witness with his own eyes the end of earth as we know it. When this period of silence is over, it will be time for the tribulation period of 3.5 years to begin.

 *And I John **saw** these things, and **heard** them*   Revelation 22:8

The impact of what John is about to see is so destructive and catastrophic that Christ warned:

[21] *For **then shall be great tribulation**, such as was not since the beginning of the world to this time, no, nor ever shall be.*
[22] *And except those days should be shortened, there should no flesh be saved: but for the elect's sake those days shall be shortened.*   Matthew 24: 21-22

We will later show when and how these two prophecies are fulfilled.

Following the silence of *about a half an hour*, a sequence of preparatory events now takes place in Heaven. ***Another angel*** (Rev 8:2), is summoned and comes to stand before the altar of God. He is given a ***golden censor*** with ***much incense, that he should offer it with the prayers of all saints upon the golden altar which is before the throne. And the smoke of the incense, which came with the prayers of the saints, ascended up before God out of the angel's hand*** (Revelation 8: 3-4).

Here is a remarkable contrast between the Old and New Testament economies. In the Old Testament, there was standing in the Holy Place a brazen altar of sacrifice upon which the

Hebrew people placed an offering of bulls and goats. This altar was to have a fire burning perpetually with hot coals. It was a function of the Levitical Priesthood to make sure the fire never went out. The coals were considered to be sacred. A sacrificial animal was killed, and the blood offered as an atoning sacrifice for sins. Except for rare divine appearances by God to his servants, and to the High Priest in the Holy of Holies on the Day of Atonement, an individual had no direct access to God. Because we are now justified by our Lord and savior, we have access to the very throne of God through our eternal High Priest, Jesus Christ.

It appears from Revelation 8: 3-4, that the prayers of New Testament saints are all collected and stored near the throne of God. How marvelous that through Jesus Christ our prayers are heard and saved by God! Sometimes we feel that our prayers are not answered, but they are always heard. These prayers are offered with *much incense* upon the true Golden Altar before God's throne in heaven; the true altar of sacrifice. Not a copy of the one that stood in the earthly tabernacle or the temple.

For it is not possible that the blood of bulls and goats should take away sins　　　　Hebrews 10:4

At this point in time another monumental event occurs in preparation for the 7 trumpets to sound.

And the angel took the censor (Revelation 8: 2-4), *and filled it with the fire of the altar, and cast it into the earth: and there were voices, and thunderings, and lightning and earthquakes* Revelation 8:5

God is announcing the last 3.5 years of this current age by heavenly signs and sounds along with earthly upheavals and earthquakes. The millions of prayers over thousands of years to vanquish Satan and start a new age are about to be answered. Judgment will be passed to the earth by 7 angels. When the 7th Seal is removed, the contents of the scroll can now be revealed. The 7 trumpets are now prepared to sound.

The 7 Trumpets

"And I saw the seven angels which stood before God ; and to them were given seven trumpets"　　Revelation 8:1

"and the 7 angels which had the seven trumpets prepared themselves to sound"

The 7 trumpet judgments represent the Wrath of Satan which will be unleashed upon Satan and all unbelievers. Not one Christian who has accepted Jesus Christ as their Lord and Savior prior to the sounding of the 7th trumpet will experience God's Wrath. As the 1st trumpet sounds, there are devastating effects upon the earth's ecology.

Trump 1 — As the first Trumpet sounds, hail, fire and blood are cast to the earth. 1/3 Of all the trees and *all* the green grass are burned up.

The first angel sounded, and there followed hail and fire mingled with blood, and they were cast upon the earth: and the third part of trees was burnt up, and all green grass was burnt up Revelation 8:7.

The famine depicted when third seal was removed (Revelation 6: 5-6) is now come. If *all* of the green grass is burned up, then no animals can graze and live for very long. It is likely that all of the world's food crops will also be burned up along with the green grass. Note for now that the conditions **predicted** at the opening of the third seal are now in force. The third seal itself did not cause these conditions, it only predicted that they would happen: The blowing the first trump did. The second angel now prepares to sound (Revelation 8: 8-9).

Trump 2 — As the second trumpet sounds, "something like a great mountain" burning with fire was thrown into the sea.

[8] *And the second angel sounded, and as it were a great mountain burning with fire was cast into the sea: and the third part of the sea became blood;*
[9] *And the third part of the creatures which were in the sea, and had life, died; and the third part of the ships were destroyed* Revelation 8: 8-9

God now causes the heavenly bodies which He created by the wave of His mighty hand to respond to His call. As the second trump is blown, it appears that a gigantic meteorite *Like a great mountain* was hurled from space into the sea, or possibly one of the oceans. The result is catastrophic. A third of all the creatures which live in the sea die instantly. A third of all seagoing vessels are destroyed, probably by a great tsunami. Not only are there effects felt worldwide from this gigantic *meteorite*, but a supernatural event now also occurs: 1/3 of *the sea* becomes blood. (Revelation 8:8). As the 3rd trumpet sounds, the heavens again respond to His call.

Trump 3 — As the third trumpet sounds, a "great star" falls from the heavens.

At the sounding of the third trump, another object falls from heaven. This object is larger and is called a *great star.*

[10] *And the third angel sounded, and there fell a great star from heaven, burning as it were a lamp, and it fell upon the third part of the rivers, and upon the fountains of waters;*
[11] *And the name of the star is called Wormwood: and the third part of the waters became*

wormwood; and many men died of the waters, because they were made bitter
Revelation 8: 10-11

As it falls from the sky, it splits and falls upon all the major continents. We know this because one third of all the rivers, streams and ***fountains of waters,*** or the subterranean water supply, is made bitter and undrinkable (Rev 8:10). We are told the name of this star; it is called **Wormwood**. The entomology of wormwood is *to curse or make like gall.* This event was predicted by the prophet Jeremiah.

Therefore, thus saith the Lord of Hosts concerning the (false) prophets; Behold I will feed them with wormwood, and make them drink the water of gall.   Jeremiah 23:15
The result is death, as predicted when the fourth seal was broken (Revelation 6:8): ***many men died of the waters, because they were made bitter*** (Revelation 8:11). The fourth trumpet is now ready to sound (Revelation 8:12).

Trump 4   **As the fourth trumpet sounds, the sun and the moon and the stars are all affected.**

As the fourth trump sounds, the heavens change the way they have operated for more than 6000 years. The cosmos begins to change, and 1/3 of the celestial bodies are affected.

A third part of the sun was smitten, and the third part of the moon, and a third part of the stars; so, as the third part of them was darkened, and the day shown not for a third part of it, and the night likewise.   Revelation 8:12

The Lord God created all of the heavens and the earth. He created the sun to determine the length of years and the seasons, and the moon was created to determine the days and the months. In the beginning God said:

Let there be light, and there was light. And God saw the light, and it was good: and God divided the light from the darkness.   Genesis 1: 3-4

And God said, let there be lights in the firmament of the heaven to divide the day from the night; and let them be for signs, and for seasons, and for days, and years   Genesis 1:14

For the 1st time since God created the earth, there will be only about 8 hours of daylight and 16 hours of darkness (Revelation 8:12). This was predicted when the 6th seal was removed (Revelation 6:12). A rather obscure passage in Daniel 7 presents a similar prophetic passage.

And he (the antichrist) *will speak great words against the Highest, and shall wear out the saints of the Highest, and think to change times and laws: And they shall be given into his hand until a time and times and the dividing of time.*   Daniel 7:25

The basic laws of nature which respond to about 12 hours of night and about 12 hours a day are based upon Genesis 1:14. The human body needs to rest at night and work during the day. The response of a human body to regular wake-sleep cycles based upon a 24-hour day of sunlight and darkness is called *Circadean Rhythm*. God created the human body, the sun, and the rotation of the earth to operate in harmony with one another and with man. It is possible that Daniel 7:25 is referring to that cycle. It is a biblical fact that *time and laws* are the very foundation of Man's existence and were a part of God's creative process: *And he changes the times and the seasons: he removes kings, and sets up kings: he giveth wisdom unto the wise, and knowledge to them that know understanding* (Daniel 2:21). Satan is always imitating God, and he may claim that this is his doing… but even through this period of great tribulation, God is in control and causes these things to happen.

Satan is evil and powerful, and to challenge God's superiority and authority he will redefine evil as good, and reward sin instead of righteousness. He will disregard natural laws of affection and encourage sinful morality as in the days of Sodom and Gomorrah (II Timothy 3:3). The actual meaning of Daniel 7:25 a can only be speculated. However, it is clear that the saints *shall be given into his hand until a time and times and the dividing of time* (1260 days). This is confirmed in both Daniel 12:7 and in Revelation 12:14.

At this point, an announcement is proclaimed from **an angel** *flying through Heaven.*

And I beheld, and heard an angel flying through the midst of heaven, *saying with a loud voice, Woe, woe, woe, to the inhabiters of the earth by reason of the other voices of the trumpet of the three angels, which are yet to sound!*   Revelation 8:13

The angel announces in a loud voice that although the first four trumpets have been disastrous, the worst is yet to come in the sounding of the last three trumpets. The *fifth, sixth and seventh trumpets* are so severe that they are called the **three woes** (Revelation 8:13). The 5th trumpet now sounds.

Trump 5 — *As the fifth trumpet sounds, Satan is given a key to the bottomless pit, and demon locusts are released to torture mankind. There are soo many the "sky is darkened".*

As the fifth trumpet sounds, we are given a glimpse of the underworld dungeons that are reserved for particularly bad demons and fallen angels (Revelation 9:1). There are several compartments of confinement mentioned in the Holy Scriptures. The place referenced here is called *Abussos*. The Aramaic word for *Abussos* is *a-bis*, and it means *very deep, bottomless*. The word *Abussos* is never used in Greek to English translation in the King James Bible. The KJV translates the word nine times. It is translated *deep* two times (Luke 8:31, Romans 10:7); it is translated *bottomless* 2 times (Revelation 9:1, Revelation 9:2); and it is translated *bottomless pit* five times (Revelation 9:11, Revelation 11:7, Revelation 17:8, Revelation 20:1 and Revelation 20:3). *Abussos* is an abode for evil spirits, but it is not their final resting place. Their final destination is the **lake of fire and brimstone**, which is translated from the Aramaic word

Gehenna. It is important that we stress this concept to identify what is happening when the fifth trumpet is blown. We are told that John sees:

I saw a star fall from heaven to earth: and to him was given the key to the bottomless pit.   Revelation 9:1

It is safe to assume that this key is given to Satan, for we can correlate this event with that given in Revelation Chapter 12.

And that great dragon was cast out, that old serpent, called the Devil and Satan, which deceives the whole world: he was cast out into the earth and his angels were cast out (of the heavens) *with him.*   Revelation 12:9

In a rather obscure statement, Christ was speaking to His disciples and He had just commissioned the 70 to go before him two-by-two into every city and proclaim the Gospel. He would also visit each city to prepare the way (Luke 10:1). Christ then empowered them to heal the sick (Luke 10:9) as a sign that He was coming. The seventy returned later with joy, reporting that **even the demons are subject to us in Your Name** (Luke 10:17). The reaction of Christ was undoubtedly a *mystery* at that time. He turned and said to them: ***I saw Satan fall like lightning from heaven*** (Luke 10:18). Christ was not impressed with their power over demons. He saw far into the future when Michael and his angels defeated Satan and all his angels and cast them all out of heaven (Revelation 12: 7-10). Satan will be in a war in the heavens, and will be defeated. His defeat will result in him and 1/3 of all the angels being cast out of heaven and onto the earth (Revelation 12: 3-4). Up until this point in time, Satan has had access to the very throne of God (Job 2:1). Satan is furious, and he now begins to persecute all who dwell upon the earth for a *time, times and half-a-time* (Revelation 12:14) as previously discussed. This event starts the tribulation period, the last half of Daniel's 70th week.

Woe to the inhabitants of the earth and of the sea! For the devil is come down unto you, having **great wrath***, because he knoweth he has but a short time*   Revelation 12:12

Revelation 12:12 is why the reign of Satan is called the *Wrath of Satan* in this book. When the 5th trumpet sounds, Satan uses the key that Christ has given to him to open the bottomless pit. When the pit (Abussos) is opened, demon locusts are released to torture mankind. There are so many demons that their appearance darkens the sunlight.

[2] *And he opened the **bottomless pit**; and there arose a smoke out of the pit, as the smoke of a great furnace; and the sun and the air were darkened by reason of the smoke of the pit.*
[3] *And there came out of the smoke **locusts** upon the earth: and unto them was given power, as the scorpions of the earth have power. And it was commanded them that they should not hurt the grass of the earth, neither any green thing, neither any tree; but only those men which have not the seal of God in their forehead*

[4] *And it was commanded them that they should not hurt the grass of the earth, neither any green thing, neither any tree; but **only those men which have not the seal of God in their foreheads.***
[5] *And to them it was given that they should not kill them, but that they should be **tormented five months**: and their torment was as the torment of a scorpion, when he stings a man.*
[6] *And in those days shall men seek death, and shall not find it; and shall desire to die, and death shall flee from them.* Revelation 9: 2-6

This passage is full of interesting information. *First*, notice that these demons are described as *locusts*. A locust is basically a grasshopper who has developed into a migratory, swarming stage. They gather by the millions, and when locusts swarm upon crops of the field they are devastating. They can strip a healthy field in a matter of hours and then move on. However, these are not ordinary locusts. These demons looked like *horses prepared for battle*; they had *crowns of gold on their head*; and they had *the faces of men*. Their teeth were like *Lion's teeth*; and their *hair like women*. They wore breastplates of iron; the sound of their wings was as *chariots rushing to battle*; and the sting was *in their tails* (Revelation 9: 7-10). These are awesome creatures that inflict pain but do not kill. The torture will be excruciating and this supernatural attack of demons will last for 5 months (Revelation 9:5).

They swarm and torment mankind but they cannot **hurt the grass** or any **tree** or any **green thing**. This is because the results of blowing the first trumpet have killed 1/3 of all the trees and all green grass. Trees make the oxygen that we breathe, and without them we would die. Grass feeds many animals, and without green grass there would be mass genocide of those species. So, no further harm is allowed to either the trees or the grass at this time. *Second*, we are told that they can torment anyone who is not sealed by God. *Who is sealed from this demonic attack?* The 144,000 Jews in Revelation 7. Third, we can be sure that the **bottomless pit** is a real place and that it now holds particularly bad demons who will emerge as scorpion-like-creatures. Satan will be bound and thrown into this subterranean chamber after the Battle of Armageddon where he will be confined for 1000 years (Revelation 20:2). We are next given another glimpse into the spirit world and its inhabitants

*And they had a king over them, which is the **angel of the bottomless pit**, whose name in the Hebrew tongue is Abaddon, but in the Greek tongue hath his name Apollyon* Revelation 9:11

In this place called the *bottomless pit* (*Abussos)* there is an angel who is called *the angel of the bottomless pit*. His name is **Abaddon** (Hebrew) or **Apollyon** (Greek). Both words mean *the destroyer*. This very strong angel is called the *king* of the demonic locust army. Evidently, Satan has many strong angels at his command, for Paul told us that there are hierarchies of demonic beasts including powerful rulers.

For we wrestle not against flesh and blood, but against principalities, against powers, against the rulers of the darkness of this world and against spiritual wickedness in high places Ephesians 6:12

Who is being persecuted as the fifth trumpet sounds? Clearly, it is anyone who does not have the **seal of God in their forehead** (Revelation 9:4). *What is this seal?* We are not told, but Revelation 14:1 suggests that it might be the name of God. We are told *who* is being divinely protected and *how* but not *why*. We have previously suggested that the 144,000 are all redeemed Jews who will inherit the promised land during the 1000-Year Millennial Kingdom.

[1] *And after these things I saw four angels standing on the four corners of the earth, holding the four winds of the earth, that the wind should not blow on the earth, nor on the sea, nor on any tree.*

[2] *And I saw another angel ascending from the east, having the **seal of the living God**: and he cried with a loud voice to the four angels, to whom it was given to hurt the earth and the sea,*

[3] *Saying, Hurt not the earth, neither the sea, nor the trees, till we have sealed the **servants of our God in their foreheads.***

[4] *And I heard the number of them which were sealed: and there were sealed an hundred and forty and four thousand of all the tribes of the children of Israel.* Revelation 7: 1-4

This seal in Revelation 7:2 is not unique. In Ezekiel 9:4 a group of righteous people in Jerusalem were sealed with a *mark* on the forehead from the massacre which was coming upon Israel. In both Revelation 7 and Ezekiel 9, a selected group is spared from the wrath to come.

A 3rd and 4th question is *why* this seal is placed upon the 144,000 Jews and *when* are each being protected? It is suggested that these 144,000 Jews….12,000 from each of 12 tribes of Israel… have been sealed to inherit the 1000-year Millennial Kingdom and fulfil the Covenant promises that God made to Abraham, Moses and King David. The Millennial Kingdom must be inhabited by real people. The 6th trumpet will bring death to 1/3 of all who remain alive on earth (Revelation 9: 18) and the 7 Bowls of God's Wrath will not fall upon this group. Hence, they must be protected from death to fulfill their purpose and destiny. The question of *when* they are sealed can also be determined. The clue is found in Revelation 6–7. They are to be sealed *before* the demon locusts are released when Trumpet 5 sounds, because in Revelation 9:4 everyone alive on the earth who has the seal of God upon their forehead will be spared. This cannot be anyone but those 144,000 in Revelation 7: 1-8. Also, the sealing of the 144,000 must take place at least 5 months prior to when the 6th and 7th trumpets are blown.

The fifth trumpet is called the ***first woe.*** There are two more *woes* to come in the sixth and seventh trumpets (Revelation 9: 12-13). The 6th trumpet now sounds.

Trump 6 — As the sixth trumpet sounds, there are 4 mighty angels released "at the River Euphrates". Thet command an army of "200 million" "horses with riders".

This is the ***second woe*** (Revelation 9:12).

[13] *And the sixth angel sounded, and I heard a voice from the four horns of the golden altar which is before God,*

[14] *Saying to the sixth angel which had the trumpet, Loose the four angels which are bound in the great river Euphrates.*

[15] *And the four angels were loosed, which were prepared for an hour, and a day, and a month, and a year, for to slay the third part of men.*

[16] *And the number of the army of the horsemen were two hundred thousand thousand: and I heard the number of them.*

[17] *And thus I saw the horses in the vision, and them that sat on them, having breastplates of fire, and of jacinth, and brimstone: and the heads of the horses were as the heads of lions; and out of their mouths issued fire and smoke and brimstone.*

[18] *By these three was the third part of men killed, by the fire, and by the smoke, and by the brimstone, which issued out of their mouths.*

[19] *For their power is in their mouth, and in their tails: for their tails were like unto serpents, and had heads, and with them they do hurt.*

[20] *And the rest of the men which were not killed by these plagues yet repented not of the works of their hands, that they should not worship devils, and idols of gold, and silver, and brass, and stone, and of wood: which neither can see, nor hear, nor walk:*

[21] *Neither repented they of their murders, nor of their sorceries, nor of their fornication, nor of their thefts*   Revelation 9: 13-21

This *second woe* is announced from one of the ***four horns of the golden altar which is before God*** (Revelation 9:13). These four horns are seen only here in the New Testament. But, in both the Old and New Testament, a *horn* is used to represent power or nations (Daniel 7:24, Daniel 8, Revelation 12:3), individuals (Psalms 75:10) or actual horns that can be blown. The antichrist was seen by Daniel as a ***little horn*** (Daniel 7:8). This is another instance of how Satan can only mimic God and Christ. The Lord is depicted as the ***horn of our salvation*** (Psalm 18: 2); and Jesus Christ is called ***a horn of salvation*** (Luke 1:69).

The Ark of the Covenant in the Old Testament had four horns, one on each corner of the Ark. The ark which Moses constructed was only a copy or replica of the true Ark which stands before the Throne of God in heaven. In context, it is better to assume that an angel in close proximity to the four horns announces what is about to occur rather than a sounding of the horns themselves. The agent of this announcement has great power, because he commands the angel which held the sixth trumpet to: ***loose the four angels which are bound in the great River Euphrates*** (Revelation 9:14). The Euphrates River forms the border between Saudi Arabia and the countries of Syria and Iraq. It was the principal water source for the great Babylonian Empire, and the headwaters of the Euphrates River were said to be formed from the river that flowed through the Garden of Eden (Genesis 2: 10-14). As the sixth trumpet sounds, we are told something quite remarkable about the four angels who are released from the river.

And the four angels were loosed, which were prepared for an hour, and a day, and a month and a year to slay the third of men.   Revelation 9:15

Imagine that! *Who can doubt the omnipresence and omnipotence of Almighty God?* He knows all, He sees all, and He controls all. These four angels are waiting until an exact hour to fulfill their destiny. Their mission is not mercy but death and destruction as predicted when the fourth seal was opened (Revelation 6:8). We are told that their army is *200 million horsemen.* The horses are similar to the demonic locusts released when the fifth trumpet sounded, but they are more frightening both in the power to kill and in their appearance.

And thus, I saw the horses in the vision, and them that sat on them, having breastplates of fire, and of jacinth, and brimstone: and the heads of the horses were as the heads of lions; and out of their mouths issued smoke and brimstone Revelation 9:17

Their command is to kill 1/3 of all mankind, and they kill by issuing fire and brimstone out of their mouths and tails. Nothing like this supernatural event has ever occurred in the history of mankind. Some have supposed that these creatures were actually attack helicopters which John saw and described as demonic horses.

By these three was the third part of men killed, by the fire, and by the smoke, and by the brimstone, which issued out of their mouths. For their power is in their mouth, and in their tails: for their tails were like unto serpents, and had heads, and with them they do hurt
Revelation 9: 18-19

Amazingly, the reaction of those attacked by the demonic hoards unleashed by the fifth and sixth trumpets is not to ask for mercy or grace; but the attitude is one of scorn and defiance.

And the rest of the men who were not killed by these plagues yet repented not of the works of their hands, that they should not worship devils, and idols of gold, and silver, and brass, and stone, and of wood: which neither can see, nor hear, nor walk. Neither repented they of their murders, nor of their sorceries, nor of their fornication, nor of their thefts
Revelation 9: 20-21

The time has come for the sounding of the seventh trumpet (Rev 11:15-19). The 7th Trumpet will announce that the 7 Bowl Judgments, which are the **Wrath of God** (Revelation 15:1, Revelation 16:1) are about to be poured out upon the earth.

Trump 7 — As the seventh trumpet sounds, the prophecies of Daniel's 70th week start to be fulfilled. The 7 Bowl judgements are imminent

[15] *And the seventh angel sounded; and there were great voices in heaven, saying,* **The kingdoms of this world are become the kingdoms of our Lord, and of his Christ; and he shall reign forever and ever.**
[16] *And the four and twenty elders, which sat before God on their seats, fell upon their faces,*

and worshipped God,

[17] *Saying, We give thee thanks, O Lord God Almighty, which art, and were, and art to come; because thou hast taken to thee thy great power, and hast reigned.*

[18] ***And the nations were angry, and thy wrath is come, and the time of the dead, that they should be judged, and that thou shouldest give reward unto thy servants the prophets, and to the saints, and them that fear thy name, small and great; and shouldest destroy them which destroy the earth.***

[19] *And the temple of God was opened in heaven, and there was seen in his temple the ark of his testament: and there were lightnings, and voices, and thunderings, and an earthquake, and great hail.*

The Kingdoms of this world become the Kingdoms of Jesus Christ   Rev 11:15

The 24 elders (Rev 4:4) fall on their faces and worship God   Rev 11:16

God's Wrath has come   Rev 11:18-a

It is time to judge the dead in Christ; and to reward his servants & prophets   Rev 11:18-b

The Temple of God is opened, and the Ark of the Covenant is seen.   Rev 11:19

Revelation 11: 15-19

The seventh angel sounds the seventh trumpet, and this gives rise to rejoicing in heaven, but on earth *the nations are angry* (Revelation 11:18). This incredible reaction on the earth is because those who are left on earth blindly and totally follow after the Antichrist and his false prophet. There will be more detailed discussions of what happens when the seventh trump is blown in Chapter 5. For now, note that when the 7th angel sounds the 7th trumpet, five important things will come to pass (Rev 7: 15-19).

Christ is about to assume His rightful place as King of this Earth (Revelation 11:15)). The Wrath of God (the 7 Bowl Judgments) is about to fall upon the earth (Revelation 11:18a). The ark of the Covenant is seen in heaven (Revelation 11:19, and *the time has arrived to reward those who have faithfully served Him and His Son Jesus Christ* (Revelation 11:18b).

Anyone who reads Revelation 11:18 without a preconceived bias would immediately recognize that all believers (living and dead) will be judged and rewarded for their faithful service to Jesus Christ while they served Him on this earth (II Corinthians 5:10). They will not be judged for condemnation but for rewards. This will take place at the *Bema Seat Judgment* following the *rapture of the church*. The rapture of all *believers* that are alive and remain as the seventh trumpet sounds is without controversy when this will occur. This conclusion will

be further justified in Chapters 6 and 7. The immediate implication of this conclusion is that if the Rapture occurs when the 7th Trumpet is blown, then those true believers who are caught up to meet the Lord in the air will escape from the 7 Bowl Judgments, which are the **Wrath of God** (Revelation 15:1, Revelation 16:1).

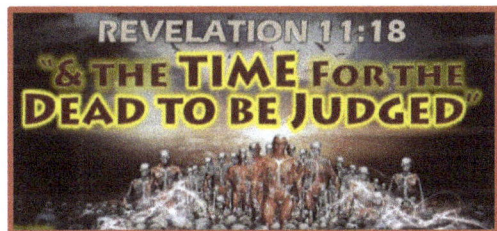

Jewish Perspectives: *Feast of Trumpets* (Rosh Hashanah or Yom Teruah)

The *Feast of Trumpets* is the 5th feast of the 7 feasts of Israel. It is always in the Fall on Tishri 1. In ancient times, it was almost exclusively called the *Feast of Rosh Hashanah* or the *Feast of*

New Beginnings. That is because the Rabbi's taught that the world was created on Tishri 1. It was also called *Yom Terua* several times in the Old Testament. Yom Terua means *sounding of a trumpet*. In later years, it began to be called the Feast of Trumpets. The ancient Jewish calendar year began on the Feast of Trumpets, Tishri 1. That was the first month in the Jewish calendar year until the exodus from Egypt. When God rescued the Jews from Egyptian slavery, He rotated the calendar months … Nisan became the 1st month and Tishri the 7th month. Nothing was really changed, only the numbering of each month as a memorial. It is interesting that all of the other 7 feasts have a meaning attached to them in the scriptures (Leviticus 23), but the Feast of Trumpets is not fully explained.

The sounding of a trumpet is a significant event to the Jews. It was to be blown on several ordained occasions for different reasons: (1) The Coronation of a King…Psalms 98:6 (2) A call to repentance…Isaiah 58:1 (3) A reminder of when the Law was given at Mt Sinai…Exodus 24 (4) A warning of impending danger or a call to war…Ezekiel 33: 4-5, Jeremiah 4:19 (5) To remember the Binding of Isaac…Genesis 22:13 (6) To warn Israel that the Day of the Lord is coming…Zepeniah 1: 14-16 (7) to remember that a day is coming in which all of Israel will be regathered into the promised land…Isaiah 27:13 (8) To remind the people that there will be a Resurrection from the dead…Isaiah 18:3. It is interesting that there will be a trumpet blown on the final Feast of Trumpets which will launch the rapture as proposed in this book, and that all of these Jewish reasons for blowing a trumpet apply to the rapture of Jews and gentiles that have died in faith. Paul revealed the *Mystery of the Rapture and resurrection.*

[**51**] *Behold,* ***I shew you a mystery****; We shall not all sleep, but we shall all be changed,*
[**52**] *In a moment, in the twinkling of an eye, at the* ***last trump****: for the trumpet shall sound, and the dead shall be raised incorruptible, and we shall be* changed   I Corinthians 15: 51-52

Paul tells the saints to whom he is speaking (and us) that ***we will all be changed***, whether we are alive or dead, at the ***last trump***. Now that is fairly specific, but: *When would the* ***last trump*** *be sounded?* The term ***last trump*** is a Jewish eschatological term which is always connected to the *Feast of Rosh Hashanah* or the *Feast of Trumpets*...which always occurs in the 7th Jewish month in the Fall on Tishri 1. Jewish people see Rosh Hashanah or the Feast of Trumpets as the beginning of a 10-day period of introspection, confession of sins and a time of repentance leading up to the *Feast of Yom Kippur* or the *Day of Atonement* on Tishri 10. There are 30 days of blowing the trumpet on each day preceding Tishri 1. Finally, a ***last trump*** is blown on the Feast of Trumpets. But there is also a trumpet blown on Tishri 10, so again…. *When is the last trumpet?* Here we must dig deeper into Jewish Rabbinical teachings. According to the ancient Jewish rabbis and teachers, the ***last trump*** is related to the ***binding of Isaac***. Recall that Abraham was called by God to sacrifice his only natural son Isaac, and he went up onto the mountain to do so. Ancient teachings say that Abraham went to where the ***Dome of the Rock*** now stands. He built an altar of sacrifice, and just as he was about to kill his son, God stayed his hand and produced a ***ram*** for a suitable sacrifice. This ram was offered as a ***burnt offering*** to the Lord and totally consumed by fire. The only thing that survived was the two ram's horns. Tradition holds that the first horn was blown when the Law was given to Moses and the people at Mt. Sinai. The second horn…. The second and ***last horn***…. is to be blown at a future ***Feast of Rosh Hashanah*** (Feast of Trumpets). The Feast of Trumpets is also called Yom Teruah …*Day of Awakening Blast*. The *awakening blast* on some future Feast of Rosh Hashanah refers to a belief that the righteous dead will be raised on this day.

The Rabbis wrote that two very important things will take place when the last trump sounds...the *second ram's horn*...on some future *Feast of Trumpets*; (1) Those who are of the seed of Abraham who have died in faith will be redeemed and will rise from the dead. (2) The resurrection of the dead will occur on this day. On the Feast of Trumpets (Tishri 1), there are actually 100 trumpet blasts. The final, long, and most significant trumpet blast is called the **last trump** and is sounded by God using the 2nd Rams Horn. The fact that the last trump in the Book of Revelation is the last in a series of 7 does not fully justify that the Rapture of all living saints and the resurrection of all dead saints will occur when the 7th trumpet sounds, but supported by Jewish beliefs it is a distinct and logical possibility. The *Jewish* beliefs concerning the *last trump* are largely unknown to Western prophecy scholars who have not studied the *7 Feasts of Israel*.

Thy dead men shall live, together with my dead body shall they arise. Awake and sing, ye that dwell in dust: for thy dew is as the dew of herbs, and the earth shall cast out the dead
    Isaiah 26:19

The *Wrath of God*

One of the keys to understanding the sequence of events in the tribulation period, and how those events relate to the rapture and resurrection of the *elect* is to understand the concept of *God's Wrath*. In Revelation 15:1, 15:7, and Revelation 16:1, we are told that the *Wrath of God* is the seven bowl judgments. We must again ask the question: *Are those who have accepted Jesus Christ as their Lord and Savior...and who remain alive on earth at this time... expected to suffer through God's wrath?* The answer is *No* from many scriptures. Several scriptural confirmations are given below.

For God hath not appointed us to wrath, but to obtain salvation by our Lord Jesus Christ.
I Thessalonians 5: 9

He that believeth on the Son hath everlasting life: and he that believeth not the Son shall not see life; but the Wrath of God abides on him   John 3:36

Much more then, being now justified by his blood, we shall be saved from wrath through him
Romans 9: 5

The prophets Isaiah and Zepeniah saw the Wrath of God coming long ago.

*Behold, the **Day of the LORD** cometh, cruel both with wrath and fierce anger, to lay the land desolate: and he shall destroy the sinners thereof out of it. Therefore, I will shake the heavens, and the earth shall remove out of her place, in the wrath of the LORD of hosts, and in the **Day of his fierce anger***   Isaiah 13: 9, 13*

***That day is a day of wrath**, a day of trouble and distress, a day of wasteness and desolation, a day of darkness and gloominess, a day of clouds and thick darkness: Neither their silver nor their gold shall be able to deliver them in the day of the LORD's wrath; but the whole land shall be devoured by the fire of his jealousy: for he shall make even a speedy riddance of all them that dwell in the land*   Zephaniah 1: 15, 18

Once again by the prophetic dual testimony of Isaiah and Zephaniah it is emphatically believed that the Day of the Lord is not extended period of time but is exactly what it implies…a single day. It is that Day when Jesus Christ will return as a conquering hero and as the King of Kings to fight the great Battle of Armageddon. This assertion is proved by Isaiah 13:9. There is no doubt that Satan will rule with God's permission for 1260 days or time, time and half-a-time or 3.5 years. Isaiah 13: 9 and Isaiah 13:13 declare without ambiguity that **He**…God almighty (by His Son) will *destroy all sinners.* Satan during his rule will not destroy those who take his mark and worship him, only those who refuse. This is an incontrovertible truth. Zephaniah further says that this is a day of *thick darkness*. He entire last 3.5 years will not be cloudy and dark…only after the 5th Bowl/vial is poured out will this happen. The conclusion is secure: The Day of the Lord is a *single day*…the Battle of Armageddon.

The seven bowls (vials) are without question the **Wrath of God** (Revelation 15:7, Revelation 15:1, Revelation 16:1). Since not one true believer is to go through the Wrath of God, all living believers will be raptured out at the sounding of the seventh trumpet, with the exception of the 144,000 Jews who have been sealed (Revelation 7: 1-8). The rapture of all living saints and the resurrection of the righteous dead will occur after 1250 days on the Feast of Trumpets Tishri 1… 10 days short of the 1260-day period which constitutes the last half of Daniel's 70th week which will end on the Feast of Yom Kippur… Tishri 10 (Revelation 12:6). Christ prophesied of this time in the Olivet Discourse.

…and unless those days be shortened, no flesh would be saved; but for the elect's sake, those days will be shortened   Matthew 24:22

The 1260 days of the Great Tribulation will not be shortened, only the last 10 days for all true believers. The *Wrath of God* is poured out upon those who have rejected salvation by not believing on his Son, Jesus Christ. Having declared that the church will not have to be subjected to God's Wrath, there needs to be a clear distinction made between *tribulation* and *wrath*. *Tribulation* is the suffering and persecution that the world and Satan will put on any true believer in Christ, while *wrath* is God's suffering and righteous justice that He will execute on unbelievers at the end of the church age. The church will be saved from God's wrath by being raptured out at the seventh trumpet. Christ has told us that we will *suffer much tribulation*, but Jesus comforted us by saying that with great tribulation comes real peace.

These things I have spoken to you, that in Me you may have peace. In the world you will have tribulation, but take courage; I have overcome the world   John 16:33

Tribulation is necessary to mature us and prepare us for the world to come, and to move us toward perfection (Romans 5:3, I Thessalonians 3:4), but we are not appointed to *God's Wrath*. The following verses reflect what the scriptures teach on this important concept.

We glory in tribulations also: knowing that tribulation worketh patience; and patience experience; and experience, hope   Romans 5: 3-4

For the Wrath of God is revealed from heaven against all ungodliness and unrighteousness of men who suppress the truth in unrighteousness   Romans 1: 18

For God hath not appointed us to wrath.   I Thessalonians 5:9

Let no man deceive you with vain words: for because of these things cometh the Wrath of God upon the children of disobedience   Ephesians 5:6

The Wrath of God: *Jewish Expectations and Confirmation*

Jewish rabbinical writings teach that the days between the *Feast of Trumpets* and the *Feast of Yom Kippur* are the *Days of Awe* (Yamim Noraim) or the *Days of Repentance*. These are the days given to Israel to prepare to meet the Lord. In the Old Testament these were 10 days of repentance and renewal that begin at sunset on Rosh Hashanah (Tishri 1) and end on the Feast of Yom Kippur (Tishri 10), the solemn *Day of Atonement*. One of the ongoing themes of *the Days of Awe* is the concept that God has *books* in which He writes our names; who will live and who will die, and who will have a good life and who will have a bad life during the next year (a type of II Peter 3:8). Actions during the *Days of Awe* can alter God's decree. In the Old Testament, the Jews believed that the actions that change the decree are *teshuva, tefilah and dakahtze…* or *repentance, prayer, and good deeds.* However, the gift of eternal life is free, and cannot be earned by works or mental attitude. All books are sealed on Yom Kippur. The Abrahamic Covenant finds its ultimate fulfillment in connection with the return of the true Messiah to rescue and bless Israel. That ultimate blessing will be the gift of eternal life to all of Israel who believe upon the Lord Jesus Christ during this 10-day period of time. They will join the 144,000 from the 12 tribes of Israel who will populate the millennial kingdom here on earth. After the 7 Bowls of God's Wrath are poured out upon all unbelievers (Revelation 5:7), Satan and the armies of the Antichrist will now be supernaturally gathered to Jerusalem for the last great Battle of Armageddon (Revelation 14: 1-20) outside of Jerusalem on the Plain of Megiddo. The Wrath of God against all unbelievers has now come.

The 7 Bowl Judgments

1	2	3	4	5	6	7
Rev. 16:2	Rev. 16:3	Rev. 16:4-7	Rev. 16:8-9	Rev. 16:10-11	Rev. 16:12-16	Rev. 16:17-21
Malignant ulcers appear on those with the mark of the Beast.	Sea turns to blood, all living creatures in the sea die.	Drinking water turns to blood, men given blood to drink.	The sun becomes extremely hot, and scorches men.	Antichrist's kingdom struck with darkness.	Euphrates river dried up, armies gathered for Armageddon.	Worldwide earthquake, cities collapse, 120lb. hailstones fall from the sky

*And I heard a great voice out of the temple saying to the seven angels: Go your ways, and pour out the vials of the **Wrath of God** upon the earth*   Revelation 16:1

[5] *And after that I looked, and, behold, the temple of the tabernacle of the testimony in heaven was opened:*
[6] *And the seven angels came out of the temple, having the seven plagues, clothed in pure and white linen, and having their breasts girded with golden girdles.*
[7] *And one of the four beasts gave unto the seven angels seven golden vials full of the **Wrath of God**, who lives for ever and ever.*
[8] *And the temple was filled with smoke from the glory of God, and from his power; and no man was able to enter into the temple, till the seven plagues of the seven angels were fulfilled.*
Revelation 15: 5-8

The true tabernacle of God has been closed but it is now opened in Heaven (Revelation 15:5). Revelation 15:6 refers to *The* 7 angels. *The* is a definite article and is used to refer to a *specific* or *particular* member of a group. In this case, it refers back to Revelation 15:1 and identifies these 7 as angels, not redeemed saints. They had been inside the Tabernacle of God awaiting this very moment. These are Holy Angels created by God, and this is *very important*. They are seen wearing *pure white linen*. It is very common for commentators to state that robes of white are reserved *only* for those saints who are save by the Blood of Jesus (Revelation 6:11). Revelation 15:6 clearly reveals that this is not true. When a man or woman is called to heaven to dwell forever with our Lord Jesus Christ, they are given robes of white to identify them with the angels, which were created Holy by God and serve Him throughout all eternity. Halleluiah!!

The Seven Bowls/Vials contain 7 plagues which will be poured out upon all Satan and all unbelievers (Revelation 15:7). The temple of God is filled with smoke which represents the power of God. *We are now told something that is extremely important* (Revelation 15:8): The Temple of God cannot be entered by until the Wrath of God is over: *No man was able to enter into the temple, till the seven plagues of the seven angels were fulfilled.* What *man* is in view here? The Greek word translated as *man* is *ouden* which is the same Greek word used in Revelation 7:9. They are all those who have just been raptured out at the 7th trump. This does not prove that the rapture occurs at the 7th trump, but it is a strong indication. A Pre-Tribulation, Mid-Tribulation or a classical Pre-wrath Rapture would spare many from both the Wrath of Satan and the Wrath of God, but those who accept Jesus Christ as their Lord and Savior over the last 3.5 years would have to experience the Wrath of God. This means that some Christians would not be spared from God's Wrath…which violates a basic assumption stated throughout this book: No Christian is destined to go through the Wrath of God, which is without controversy the 7 Bowl Judgments (Revelation 15:1, Revelation 15:7 and Revelation 16:1). The only rapture that will not violate scripture is at the 7th trumpet just before the Wrath of God is poured out.

[1] *And I heard a great voice out of the temple saying to the seven angels, go your ways, and pour out the vials of the **Wrath of God** upon the earth*   Revelation 6:1

| Bowl 1 | | The first bowl is "poured out"……. "A foul and loathsome sore comes upon all who had the mark of the beast, and those who worshipped his image"   Rev 16:2 |

[2] *And the first* (angel) *went, and poured out his vial* (bowl) *upon the earth; and there fell a noisome and grievous sore upon the men which had the mark of the beast, and upon them which worshipped his image*　　　　Revelation 16:2

The first bowl persecutes those who have followed after Satan, the Antichrist and the False Prophet. Note that not one believer in Christ is mentioned in this verse. When the 7th trumpet was blown all living and dead believers are seen in heaven being rewarded for their works.

And the nations were angry, and thy wrath is come, and the time of the dead, that they should be judged, and that thou shouldest give reward unto thy servants the prophets, and to the saints, and them that fear thy name, small and great; and shouldest destroy them which destroy the earth　　　　Revelation 11:18

Note that the 7th trumpet also announces that the **Wrath of the Lord** has come (Revelation 15:1, Revelation 16:1). This was predicted when Christ opened and removed the 6th seal. This is totally consistent with what has been previously presented. It is now time for God to reclaim His earth which has been ruled by Satan for over 6000 years.

The first judgment upon the earth and all unbelievers corresponds to Bowl 1.

Bowl 1 brings misery in the form of *foul and loathsome sores.* It is interesting that these sores only affect those who have received the *mark of the beast* in either their forehead or their right hand (Revelation 16:2, Revelation 13:16-18). These are all unbelievers… anyone who receives this mark will be condemned to the *2nd death* and will be tormented in the lake of Burning Fire forever. I did not say this… John did.

And the beast was taken, and with him the false prophet that wrought miracles before him, with which he deceived them that had received the mark of the beast, and them that worshipped his image　　　　Revelation 19:20

This action will condemn any recipient to eternal damnation... The decision to take the mark will be final and eternal (Revelation 20:15). They *worshipped his image. What is this image?*

[15] *And he had power to give* **life unto the image of the beast**, *that the image of the beast should both speak, and cause that as many as would not worship the image of the beast should be killed.*
[16] *And he causes all, both small and great, rich and poor, free and bond, to receive a mark* **in their right hand, or in their foreheads**　　　　Revelation 13: 15-16

There will be an image made of the Antichrist that will actually think and speak (Revelation 13:15). Anyone who does not take the Mark of the Beast will be martyred (Revelation 13:15). Contrary to popular belief, the scriptures do not identify this mark...only where it will be placed and who will demand that it be taken. The precedent to the personal pronoun *he* in Revelation 13:15a is the *other beast* in Revelation 13:11. The personal pronoun *he* in Revelation 13:15a is the *False Prophet* who serves the *First Beast* in Revelation 13:1. This First Beast is the *Antichrist*. The False Prophet will force all people on earth who do not worship his image to *receive a mark in their right hand or on their forehead,* and without this mark, no one can *buy or sell anything* (Revelation 13: 16-17).

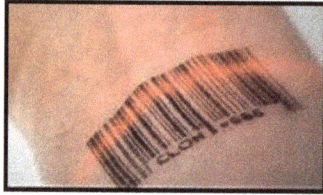

It is almost universally taught that this *mark* is the number 666, but the number 666 is not a mark but the *number of a man* who is the Antichrist. Those who worship Satan as the Antichrist will receive a mark which is either His name or the number of his name (Revelation 13:19). In the Greek alphabet, every vowel or consonant is assigned a number. The Antichrist will evidently have (an undisclosed) name, and if the numerical values of each letter in his name are added up…they will total to 666.

It is important to recognize again not only *what* is the Wrath of God but upon *who* the Wrath of God will be poured out. As the 1st Bowl is poured out, the Rapture has just occurred as the 7th Trumpet sounded and there no true believers who remain on earth…. The only people on earth who still remain are unbelievers.

*And the first went, and poured out his vial upon the earth; and there fell a noisome and grievous sore **upon the men which had the mark of the beast, and upon them which worshipped his image*** Revelation 16:2

As the 1st Bowl is poured out upon the earth, a *grievous sore* comes upon all unbelievers. In the Greek, this term is identified as resembling an inflamed wound or location which refuses to heal. This is identical to the 6th plague which God brought upon the Egyptians when the Pharaoh refused to "let my people go" (Exodus 9: 9-11). The reaction of all unbelievers to this plague is predictable: *They cursed God and refused to repent* (Revelation 16:11).

The church is gone, having been raptured out at the seventh trumpet. The only believers in Jesus Christ who remain have been divinely protected from God's Wrath by a mark on their wrist or forehead (Revelation 7:3). This group is all Jewish: There is not one gentile believer in the entire 144,000 (Revelation 7:4). *Why are they still on the earth*? The answer to this question is simple once one understands the covenant that God made with Abraham in Genesis 15.

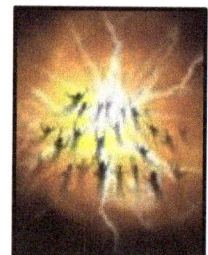

The Lord made a covenant with Abram, saying, unto thy seed have I given this land, from the River of Egypt to the River Euphrates Genesis 15:18

The purpose of the Millennial Kingdom is to establish Jesus Christ as King of Kings (Luke 1: 32-33). He will rule and reign from His new throne which will be built just north of where the Herod's Temple once stood. King David will be resurrected and installed as co-regent over

Israel, ruling the Millennial Kingdom with Jesus Christ as promised long ago (Jeremiah 30:9, Ezekiel 37:24). These things will fulfill the covenant promises concerning the land that God has made to Israel.

The *Abrahamic Covenant* has been of primary importance to the Hebrew nation. It has always been understood that God promised them all of the land from the Nile River to the Euphrates River; and from the great sea (Mediterranean) to the lesser sea (Galilee). Even under the leadership of Joshua, David and Solomon; this promise was not fulfilled. Nevertheless, God's unconditional, covenant promises are eternal and Israel as a nation will possess the land in the future. Numerous Old Testament passages anticipate the future blessing of Israel and her possession of the land as promised to Abraham. Ezekiel envisions a future day when Israel is restored to the land (Ezekiel 20:33–37, 40–42; 36:1–37:28). During the Millennial Kingdom, the Jewish nation will finally inherit and live in the land promised to them long ago. The Jewish remnant that will possess and initially populate the land are the 144,000 and their progeny. It is also important to understand that Abraham was promised many descendants. He was to produce through his loins three **seeds.** The *first* is **Jesus Christ**, the savior of the world (Galatians 3:16, Genesis 12:7).

Now to Abraham and his seed were the promises made. He saith not, and to seeds, as of one, and to thy seed, which is Christ   Galatians 3:16

The *second* is an **earthly seed**, which will inherit the earth (This is composed of the 144,000 In Revelation 7, and those who accept Christ as their Savior and survive the trumpet and bowl judgments. Those 144,000 who have been sealed and protected (Revelation 7) will inherit and populate the Promised Land during the Millennial Kingdom. Members of the body of Christ will live above the City of Jerusalem in a glorious city with Christ which is called the New Jerusalem (Revelation 22: 1-5). The reconstituted nation of Israel will be ruled over by King David on the earth (Ezekiel. 37: 24-25). These constitute the **dusty seed** of Abraham…. the seed of the earth.

For all the land which you see, to thee will I give it, and to thy seed forever. And I will make thy seed as the dust of the earth: so that if a man can number the dust of the earth, then shall thy seed also be numbered   Genesis 13: 15-16

The *third* is a **Heavenly seed**. There have been many who have believed on the name of Jesus Christ down through the ages: Those of promise from the Old Covenant… who believed the prophets when they spoke of a coming Messiah… and those Jews born-again under the New Covenant (John 3: 1-7). These are the **starry seed** of Abraham; they (living or dead) will join the body of Christ and be resurrected at the 7th trump.

For by one Spirit are we all baptized into one body, whether we be Jews or Gentiles, whether we be bond or free; and have been all made to drink into one Spirit   I Corinthians 12:1

And it shall come to pass in that day, that the great trumpet shall be blown, and they shall come which were ready to perish in the land of Assyria, and the outcasts in the land of Egypt, and shall worship the LORD in the holy mount at Jerusalem.   Isaiah 27:13

And in mercy shall his throne be established: and he shall sit upon it in truth in the tabernacle of David, judging, and seeking judgment, and hasting righteousness   Isaiah 16:5

The time has now arrived for the *second bowl* to be poured out.

Bowl 2	The second bowl is "poured out"....... The sea is turned to blood and everything in the sea dies. Rev 16:3

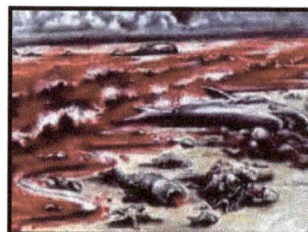

And the second angel poured out his vial upon the sea; and it became as the blood of a dead man: and every living soul died in the sea   Revelation 16:3

As the second Bowl is poured out, every living creature in the sea dies as the seas (oceans) of the earth turn to blood.   The world today lives off of the fruits of the sea. Billions of tons of fish are consumed every day. When the second bowl is poured out, *every creature in the sea dies*. As they wash ashore, the stench will be unbearable and disease will rapidly spread from decaying bodies. When the *third bowl* is poured out upon the earth, an event takes place which is so catastrophic that just the thought of it occurring is unbelievable.

Bowl 3	The third bowl is "poured out"....... All of the fresh water turns to blood. Rev 16:4

*And the third angel poured out his vial upon the **rivers and fountains of waters**; and they became blood*   Revelation 16:4

All fresh water turns to blood. Water is the element that is most required to sustain life. Man can go without food for long periods of time, but without water one will die in a matter of days. The only fresh water left to sustain life after the third bowl is poured out upon the earth is bottled water, and it will not last long. In addition, every plant and creature are now doomed. There are many prophecy teachers who teach that the bowl judgments will take place over all of the last half 3.5 years of Daniel's 70th week. These teachers are not reading the scriptures very carefully. The end is near, possibly a matter of days when the bowls are poured out. The torture of men continues when the contents of the *fourth bowl* is poured out.

Bowl 4	The fourth bowl is "poured out"....... The contents of this bowl are poured on the sun, The angel who pours this bowl "scorched men with fire" Rev 16:8

"And men were scorched with great heat, and blasphemed the name of God, which hath power over these plagues: and they repented not to give him glory."
-Revelation 16:9

... and men were scorched with great heat, and they blasphemed the name of God who has power over these plagues, and they did not repent and give Him glory   Revelation 16:9

The angel in charge of this bowl takes its contents and *pours it upon the sun*. This symbolically represents the power given to him by God to *scorch men with fire.* The results are predictable.

One would think that the reaction of men to divine judgment would be to repent and ask God to spare them of this torture. But man is *deceitfully wicked*, and even as God is destroying the earth and all of its fresh water, they will again refuse to repent of their sins nor ask for mercy.

We know that whosoever is born of God sins not; and he that is begotten of God keeps himself from sinning, and that wicked one touches him not. We know that we are of God, and the whole world lies in wickedness   1 John 5: 18-19

Remember that every living Christian who has accepted Jesus Christ as his/her savior has been raptured out before seven angels were given the seven bowls of God's Wrath. We will see in Chapter 5 that the seven bowl judgments will be poured out in rapid succession over a 10-day period between the Jewish *Feast of Trumpets* on Tishri 1, and the *Feast of Yom Kippur* on Tishri 10. Jewish tradition calls these days the *Days of Awe* and the *Days of Repentance*. This is not a second chance for salvation but *the last chance*. One should carefully study the prophetic significance of the last three fall Feasts of Israel (Rosh Hashanah, Yom Kippur and Tabernacles) and the 10-days between Tishri 1 (Rosh Hashanah) and Tishri 10 (Yom Kippur) ... (Phillips: The Book of Revelation: *Mysteries Revealed*). The earth is *reeling* as the *fifth bowl* is now poured out

| Bowl 5 | The fifth bowl is "poured out"....... The contents of the 5th bowl are poured out upon "the throne of the beast (the Antichrist). His kingdom is thrown into darkness.   Rev 16: 10 |

[10] *And the fifth angel poured out his vial upon the seat of the beast; and his kingdom was full of darkness; and they gnawed their tongues for pain,*
[11] *And blasphemed the God of heaven because of their pains and their sores, and repented not of their deeds*   Revelation 16: 10:11

As the 5th bowl is emptied, the prophecies of Joel will finally come to pass.

*The sun shall be turned into darkness, and the moon into blood, **before** the great and the terrible **Day of the Lord** come*   Joel 2:31

The moon turning to blood has already been predicted as the sixth seal was removed from the 7-sealed scroll. Note that the removal of the sixth seal predicts catastrophes which will occur *very near* the end of the 1260-day period of tribulation, and *NOT before* the seven bowl judgments are executed as the majority of prophecy teachers maintain. This is because they fail to recognize that the seals provide only an *overview* of the tribulation period and show general conditions and several specific events which will exist over the last 3.5 years. The seals *do not* represent a sequence of events which *precede* the seven trumpets and the seven bowl judgments. They preview the devastation and catastrophes that the 7 trumpets and the 7 bowls bring during the Wrath of Satan and the Wrath of God. It is consistent and biblical to again point out that if Joel is to be believed, it is clear that the *Day of the Lord* is *not* an extended period of time as all pretribulation prophecy teachers maintain, but it is a single day....as it should be.

As darkness falls upon the Kingdom of the Beast, the followers of Satan blasphemed God, cursed Him and failed to repent. Bowl 6 is about to be poured out upon the earth.

And the sixth angel poured out his vial upon the great
river Euphrates; and the water thereof was dried up, that the way of the kings of the east can
assemble in.   Revelation 16:12

As the *6th bowl* is poured out, the River Euphrates is dried up to prepare the way for Satan and the armies of the east to march upon Jerusalem.

Bowl 6   The sixth bowl is "poured out".......
The contents of this bowl are poured
out upon the River Euphrates, and its waters
are dried up.
Rev 16:12-16

The region around the Euphrates River is known as *Mesopotamia*. This area, where the invention of writing and the wheel occurred, is the cradle of civilization. Abraham was born in that area and was called out of Ur of the Chaldees. Mesopotamia eventually became the heartland of the Babylonian and Assyrian world empires. That area is near the border of Turkey and Iraq. The Euphrates River dries up *so that the way of the kings from the East might be prepared* (Revelation 16:12). There is another remarkable, supernatural event which takes place as the Euphrates River is being dried up. Three *unclean spirits* arise out of the mouths of Satan, the antichrist and the False Prophet and gather all unbelievers to march upon Jerusalem. These are the main land armies of the Antichrist. The great *Battle of Armageddon* has arrived. All who have taken the mark of the beast will join this campaign. They will be supernaturally gathered from all over the world.

[13] *and I saw three unclean spirits like frogs coming from the mouth of the dragon* (Satan), *out of the mouth of the beast (antichrist) and out of the mouth of the false prophet* (Beast out of the sea).
[14] *For they are spirits of demons, performing signs, which go out to the kings of the earth, and of the whole world, to gather them to the battle of the great day of God Almighty*
Revelation 16: 13-14

Satan will think that *he* is gathering his armies to this great final battle, but in reality, it is being done to fulfill the eternal plan of God. We call this the *Armageddon Campaign*. The word *Armageddon* appears only once in the entire Bible and is found in Revelation 16:16. No place on earth actually bears the name Armageddon. The Greek is most commonly thought to be a transliteration of the Hebrew words *Har Megiddo...* literally, *Mountain of Megiddo*. The Mount of Megiddo is actually a *tell* or a high hill overlooking the plain of Esdraelon or Jezreel, which is a valley fourteen by twenty miles in size located to the southwest of Nazareth. Here, it is thought by many, that the great final battle of Armageddon will be fought.

The seventh and last bowl is about to be poured out. The 2nd advent of Christ who descends from heaven to fight the Battle of Armageddon his will terminate both the 70-Week Prophecy of Daniel and the worldwide reign of the Antichrist.

The seventh and last bowl is about to be poured out. This will terminate both the 70-Week Prophecy of Daniel and the worldwide reign of the Antichrist. The 7th Bowl judgment is about to take place which will trigger the *Battle of Armageddon.*

[16] *And he gathered them together into a place called in the Hebrew tongue Armageddon*

> Bowl 7 The seventh bowl is poured into the air........

[17] *And the seventh angel poured out his vial into the air; and there came a great voice out of the temple of heaven, from the throne, saying,* **It is done**.
[18] *And there were voices, and thunders, and lightnings; and there was a great earthquake, such as was not since men were upon the earth, so mighty an earthquake, and so great.*
[19] *And the great city was divided into three parts, and the cities of the nations fell: and great Babylon came in remembrance before God, to give unto her the cup of the wine of the fierceness of his wrath.*
[20] ***And every island fled away, and the mountains were not found.***
[21] *And there fell upon men a great hail out of heaven, every stone about the weight of a talent: and men blasphemed God because of the plague of the hail; for the plague thereof was exceeding great* Revelation 16: 16-21

When the seventh angel pours out the seventh bowl, a loud voice from out of the temple in heaven is heard from the Throne. This voice loudly proclaims that: **It is done** (Revelation 16:17). There is immediately widespread destruction upon the earth. Although it is not revealed to us who issues this proclamation, it is altogether appropriate that the declaration *It is done* will probably come directly from God himself.

After all, it was the voice of God who brought the world into existence, and it was the voice of God who initiated the seven bowl judgments… only He can wreak such devastation and destruction upon His earth. It is also appropriate that the voice should come directly from His holy temple. Only one other place in the book of Revelation is the temple and the throne of God mentioned together, and that is in Revelation 7:15 when the saints of all ages are seen assembling before God. It is appropriate that this is so. God sent His only begotten Son to save all who would believe upon Him, and both the work of the cross and the work of battle at Armageddon are testimonies to his majesty. However, we should not try to assign too much spiritual meaning to this declaration. The most obvious meaning is that the seven bowl judgments which is Wrath of God are completed and they were initiated at His word.

The occurrence of ***thunder, lightning, earthquakes and hail*** are not unique during the last 3.5 years of the tribulation period. In fact, recall that after the seventh trumpet was blown

(Revelation 11:19) similar events were recorded. This was all predicted and shown to John as Jesus Christ removed the 6th seal (Revelation 6:12). This is proof that the events of the 6th seal reveal what will happen after the 7-sealed scroll has been opened and not before.

Then the temple of God was opened in Heaven and the Ark of the Covenant was seen in His temple. And there were lightening, noises, thunderings, an earthquake and great hail
Revelation 11:19

This scene is not difficult to correlate with Revelation 16: 18-19 as the 7th trumpet was blown. Many prophecy students have used the scene after the seventh trumpet is blown to *prove* that the seven bowl judgments *telescope* or emerge from the seventh trumpet. While there may be some apparent truth to this theory, it is clear that God himself initiates both the trumpet and bowl sequences. They are chronologically linked and occur successively over the last 3.5 years. The seven trumpet judgments take place during the persecution of Satan, the antichrist and the false prophet. The 7 Bowl judgments take place immediately following the 7 Trumpet judgments. While these two successive judgments are similar in structure, they are vastly different in terms of severity.

The first three **Trumpet Judgments** destroy 1/3 of all the trees (Revelation 8:7), all of the green grass (Revelation 8:7), 1/3 of sea turns to blood (Revelation 8: 8-9), 1/3 of all sea creatures die (Revelation 8: 8-9), 1/3 of all ships are destroyed (Revelation 8: 8-9), 1/3 of all fresh water turns bitter (Revelation 8: 10-11), 1/3 of the sun ceases to give light (Revelation 8: 10-11), 1/3 of the moon ceases to shine (Revelation 8: 10-11), 1/3 of all stars disappear (Revelation 8: 10-11) and 1/3 of mankind is killed with fire and brimstone (Revelation 9: 13-21). The Temple of God was opened (Revelation 11: 19a), and there are voices, lightning, thunder, an earthquake and hail (Revelation 11:19).

The 7th Bowl Judgment causes **all** sea water to turn to blood (Revelation 16:3) and **all** sea creatures die (Revelation 16:3). **All** fresh water turns to blood (Revelation 16: 4) which will kill **all** freshwater fish. **All** men are tortured by sores (Revelation 16:2), fire (Revelation 16: 8-9) and pain (Revelation 16:10). There are voices, thunder, and lightning (Revelation 16:18) but the earthquake which occurs at bowl seven is the granddaddy of all earthquakes!

...and there was a great earthquake, such as was not since men were upon the earth, so mighty an earthquake, and so great   Revelation 16:18-b

As the 7th bowl is poured out, another unprecedented event occurs

| 👑 | Hail about 100 pounds apiece fall | (Rev 16:21) |

And there fell upon men a great hail out of heaven, every stone about the weight of a talent: and men blasphemed God because of the plague of the hail; for the plague thereof was exceeding great   Revelation 16:21

Gigantic hail *fell upon men* and *every hailstone was about the weight of a talent* (Revelation 16:21). The weight of a talent is about 100 pounds. It is likely that hail of that size has never fallen on the earth. The reaction of man is unbelievable. It had never changed since the sixth trumpet sounded (Revelation 9: 20-21).

And man blasphemed God because of the plague of the hail, since that plague was exceedingly great   Revelation 16:21-b

The next result of pouring out the seventh bowl is that the cities of the world fall apart.

…and the cities of the nations fell…   Revelation 16:19a

As we approach the end of the church age in this 21st century, the cities of the world spiral further and further into Satan's grasp. It is true that there are many mega churches and active congregations in every major city, but Christianity and living for Christ is definitely in the minority. Drugs, alcohol, prostitution, adultery and crime are everywhere. Recent studies have shown that only 5% of youth under the age of 18 will follow Christ and regularly attend church.

At the seventh bowl, we are told that *the cities of the nations fell* (Revelation 16:19). We are not told just what is meant by *fell,* but it is almost certain that due to natural or supernatural causes, multi-story buildings and all skyscrapers will collapse in piles of rubble.

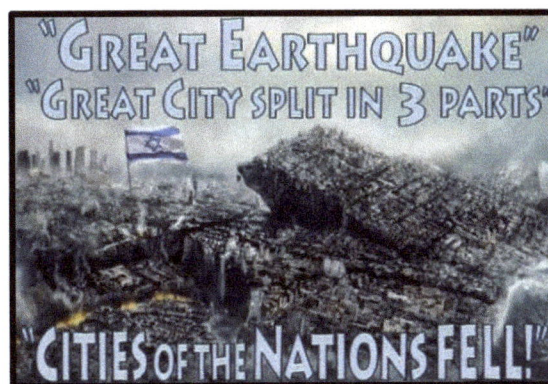

John also records that he saw *the great city divided into three parts* (Revelation 16:19). There is no doubt that this great city is Jerusalem, because in Revelation 11:8 we are told that the dead bodies of the two witnesses that testify for 1260 days *will lie in the street of the great city which spiritually is called Sodom and Egypt where also our Lord was crucified.* We are given no details as to how Jerusalem will be divided, but since the city will be divided into three parts (Revelation 16:19), it is possible that the epicenter of the *great earthquake* in Revelation 16:18 might occur there and divide the city with great chasms. The destruction of cities around the world and the division of Jerusalem into three parts indicate extensive, worldwide destruction. The shock and aftershock will be supernaturally felt worldwide. Devastation is also indicated for a city called *Babylon* (Revelation 16:19), which is the seat of Satan's world empire. It will be destroyed by a great *millstone* (Revelation 18:21). The end of both physical and spiritual Babylon will not be detailed here, but two entire chapters (Chapters 21-22) describe this destruction in Phillips, The Book of Revelation: *Mysteries Revealed.* For now, it is sufficient to say that there is no need to doubt that since Jerusalem has been mentioned by name immediately preceding this prophecy, that *Babylon* is the actual name of a city which has been rebuilt and occupied in the land of Shinar (Zachariah 5:1-11). There is no need to spiritualize the name Babylon to secretly camouflage Rome, Jerusalem or any other city. Babylon will be rebuilt in the end times and it will be completely and utterly destroyed by God at the end of the age (Revelation 16). It is true that the ancient city of Babylon that Nimrod built was destroyed by God and the people scattered all over the world after **confounding their language** (Genesis 11:1-9). It is also true that the city of Babylon that Nimrod built was also a seat of political and military power when the Babylonian Empire held sway over the entire known world. It held the throne of Nebuchadnezzar I, King of Babylon. The city of Jerusalem was Conquered by the Medo-Persian empire and served as the capital city once again. However, it was eventually destroyed by invading forces. Isaiah and Jeremiah had a great deal to say about the fall of Babylon (Jeremiah 50 and 51, Isaiah 13 and 14). Literalists argue that the Scriptures indicate a sudden destruction of Babylon whereas history records no such sudden destruction by which that city became desolated. Isaiah 47, for example, indicates that the *mistress of kingdoms* would one day suffer loss of children, and widow every man *in one day*. Furthermore, Babylon will be destroyed **as when God overthrew Sodom and Gomorrah** (Isaiah 13:19). Babylon's destruction will be brought about suddenly, and the weapons of judgment are to be by fire just as Sodom and Gomorrah was destroyed *in a moment by fire* (Genesis 19). The heavens and earth will come apart, and water will swallow up the site upon which the city stands (Isaiah 13:13, Jeremiah 51:42). The result of all this is found in the prophecies of Jeremiah.

It shall never be inhabited, neither shall it be dwelt in from generation to generation: neither shall the Arabian pitch tent there; neither shall shepherds make their flocks to lie down there.
Isaiah 13:20   (Jeremiah 50:3, 51:26)

Although Babylon has been inhabited since Babel, it now lies mostly abandoned. Babylon is still being used by a few people and is partially inhabited. The above prophecy makes it clear *no tent will ever be pitched there* and it will be perpetually uninhabited. That is yet to be fulfilled, but it will happen at the end of this age.

Recall that as the sixth seal was broken, the vision that John saw predicted that: **every mountain and island was moved out of its place** (Revelation 6:14). As the effects of the seventh bowl are concluding, John now sees the fulfillment of that vision. Not only is every island and mountain moved *out of its place,* John now testifies that **every island fled away, and the mountains were not found** (Revelation 16:20). Anyone who lived on an island or on a mountain is instantly killed. This will cause destruction and death in rural areas comparable to that which occurs as *the cities of the nations fell* (Revelation 16:19). Although not specifically stated, it appears that only those people living on the plains or in isolated rural areas might be spared. However, they will not escape all of God's wrath.

The Battle of Armageddon: *Gog and Magog*

At this point, we would like to clarify that the great battle of Armageddon is described in Ezekiel 38-39. There is an ongoing debate among Biblical scholars as to whether Ezekiel 38-39 is a description of the battle of Armageddon described in Revelation 19:19-21 or whether it describes the last great battle following the 1000-year millennial reign described briefly in Revelation 20:7-10. We are indebted to the following source of information for portions of this critique: http://www.gotquestions.org/Gog-Magog.html .

> The confusion that has resulted is in the use of the terms **Gog and Magog** in both Ezekiel 38: 1-2 Ezekiel 39:39; and in Revelation 20:8. The assumption is often that all these passages refer to the same battle This is, however, just an illusion. *Magog* was a grandson of Noah (Genesis 10:2). The descendants of Magog settled to the far north of Israel, likely beyond the Black Sea just south of current day Russia. They migrated into parts of Germany, and may have even settled in southern Russia. It is important to recognize that the Gog and Magog of Ezekiel 38-39 are different from the Gog and Magog mentioned in Revelation 20:7-8. *Gog* is a title, just as *prince* is a title.

Below are a few of the more obvious reasons why Ezekiel 38-39 *cannot* describe the final great battle *following* the Millennial Kingdom.

1. In the battle of Ezekiel 38-39, the armies come primarily from the north and involve only a few nations of the earth (Ezekiel 38:6, Ezekie15; Ezekiel 39: 2). The battle in Revelation 20: 7-9 will involve all nations, so armies will come from all directions, not just from the north.
2. There is no mention of Satan in the context of Ezekiel 38-39. In Revelation 20:7 the context clearly places the battle at the end of the millennium with Satan as the leader of this invasion and battle.
3. Ezekiel 39: 11-12 states that the dead will be buried for seven months. There would be no need to bury the dead if the battle in Ezekiel 38-39 is the one described in Revelation 20:8-9, for immediately following Revelation 20: 8-9 is the Great White Throne judgment (Revelation 20: 11-15) and then the current or present heaven and earth are destroyed, replaced by a new heaven and earth (Revelation 21:1). There obviously will be a need to bury the dead if the battle takes place on the last day of the Great Tribulation, for the land of Israel will be occupied for another 1,000 years, the length of the Millennial Kingdom (Revelation 20: 4-6).
4. The prophecies of Ezekiel in Ezekiel 38-39 are immediately followed by an extensive description of the Millennial Kingdom in Chapters 40-44. Chronologically, this eliminates the battle described in Revelation 21:8-9, since the prophecies contained in Ezekiel 40-44 clearly occur after the Millennial Kingdom has run its 1000-year course (Revelation 21:7).

We will not devote any more time or space to this important issue at this time. However, the entire content of Chapter 26 in the book by Phillips (Revelation: *Mysteries Revealed*) is devoted to the proper identification of the battles described in Ezekiel 38-39 and Revelation 21.

Conclusions

We have discussed the *seven seals*, the *seven trumpets* and the *seven bowls*. The seven seals bind the outside of the scroll held by God, and as they are broken several things which will take place over the 1260-day tribulation period are *previewed. The seven seals function exactly as the preface to a good book.* The seven trumpets represented the **Wrath of Satan** on those who refuse to worship him or his image that will stand in the rebuilt temple in Jerusalem, or those who have refused to take the *mark of the beast*. These judgments are allowed by God. *Why does God allow this persecution of all who dwell upon the earth* (believers and unbelievers) *to take place after Satan is cast down?* The purpose of the tribulation period is to fulfill Daniel's 70th week, and to bring Israel back into a covenant relationship with God by showing Israel that their long-awaited Messiah is none other than his only begotten Son, Jesus Christ. The *seven trumpets* serve to purify and refine both the precious wheat (the church) and the nation of Israel who will inherit the land during the millennial kingdom. The *seven bowls* represented the **Wrath of God** poured out upon Satan and all of his followers, following the rapture of the church at the sounding of the seventh trumpet before the seven bowl judgments occur. The seven trumpets are blown over a 1250-day period of time. Some call this period *the Time of Jacob's Trouble* (Jeremiah 30:7), but this is incorrect. A careful study of Jeremiah 30 and Joel 1-3 will establish that the phrase **Time of Jacob's Trouble** is referring to the last 3.5 years of this age which will include both the **Wrath of Satan** (the seven trumpet judgments) and the **Wrath of God** (the seven Bowl Judgments). During this period of time the Old Testament prophets spoke of days (Plural). but the **Day of the Lord** (singular) is exactly what it says…. The day that our Lord returns to fight the *Battle of Armageddon*. This *day* will conclude the *days* of Jacob's Trouble. The last 10 days between the **Feast of Trumpets** on Tishri 1 and the Feast of Yom Kippur on Tishri 10 will conclude the 1260 days that Satan is confined to the earth. Christ referred to these 10 days as one of **great tribulation**.

For then shall be great tribulation, such as was not since the beginning of the world to this time, no, nor ever shall be.   Matthew 24:21

Finally, note from Revelation 16:14 that the armies of the world are gathered to the Battle of Armageddon. As previously stated, it is time for the **Day of the Lord**. The Day of the Lord is not a protracted period of time consisting of 7 years or even 3.5 years… it is exactly what the scriptures say it is…. *One day.* The Day of the Lord is widely misunderstood and misinterpreted by almost all prophecy teachers. *It is a literal Day, the day of Christ's Second Advent*, when He will return to fight the Battle of Armageddon. The source of confusion is universally attributed to Revelation 6:17, which specifically states that as the sixth seal is broken, the Day of Lord has come.

For the great day of the Lord has come, and who is able to stand.   Revelation 16:17

The seventh bowl judgment which initiates the Battle of Armageddon will *terminate* the 70th week of Daniel. The 7 bowl judgments are so severe that they will be poured out over a very short period of time. This short period of time will be *ten consecutive days* between when the Church is raptured out at the *Feast of Trumpets* on Tishri 1, and when the Battle of Armageddon occurs on the *Feast of Yom Kippur* on Tishri 10. Chronologically, the two chosen men of God will start witnessing in the Jerusalem Temple three days *before* Satan is cast down and starts his 1260-day reign of terror. They are slain after 1250 days on the *same day* that the church is raptured out (Phillips; Daniel's 70th Week: *The cornerstone of all prophecy*). *No living Christian remains on this earth immediately after the rapture occurs, but during this short 10-day period of time… during which the seven bowls are poured out… salvation will be offered to all those who* remain. This is not a second chance to be saved...it is the last chance. It appears that many will not repent,

And they (who remained and follow Satan) *blasphemed the God of heaven... And did not repent of their deeds.*　　　　Revelation 16:11

It is important to recognize that the 10-day period of time in which a last chance for salvation will be offered is totally consistent with the scriptural *Pattern of the Harvest*. The rapture of the church is the *Great Wheat Harvest* (Revelation 14: 14-16) that Christ predicted at the end of the age in the *Parable of the Wheat and Tares* as He was speaking to the Jews (Matthew 13: 24-43).

[30] *Let both grow together until the harvest: and in the time of harvest, I will say to the reapers, gather ye together first the tares, and bind them in bundles to burn them: but gather the wheat into my barn*　　　　Matthew 13:30
[39] *The enemy that sowed them is the devil; the harvest is the end of the world; and the reapers are the angels.*　　　　Matthew 13:39

[14] *And I looked, and behold a white cloud, and upon the cloud one sat like unto the Son of man, having on his head a golden crown, and in his hand a sharp sickle.*
[15] *And another angel came out of the temple, crying with a loud voice to him that sat on the cloud, Thrust in thy sickle, and reap: for the time is come for thee to reap; for the harvest of the earth is ripe*　　　　Revelation 14:14

Wheat is the crop that sustained and fed the nation of Israel. It is such an important staple, that one would assume that it would be harvested very carefully, leaving none behind. However, when the harvest was completed, a strange thing was commanded by God which was a spiritual Mystery under the old covenant.

And when ye reap the harvest of your land, thou shalt not wholly reap the corners of thy field, neither shalt thou gather the gleanings of thy harvest.　　　　Leviticus 19: 9

In the Book of Ruth, when Ruth came to Boaz seeking redemption, it was *following* the main harvest. Ruth came to pick the *gleanings* that were left in the field, but wound up being saved... her and her entire family... by Boaz, the kinsman redeemer. The entire story of Ruth and Boaz is prophetic and foreshadowed the restoration and salvation of Israel.

The prophetic truth of this story is that the remnants of the nation of Israel that enter into the bowl judgments are the *gleanings* of the main harvest at the seventh trumpet. They have not been raptured out due to disbelief, but God in His mercy will give them 10 more days to recognize Christ as their Messiah and fulfill the words of the prophet Isaiah. These 10 days are between the *Feast of Trumpets* (Rosh Hashanah) on Tishri 1 and the *Feast of Yom Kippur*. These 10 days are called the *Time of Travail*.

Who hath heard such a thing? who hath seen such things? shall the earth be made to bring forth in one day? or shall a nation be born at once? for as soon as Zion travailed, she brought forth her children　　　　Isaiah 66:8

The *time of travail* is the last 10 days of the Church Age and the final time of redemption under the New Covenant promises: According to Jewish tradition, Rosh Hashanah is called the *Day of Judgment* in which God opens up the Books of Life and Death for the year. Yom Kippur is the Jewish *Day of Atonement*. The focus of these 10 days is to highlight their need for forgiveness and reconciliation with God. **Yom Kippur is the holiest day of the year and is a day of fasting to express their repentance and need for forgiveness.** This will be *the time of restoration for the Nation of Israel.* It is at this time… when there is apparently no hope… that hope and grace will be found. Our hope and salvation are only in Jesus Christ. A non-believing Jewish remnant will finally accept Jesus Christ as their long-awaited Savior and Messiah.

For I would not, brethren, that ye should be ignorant of this mystery, lest ye should be wise in your own conceits; that blindness in part is happened to Israel, until the fullness of the Gentiles be come in. And so, all Israel shall be saved: as it is written, There shall come out of Sion the Deliverer, and shall turn away ungodliness from Jacob.   Romans 5:26

In Chapter 5, we will now show that a great deal if not all of spiritual confusion in the Book of Revelation results from not recognizing that the seals, trumpets and bowls are *not successive events occurring over a seven-year period of time,* but that the seals are a *preview of conditions which will exist* during a total tribulation period of 3.5 years or 1267 days. The sixth seal is predicting those events which occur immediately preceding the Battle of Armageddon (Revelation 6: 12-17). We are now ready to show how the trumpets and bowls fit together chronologically, and how the 1267 days are allocated to the trumpet and bowl judgments. The following diagram illustrates how the *Feast of Trumpets* on Tishri 1 and the *Feast of Yom Kippur* on Tishri 10 are related to the last half of Daniel's 70th Week.

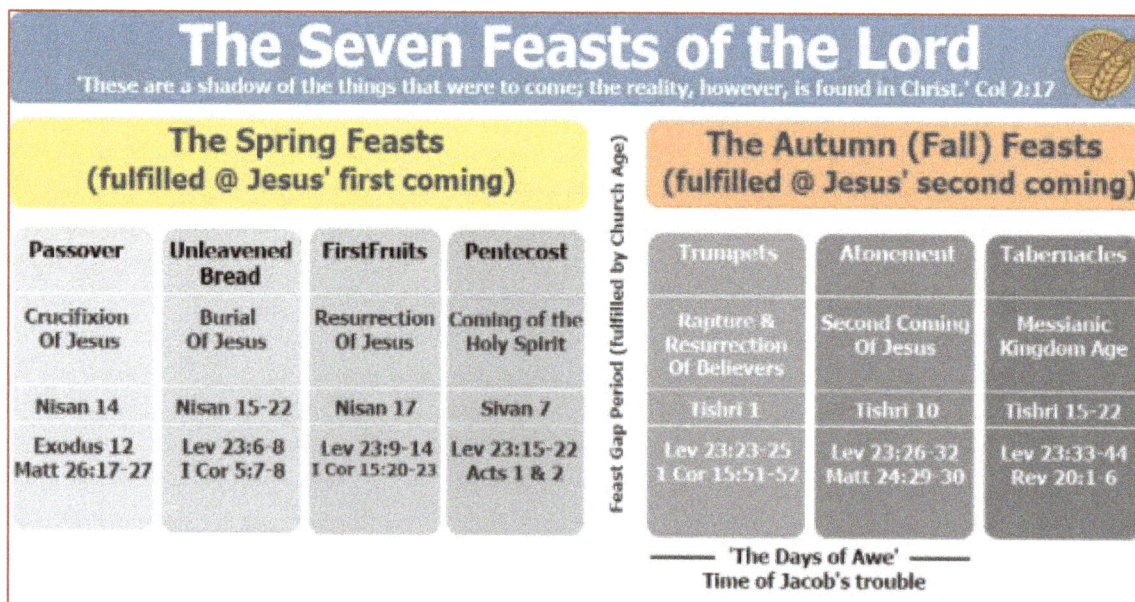

The Seven Feasts of the Lord
'These are a shadow of the things that were to come; the reality, however, is found in Christ.' Col 2:17

The Spring Feasts (fulfilled @ Jesus' first coming)				Feast Gap Period (fulfilled by Church Age)	The Autumn (Fall) Feasts (fulfilled @ Jesus' second coming)		
Passover	Unleavened Bread	FirstFruits	Pentecost		Trumpets	Atonement	Tabernacles
Crucifixion Of Jesus	Burial Of Jesus	Resurrection Of Jesus	Coming of the Holy Spirit		Rapture & Resurrection Of Believers	Second Coming Of Jesus	Messianic Kingdom Age
Nisan 14	Nisan 15-22	Nisan 17	Sivan 7		Tishri 1	Tishri 10	Tishri 15-22
Exodus 12 Matt 26:17-27	Lev 23:6-8 I Cor 5:7-8	Lev 23:9-14 I Cor 15:20-23	Lev 23:15-22 Acts 1 & 2		Lev 23:23-25 1 Cor 15:51-52	Lev 23:26-32 Matt 24:29-30	Lev 23:33-44 Rev 20:1-6

—— 'The Days of Awe' ——
Time of Jacob's trouble

Chapter 5

The 7 Seals: Correct Chronology

In Chapter 4, the seals, trumpets and bowls which are revealed in the Book of Revelation were summarized and described. The 7 Trumpet Judgments parallel the reign and Wrath of Satan, and the 7 Bowl Judgments are the Wrath of God. We will now show that the seals, trumpets and bowls are *not* all sequential through time. The 7 seals are broken to gain access and reveal the contents of a scroll. The purpose of Chapter 4 is to show beyond reasonable doubt that as the 7 seals are broken by Jesus Christ, John was shown visions of the future which would later be fulfilled. The 7 seals only predict conditions (Seals 1-4) and specific important events (Seals 5-6) which will later take place during the Great Tribulation. The 7 seals are analogous to the *Preface* of a good book. A Preface always precedes the contents and details of a book.

The 7 seals prophesy of things which will take place as the 7 trumpets are blown and the 7 bowls are poured out. However, there is a direct relationship between the seals, bowls and trumpets. The seals span the entire period of time during which the 7 Trumpets and the 7 Bowls will take place. Note that the 7 trumpets and the 7 Bowls are each delivered to the earth from heaven by angels (Revelation 8:2, Revelation 15:1). The 7 seals are broken/ removed by Jesus Christ (Revelation 5:5).

Even though there is a direct relationship between the seals, bowls and trumpets…there is a distinct difference between the seals and both the trumpets and bowls. The 7 seals only reveal things to come: The 7 trumpets and the 7 bowls actually cause things to happen. The seals are 7 in number and they have been placed upon a royal document called a *scroll*. The scroll was being kept by God, and when it came time to reveal its contents only Christ was worthy to reveal its mysteries (Revelation 5: 1-8). John was actually to see visions of its contents as it is unrolled. This scroll contains the eternal plan of God to fulfill all of His covenant promises to the nation of Israel. He had promised His beloved nation of Israel that one day He would place them in the land of promise where they would be ruled again by King David, and that they would dwell there forever. This event will begin the 1000-year Millennial Kingdom. The purpose of the Great Tribulation is to fully restore the Jews into an intimate and personal relationship with God as He intended all along. Only God can do this, and He will do it to exalt and honor His Son Jesus Christ.

[18] *But those things, which God before had showed by the mouth of all his prophets, that Christ should suffer, he hath so fulfilled.*
[19] *Repent ye therefore, and be converted, that your sins may be blotted out, when the times of refreshing shall come from the presence of the Lord;*
[20] *And he shall send Jesus Christ, which before was preached unto you:*
[21] Whom *the heaven must receive until the times of restitution of all things, which God hath spoken by the mouth of all his holy prophets since the world began*   Acts 3: 18-21

Breaking the 7 Seals

John has been in exile on the Island of Patmos for boldly proclaiming the gospel of Christ in Roman provinces. As he was praying *in the spirit* (Revelation 1:10) the reincarnated Christ came to him and spoke (Revelation 1: 11-20). John was then commanded to write 7 Letters to the *angelos* (angel or messenger) in each of 7 churches in Asia Minor (Revelation 2-3). After obeying this command, he was then called to heaven where he stood before the Throne of God (Revelation 4:2) and was told to write the prophetic Book of Revelation. Only Jesus Christ is worthy to take the scroll, break the 7 seals and reveal its contents (Revelation 5: 4-5).

[1] *And I saw in the right hand of him that sat on the throne a book written within and on the backside, sealed with seven seals.*
[2] *And I saw a strong angel proclaiming with a loud voice, who is worthy to open the book, and to loosen the seals thereof?*   Revelation 5: 1-2

John has been taken to heaven in the spirit (Revelation 4: 1-2) and he is standing before the throne of God (Revelation 4: 2-11). As he beholds the majesty and splendor of God's Throne Room, he saw God holding a scroll with 7 seals that was written on front and back (Revelation 5:1). A *strong angel* appeared and in a loud voice asked who was worthy to open the scroll...and he found no man worthy to open the scroll. John *wept bitterly* since no man was found in the heavens or in the earth (Revelation 5: 3-4).

[3] *And no man in heaven, nor in earth, neither under the earth, was able to open the book, neither to look thereon.*
[4] *And I wept much, because no man was found worthy to open and to read the book, neither to*

look thereon.
[5] And one of the elders saith unto me, Weep not: behold, the Lion of the tribe of Juda, the Root of David, hath prevailed to open the book, and to loosen the seven seals thereof
        Revelation 5: 3-5

Suddenly the lamb of God appeared and He takes the scroll from God and all of heaven rejoices because He is worthy. The voice of many angels, the four beasts and the elders praise and honor Jesus Christ …because He is the only creature in heaven or in earth that could open the scroll. We are given a glimpse of how many angels are in heaven; the number of them was ten thousand times ten thousand, and thousands of thousands, which are at least 100 trillion angels. Just think, one day soon we will join these ranks of heavenly creatures and serve God forever….what a glorious day it will be.

As Christ began to remove the 7 seals, John began to see what would take place as this age comes to an end. The first vision comes as the 1st seal is removed.

[1] And I saw when the Lamb opened one of the seals, and I heard, as it were the noise of thunder, one of the four beasts saying, Come and see.
[2] And I saw, and behold a white horse: and he that sat on him had a bow; and a crown was given unto him: and he went forth conquering, and to conquer   Revelation 6: 1-2

First Seal
Rider on White Horse

Rider has a bow
Rider wears a crown
Rider goes forth
    Conquering

Revelation 6: 1-2

As Christ breaks the 1st seal, one of the 4 beasts that stand before the throne of God tells John: *Come and see* (Revelation 6:1). As John obeys, he sees a white horse and a rider which has a bow but no arrows. He comes forth to conquer (Revelation 6:2). The rider n This rider has long been debated. Many have identified the rider of this hose as Jesus Christ, but this is entirely out of context with the horses that will appear as Seals 2-4 are broken. This rider will conquer with military power as well as political cunning. It is not Jesus Christ who rides forth on a white horse. It is not Satan, and in context with the other three riders it cannot be exclusively the Antichrist. All 4 horses and riders personify and represent both supernatural and devastating forces that will be at work during the Great Tribulation. After careful consideration, it is suggested and concluded that this rider represents political and military power of Satan during the Great Tribulation. Satan will conquer by using the military power of the final 10-nation confederacy, and by political deception because he has a bow but no arrows. His instruments of power and destruction will be the Antichrist and the False prophet (Revelation 13: 1-18).

For there shall arise false Christs, and false prophets, and shall shew great signs and wonders; insomuch that, if it were possible, they shall deceive the very elect.   Matthew 24:24

The Antichrist, false Prophet and Satan will fulfil these words of Christ, deceive many, and lead those who reject Christ as their Lord and Savior to everlasting punishment in the Lake of Fire. This will be manifested throughout the duration of the Great Tribulation accompanied by what each of the first 4 horseman represents: *Destruction, Wars, Famine*, and *Death*.

Second Seal

Rider on Red Horse

Rider has a Great Sword
Rider has power to take
Peace from World

Revelatiion 6: 3-4

As the second seal is broken/removed, John is again commanded to *come and see,* and he sees a rider on a Red Horse.

[3] *And when he had opened the second seal, I heard the second beast say, Come and see.*
[4] *And there went out another horse that was red: and power was given to him that sat thereon to take peace from the earth, and that they should kill one another: and there was given unto him a great sword*
Revelation 6: 3-4

This rider is given a great sword. This sword represents the instrument by which peace will be removed from all of the earth. Men will war against one another and kill one another. *Is this horse and great sword the only instrument of war?* Likely not. In the 1st century there were no helicopters, tanks or airplanes and John is conveying the instruments of war which will be used over 2000 years later as best he can. It is better to interpret the sword which takes peace from the world as a symbol of destruction and death over an extended period of time…. characterized by conflict, terror and bloodshed. The fact that there have been wars and rumers of wars throughout recorded history cannot be challenged. However, the prophetic nature of the scroll itself demands that this imagery applies to a future period of death and destruction that will surpass anything yet recorded in history. The 3rd seal is now removed.

Third Seal

Rider on Black Horse

Rider has scales in his hands
Rider brings famine
and shortage of food

Revelation 6: 5-6

[5] *And when he had opened the third seal, I heard the third beast say, Come and see. And I beheld, and lo a black horse; and he that sat on him had a pair of balances in his hand.*
[6] *And I heard a voice in the midst of the four beasts say, A measure of wheat for a penny, and three measures of barley for a penny; and see thou hurt not the oil and the wine*   Revelation 6: 5-6

When Jesus Christ opens the 3rd seal. John is told to *come and see* A black horse appears with a rider which has a scale in his right hand. This scale is one which was commonly once used to weigh grain. the counterweight was used to determine the purchase price. The rider clothed in black and the scales indicate that a time is coming of sorrow and suffering due to a shortage and scarcity of food. *What could cause such a worldwide lack of food?*

This is a prediction of what will occur when Trump 1 and 2 sounds. When Trump 1 sounds *all* green grass is burned up along with 1/3 of all the trees (Revelation 8:7). If something burns up *all* the green grass, crops will largely be burned up also. There will not only be devastating fires, but when the 3rd trumpet sounds, 1/3 of all the fresh water will be polluted in some way (Revelation 8:10). The devastation of crops and food when Trump 1 and Trump 2 are blown is bad enough, but later when the 3rd Bowl is poured out, *all* fresh water rivers, streams and wells (fountains of water) turn to blood. The 3rd Bowl in a sequence of seven will obviously be poured out upon all the earth very near the end of the Tribulation period. Man can be denied food for an extended period of time, but water is necessary to sustain all life. Medical doctors have stated that the average person can live only 3-4 days without water. With access to bottled water, mankind might survive up to 1-2 weeks. The 4th seal is now removed.

Fourth Seal
Rider on Pale Horse

Rider is Death
Hell closely follows
Power is given to rider to
   kill 1/4 of all people

Revelation 6: 7-8

[7] *And when he had opened the fourth seal, I heard the voice of the fourth beast say, Come and see.*
[8] *And I looked, and behold a pale horse: and his name that sat on him was Death, and Hell followed with him. And power was given unto them over the fourth part of the earth, to kill with sword, and with hunger, and with death, and with the beasts of the earth*   Revelation 6: 7-8

As the 4th seal is broken, John turns to see a pale horse. In the Greek, the phrase translated as pale horse (KJV) means a sickly, yellowish-green color. This horse is ridden by death. The 1st seal has brought war....and war always brings famine and devastation. War and famine always result in death. This is a serious revelation of what is about to take place as the Great Tribulation begins. Satan will be cast out of heaven and he will be furious with rage. He will totally dominate and inherit the body of the slain European world leader and arise as the Antichrist. He will break a peace treaty with Israel which has allowed them to build a new temple in Jerusalem and resume Temple worship. Isaiah called this the *Covenant of Death.*

Because ye have said: We have made a covenant with death, and with hell are we at agreement; when the overflowing scourge shall pass through, it shall not come unto us: for we have made lies our refuge, and under falsehood have we hid ourselves   Isaiah 28:15

Israel will be deceived and think that they are living in peace and safety. Suddenly, Satan as the Antichrist will turn upon Israel and annul the Covenant of Peace which was in reality a Covenant of Death.

And your covenant with death shall be disannulled, and your agreement with hell shall not stand; when the overflowing scourge shall pass through, then ye shall be trodden down by it
Zachariah 28:18

[1] *Behold, the day of the LORD cometh, and thy spoil shall be divided in the midst of thee.*
[2] *For I will gather all nations against Jerusalem to battle; and the city shall be taken, and the houses rifled, and the women ravished; and half of the city shall go forth into captivity, and the residue of the people shall not be cut off from the city.*
[3] *Then shall the LORD go forth, and fight against those nations, as when he fought in the day of battle.*
[4] *And his feet shall stand in that day upon the mount of Olives, which is before Jerusalem on the east, and the mount of Olives shall cleave in the midst thereof toward the east and toward the west, and there shall be a very great valley; and half of the mountain shall remove toward the north, and half of it toward the south.*
[5] *And ye shall flee to the valley of the mountains; for the valley of the mountains shall reach unto Azal: yea, ye shall flee, like as ye fled from before the earthquake in the days of Uzziah king of Judah: and the LORD my God shall come, and all the saints with thee.*
[6] *And it shall come to pass in that day, that the light shall not be clear, nor dark:*

[7] *But it shall be one day which shall be known to the LORD, not day, nor night: but it shall come to pass, that at evening time it shall be light.*

[8] *And it shall be in that day, that living waters shall go out from Jerusalem; half of them toward the former sea, and half of them toward the hinder sea: in summer and in winter shall it be.*

[9] *And the LORD shall be king over all the earth: in that day shall there be one LORD, and his name one.*

[10] *All the land shall be turned as a plain from Geba to Rimmon south of Jerusalem: and it shall be lifted up, and inhabited in her place, from Benjamin's gate unto the place of the first gate, unto the corner gate, and from the tower of Hananeel unto the king's winepresses.*

[11] *And men shall dwell in it, and there shall be no more utter destruction; but Jerusalem shall be safely inhabited.*

[12] *And this shall be the plague wherewith the LORD will smite all the people that have fought against Jerusalem; Their flesh shall consume away while they stand upon their feet, and their eyes shall consume away in their holes, and their tongue shall consume away in their mouth.*
Zachariah 14: 1-12

Satan will attack Jerusalem in what we have called the *Jerusalem Campaign*. He will pursue a fleeing remnant of Jews into the wilderness (Revelation 12: 14-15). Just as all hope seems to be lost, God will miraculously save these people with what appears to be a great earthquake (Revelation 12: 14-15). Satan will be furious (Revelation 12:17a). He will then turn on all Jews and Christians (Revelation12: 17b). During his 3.5 years reign of terror, he will kill 2/3 of all Jews (Zachariah 13: 8-9). In Zachariah Chapter 14, the Prophet jumps ahead 3.5 years and describes things which will happen just prior to the Battle of Armageddon…. Which will take place at the Second Advent of Christ. If one will carefully read Zachariah 14:1-12 there can be no doubt that this is true. It is also true that the *Day of the Lord* is exactly what we have said it is… one day (compare Zachariah 14: 1-3 to Zachariah 14:7).

As the Battle of Armageddon is about to be fought, Satan and his army will attack Jerusalem. We call this the *Armageddon Campaign*. In Zachariah 14:2 the prophet writes that as Satan invades Jerusalem, ½ of all the people will be taken into captivity. After desecrating the new Jewish temple, he will sit in the temple declaring himself to be God (Matthew 24:15, Daniel 11:36, II Thessalonians 2: 3-4). A False Prophet will arise who is just another instrument of destruction and tribulation for Satan and the Antichrist (Revelation 13: 11-18). He will construct an image which will actually speak and think (Revelation 13:15). The image will demand that all people worship the Antichrist/Satan as God and take the mark of the beast. Those who capitulate will take the mark of the beast in either their right hand or forehead (Revelation 13:16). Failure to worship the beast (Antichrist) or his image and take his mark will result in instant death (Revelation 11:15). A timeline for these events is presented in Chapter 6.

There seems to be a paradox in Zachariah 14:2 (compare to Zachariah 13: 8-9). There is no paradox, Zachariah 13: 8 is speaking of the entire 3.5-year tribulation while Zachariah 14:8 is referring to the Jerusalem Campaign. When the 4th seal is opened, this is a prediction of things that will soon happen (Revelation 1:19c). Be sure about it……The 4th seal did not cause these things to happen ……they will take place as the 7 trumpets and the 7 bowls take place over the last 3.5 years of the Church Age. It is time for Christ to remove the 5th seal.

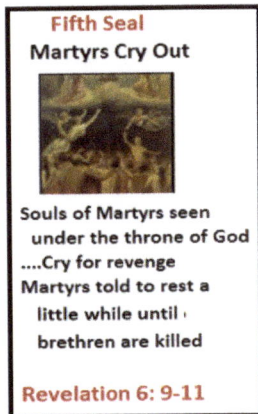

Fifth Seal

Martyrs Cry Out

Souls of Martyrs seen under the throne of God ....Cry for revenge Martyrs told to rest a little while until brethren are killed

Revelation 6: 9-11

[9] *And when he had opened the fifth seal, I saw under the altar the souls of them that were slain for the word of God, and for the testimony which they held:*

[10] *And they cried with a loud voice, saying, How long, O Lord, holy and true, dost thou not judge and avenge our blood on them that dwell on the earth?*

[11] *And white robes were given unto every one of them; and it was said unto them, that they should rest yet for a little season, until their fellow-servants also and their brethren, that should be killed as they were, should be fulfilled* Revelation 6: 9-11

As the 5ᵗʰ seal is broken, John is shown a remarkable vision concerning the Christians who have been martyred rather than deny Jesus Christ. The death and destruction predicted as the first four seals are broken will prove to be the ultimate test of faith to many Christians who will not bow down to the Antichrist. They will stand tall and be put to death for Christ. Once again, it should be clear that the opening of the 5ᵗʰ seal is not an *event* that will happen all at once, but something that will happen *throughout the duration* of the last 3.5 years of this age. This is a remarkable prophecy.... the souls of all faithful martyrs are seen *beneath the throne of God* (Revelation 6: 9-11). Their suffering and faith to the death is evidently so great that when they are martyred for Christ they are immediately taken to a place beneath the heavenly throne of God. They cry out for vengeance:

And they cried with a loud voice, saying, how long, O Lord, holy and true, dost thou not judge and avenge our blood on them that dwell on the earth? Revelation 6:10

The response to this plea is both revealing and immediate.

And white robes were given unto every one of them; and it was said unto them, that they should rest yet for a little season, until their fellowservants also and their brethren, that should be killed as they were, should be fulfilled Revelation 6:11

This scene is captured completely by the words of Robert L. Thomas.

> These words were spoken by Jesus Christ to the souls under God's throne. These words give them complete assurance that He will avenge their blood, but the time has not yet arrived for the culmination of that vengeance. There must still be others who will be tested, tried and martyred for Christ. Death will take an even greater toll on those on the earth before Christ returns. Until then, those who have already been martyred can rest in the assurance that they will be avenged and attain eternal life.

A question which must be asked is: *From what dispensation of time did these martyrs come from?* Revelation 6:9 tells us that: *I saw under the altar the souls of them that were slain for the word of God, and for the testimony which they held.* This seems to indicate that these martyrs come from when Adam fell to the 2ⁿᵈ advent of Christ. Men of God, prophets in the Old Testament, and New Testament witnesses for Jesus Christ have been slain through recorded time. This holy and blameless group of martyrs will not be complete until the 3.5 years of Satans reign of terror have come to an end. It appears that they will be raised in a special resurrection just before the 1000 Millennial kingdom begins (Revelation 20: 1-5).

...and I saw the souls of them that were beheaded for the witness of Jesus, and for the word of God, and which had not worshipped the beast, neither his image, neither had received his mark upon their foreheads, or in their hands; and they lived and reigned with Christ a thousand years.
Revelation 20: 4b

We have shown mounting evidence that the 7 seals are not in lock-step with the 7 Trumpets and 7 Bowls, but they only prophecy and overview things which will take place during the last 3.5 years of the Church Age. The seals consume no time and do not precede the Trumpet or bowl judgments in lock-step time delays as is commonly taught. When the 6th seal is broken *possibility* becomes *certainty*.

Sixth Seal
Celestial and Earthly Disturbances

There is a Great Earthquake
Sun becomes black
Moon is blood red
Stars fall from sky
Heaven rolls up like a scroll
Every mountain and island
    moved out of place
Men hide in caves
Great Day of Wrath of Lamb is come

Revelation 6: 12-17

[12] *And I beheld when he had opened the sixth seal, and, lo, there was a great earthquake; and the sun became black as sackcloth of hair, and the moon became as blood;*
[13] *And the stars of heaven fell unto the earth, even as a fig tree casts her untimely figs, when she is shaken of a mighty wind.*
[14] *And the heaven departed as a scroll when it is rolled together; and every mountain and island were moved out of their places* Revelation 6: 12-14

When the 6th seal is broken unprecedented heaven and earthly disturbances are prophesied. (1) The sun becomes black (2) The moon turns blood red (3) Stars fall from the sky (4) Heaven rolls up like a scroll. *When do these things occur in the Period of Great Tribulation?* This question was answered by the prophet Joel.

[1] *Blow ye the trumpet in Zion, and sound an alarm in my holy mountain: let all the inhabitants of the land tremble: for the **Day of the LORD** cometh, for it is nigh at hand;*
[2] *A Day of darkness and of gloominess, a day of clouds and of thick darkness, as the morning spread upon the mountains: a great people and a strong; there hath not been ever the like, neither shall be any more after it, even to the years of many generations* Joel 2: 1-2

[2] *I will also gather all nations, and will bring them down into the valley of Jehoshaphat, and will plead with them there for my people and for my heritage Israel, whom they have scattered among the nations, and parted my land.* Joel 3:2

[14] *Multitudes, multitudes in the valley of decision: for the **Day of the LORD** is near in the valley of decision.*
[15] The sun and the moon shall be darkened, and the stars shall withdraw their shining.
[16] *The LORD also shall roar out of Zion, and utter his voice from Jerusalem; **and the heavens***

and the earth shall shake: but the LORD will be the hope of his people, and the strength of the children of Israel.   Joel 3: 14-16

Joel clearly says that the **Day of the Lord** is coming and that it will be a day of darkness and gloom. A day of earthquakes in which the sun will be darkened and the stars cease to shine. There can be no doubt that this Day of the Lord is the **Battle of Armageddon** (Compare Joel 3: 14-16 to Revelation 6: 12-14). If Joel can be believed (and he can) that day will not be months and years but a single day. The Battle of Armageddon (Joel 3:2), will be fought following the 7 bowl judgments (Wrath of God) on the last day of the Great Tribulation. He then writes of an army of demon horsemen in Joel 2: 3-11 who will arise shortly before the battle.... exactly as described in Revelation 9: 13-21. The prophet Joel also accurately describes what will happen immediately preceding the Battle of Armageddon.

[30] *And I will shew wonders in the heavens and in the earth, blood, and fire, and pillars of smoke.*
[31] *The sun shall be turned into darkness, and the **moon into blood,** before the great and the terrible day of the LORD* come   Joel 2: 30-31

This should settle three key issues: (1) This exactly describes the same events which Christ prophesied and revealed as He broke the 6th seal in Revelation 6: 12-14. Do not fail to recognize the significance of the 2nd observation. (2) The things shown to John as the 6th seal is broken *coincide* with the pouring out of the 7th bowl. Are we to believe that these things will happen twice as necessitated by all Pre -Tribulation teachers? (3) The *Day of the Lord* is not a protracted period of time necessitated by a Pre-Tribulation theology or a Pre-Wrath theology but *one day*.

This is convincing evidence that the 6 seals when broken by Christ are a preview of things to come and will either span the entire last half of Daniel's 70th week (Seals 1-5), or specific events which will occur at the 2nd advent of Christ (Seal 6). It is now time to present the most convincing evidence of all. As Christ breaks the 6th seal, the following picture of things to come are revealed to John.

*And the heaven departed as a scroll when it is rolled together; and **every mountain and island were moved out of their places***   Revelation 6: 14

This is a specific, devastating event which will occur at only one moment in time. ***Every*** mountain and island will be moved and possibly disappear. Such an event cannot be comprehended and even imagined. *Can we determine exactly when this will happen?...* YES. When the 7th and last bowl is poured out just prior to the Battle of Armageddon.

And every island fled away, and the mountains were not found.   Revelation 16:20

Now, once again apply scriptural evidence and common sense to the Revelation Record. *Are we to believe that this incredible event will happen twice? ...Once when the 6th seal is broken and again at the end of the tribulation period??* Such a conclusion cannot possibly be believed or sustained!!! The conclusion .... beyond any reasonable doubt....is that when the 6th seal is broken by Christ, John is shown what will happen just before Christ returns a 2nd time as King of Kings and Lord of Lords....not as a suffering servant but as a conquering King....Praise God Forever. Finally note that a great earthquake will happen at that time, so great that such has never occurred since time began.

*And I beheld when he had opened the sixth seal, and, lo, there was a **great earthquake**;*
Revelation 6: 12a

This *great earthquake* which was predicted as the 6th seal is removed (Revelation 6:12). It will occur as the 7th and last bowl/vial is poured out (Revelation 16:18).

[17] *And the seventh angel poured out his vial into the air; and there came a great voice out of the temple of heaven, from the throne, saying, It is done.*
[18] *And there were voices, and thunders, and lightnings; and there was a **great earthquake**, such as was not since men were upon the earth, so mighty an earthquake, and so great*
        Revelation 16: 17-18

The 7th and final seal is now broken and removed by Christ.

And when he had opened the seventh seal, there was silence in heaven about the space of half an hour   Revelation 8:1

The scroll which belonged to God can now be completely unrolled. It is written on both sides and contains a detailed description of end-time events. As Christ breaks the 7th seal, a sequence of events can be seen by John which are so incredible and devastating that heaven falls completely silent for about *half an hour*. We can only guess the duration of this period of time. It is to allow several events to take place when the church age begins its last 3.5 years. These will be discussed in Chapter 5.

The contents of the 7 sealed scroll can now be revealed to John, who will write them to us in the last book of our holy Bible: The *Book of Revelation*. John will actually *see* things which take place in the distant future (Revelation 22:8).

[2] *And **I saw** the seven angels which stood before God; and to them were given seven trumpets.*
[3] *And another angel came and stood at the altar, having a golden censer; and there was given unto him much incense, that he should offer it with the prayers of all saints upon the golden altar which was before the throne.*
[4] *And the smoke of the incense, which came with the prayers of the saints, ascended up before God out of the angel's hand.*
[5] *And the angel took the censer, and filled it with fire of the altar, and cast it into the earth: and there were voices, and thunders, and lightnings, and an earthquake.*
[6] *And the seven angels which had the seven trumpets prepared themselves to sound*
Revelation 8: 2-6

Revelation 8:2 implies that God Himself gives a trumpet to each of 7 mighty angels. Before the 7 trumpets can sound, another mighty angel appears with a golden censor which is filled with much incense. This reminds us of the Altar of Incense which stood before the Holy of Holies in the Tabernacle of Moses, which was only a copy of the true Altar of Incense that is before God's throne in heaven. A remarkable event is then shown to John. The incense is poured out of the golden censor and placed on the Altar of Incense. This mighty angel then takes the prayers of the saints and offers both up to God. *Where did these prayers come from*? They were identified when the scroll of truth was given to Jesus Christ to break the 7 seals and disclose its contents (Revelation 5: 6-8). What an astounding revelation! Evidently when a Christian prays to God, those prayers are recorded and kept by the 4 living beasts (zoa) and the 24 elders which stand before the throne of God. When this angel placed his incense upon the alter, the smoke of the burning incense and the prayers of the Saints ascended up to God. The next event is even more incredible and revealing. The angel takes the censor previously full of incense, and fills it with coals from the Golden Altar. He then casts these burning coals to the earth and there were voices, and thunders, and lightnings, and an earthquake.

This is exactly what happens 3. 5 years later as an angel pours out the 7th and final bowl upon the earth.

[17] *And the seventh angel poured out his vial into the air; and there came a great voice out of the temple of heaven, from the throne, saying: It is done.*
[18] *And there were voices, and thunders, and lightnings; and there was a great earthquake, such as was not since men were upon the earth, so mighty an earthquake, and so great*
        Revelation 16: 17-18

Evidence Demands a Verdict

The scroll which was in the right-hand of God and was given to Jesus Christ contains a record of the sequence of events which will terminate the Church Age. Jesus Christ will rapture out all who will accept Him as Lord and Savior; defeat Satan, the Antichrist, and the False Prophet at the Battle of Armageddon; initiate the 1000-year Millennial kingdom; and finally, usher in eternity. The events which will take place during the Tribulation cannot be shown to John until all of the Seals are broken and removed by Jesus Christ. As Christ breaks and removes each seal, conditions (Seals 1-4) and specific events which will take place (Seals 5-6) over the next 3.5 years are shown to John. The scroll was sealed with 7 seals which when broken will predict and preview conditions (Seals 1-4) and events (Seals 5 and 6) which will take place at some time(s) over the next 3.5 years. The Great Tribulation or the last half of Daniel's 70th week will begin when Satan is cast down to earth by Michael and the holy angels (Revelation 12: 7-8). The 7 trumpet judgments will start (Wrath of Satan), followed immediately by the 7 Bowl Judgments (Wrath of God). The last great event to take place is the Battle of Armageddon. We will now discuss the Mysterious Numbers in the Book of Revelation (Chapter 6) and when the rapture of all saints…living and dead will take place (Chapter 7).

Chapter 6

The Mysterious Numbers in The Book of Revelation

The *Book of Daniel* in the Old Testament and the *Book of Revelation* in the New Testament are the two book-ends of Prophecy. It is generally conceded that one cannot be fully understood without understanding the other. Both the Book of Daniel and the Book of Revelation contain specific references to periods of time which define the duration of specific events. There are three different times mentioned in the Book of Revelation: (1) 1260 days (2) 42 months and (3) A time, times and half a time. The Book of Daniel specifically mentions a time, times and half-a-time.

The Book of Daniel

- *And he shall speak great words against the most High, and shall wear out the saints of the most High, and think to change times and laws: and they shall be given into his hand until a **time and times and the dividing of time*** Daniel 7:25
- *And I heard the man clothed in linen, which was upon the waters of the river, when he held up his right hand and his left hand unto heaven, and swore by him that lives forever that it shall be for a **time, times, and half***; *and when he shall have accomplished to scatter the power of the holy people, all these things shall be finished*   Daniel 12:7

Daniel 7:25 reveals that he (the antichrist) will persecute and kill the saints of the *most high* for a period of *time and times and a dividing of time* which is 3 1/2 years. Daniel 12:7 reveals that Satan (Daniel 12: 1-6) will rule persecute Christians and Jews for a *time, times and a half*, which is also 3 ½ years.

The Book of Revelation

- *But the court which is without the temple leave out, and measure it not; for it is given unto the Gentiles: and the holy city shall they tread under foot **forty and two months***   Revelation 11:2

- *And I will give power unto my two witnesses, and they shall prophesy **a thousand two hundred and threescore days**, clothed in sackcloth*   Revelation 11:3

- *And the woman fled into the wilderness, where she hath a place prepared of God, that **they** should feed her there a **thousand two hundred and threescore days***   Revelation 12:6

- *And to the woman were given two wings of a great eagle, that she might fly into the wilderness, into her place, where she is nourished for a **time, and times, and half a time**, from the face of the serpent* (Satan) Revelation 12:14

- *And there was given unto him a mouth speaking great things and blasphemies; and power was given unto him to continue **forty and two months***   Revelation 13:5

Revelation 11:2 reveals that the rebuilt Jewish Temple would be invaded and desecrated by the Gentiles for 42 months. Revelation 11:3 is referring to two witnesses that will stand and prophesy for 1260 days. Revelation 12:6 is referring to a beautiful sun-clothed woman (Revelation 12:1) which has just given birth to a Man-Child (A Firstfruit harvest of Jews who have accepted Jesus Christ as their Savior). This woman represents a Jewish remnant who has accepted Jesus Christ as their Lord and Savior. Revelation 12:6 and Revelation 12:14 are separated by 7 verses but they actually belong together. We will discuss this at length later. The believing remnant (Revelation 12:17) will flee Jerusalem as it is being attacked by Satan and his forces (Revelation 12: 13-17). The fleeing remnant will be protected by God in an unknown wilderness location for *a time, and times, and half a time.* Revelation 12:6 refers to a time period of 1260 days, but Revelation 12:16 refers to a time period of *time, times and half-a-time…* We will subsequently show that these two time periods are not identical and explain why. Revelation 13:5 reveals that he Antichrist (*him*) will speak against both Christians and Jews for a period of *42 months.*

An overwhelming number of prophecy students, teachers and seminary professors have taught that the references to 3 different designations of time: (1) A thousand, two hundred and three score days (2) 42 months (3) and time, times and half a time… all equate to 1260 days. It will now be proposed that this is not correct.

All agree that that the Daniel 70-week prophecy equates 70 weeks to 490 years using a one-day for one-year principle (70 times 7=490 days). It is then assumed that the phrase *time, times and half a time* denotes 3.5 years. *But how long is 3.5 years*? The length of a year depends upon whether a year is a 360-day *prophetic year* or a *standard vernal equinox year* of 365.2424 days. Hence, one biblical scholar might say that 70 years are 25,200 days (70*12*30) and another might say that 70 years are 25,567 days (70*12* 365.2424). In the Book of Revelation, these two systems would result in a 7-year Tribulation equal to 2520 days (prophetic year) or 25,567 days (calendar year). Revelation 11:2 records that the *City of Jerusalem* and *the Temple* would be overrun by Gentiles for 42 months, and Revelation 11:3 reveals that *two witnesses* sent by God will testify for 1260 days. All teachers of prophecy say that *both* periods of time are 1260 days long. *But are they????* Consider the construction of the Hebrew calendar. To keep the 1st of each month in sync with a 29.54-day Lunar Month, and to keep the calendar in sync with a 365.2422-day solar year, days are selectively added to designated months and 7 times in a 19-

year cycle an extra month of 30 days is added to the Calendar year. The Hebrew calendar years of 13 months are called *Leap years*. This results in a calendar year of 354, 355 or 356 days (normal year) or 383 or 385 days (leap year). Both Anderson and Hoehner declared that the 490-year prophecy given to Daniel was not based upon calendar years of 365.2425 years as defined by God, but on 360-day *Prophetic years*. Both based their belief upon the flood account in Genesis 7 and Genesis 8. Both had no choice but to define 42 months, and a time, times and half a time in the Book of Revelation to be 3.5 years or 1260 days.

The Book of Daniel was written about 164 BC while Israel was in Babylonian exile. It was written by Daniel…a Jew…to the Jewish people. Its purpose was to reveal to Daniel what was going to happen to God's chosen people in future years. It is almost certain that the calendar in use at that time was the same calendar in use today. God instituted the Jewish Calendar when He gave the Law and the *7 Feasts of Israel* to Moses after they crossed the Red Sea at Mt. Sinai. We know this because God was very specific about when each Feast was to be observed.

אֵלֶּה מוֹעֲדֵי יְהוָה מִקְרָאֵי קֹדֶשׁ אֲשֶׁר־תִּקְרְאוּ אֹתָם בְּמוֹעֲדָם׃

These are the set times of the LORD, the sacred occasions, which you shall celebrate each at its appointed time. - Leviticus 23:4

What determines the appointed times? The calendar that God gave Israel was to make sure that the 7 feasts of Israel and the new moon festivals were to be kept at their appointed time each year. The Jewish calendar is a remarkable Lunar-Solar calendar. The lunar (new moon to new moon) cycles were to determine the new moon festivals and the 7 Feasts of Israel. The 7 feasts of Israel were to b observed according to the Solar cycles of seasons and the equinoxes. The Jewish calendar is a remarkable instrument which balances the Lunar Cycles with the Solar cycles. It is known as a lunar-solar calendar and is still in use today. There are usually 12 months in every year, and each month in a lunar calendar always begins with a *New Moon*. The Feast of Passover was ordained by God to occur on the 1st full moon of the 1st Month… Nisan (Nisan 14) … in the *Spring*. The next three Feasts of Unleavened Bread, Firstfruits and Feast of Shavuot are all determined from Nisan 1. The lunar cycle of New Moon to Full Moon and then back to a New Moon is very stable and is now known to be 29.53 days. Since one cannot use a fraction of a day to mark a month, the *basic* Jewish month would alternate between 29 and 30 days over a basic 12-month year. If all 12 months in a year were 30 days, the year would be 360 days long. But, the length of a Solar year is 365.25 days long and if 360-day years were perpetually used to determine the length of each year, a Lunar year of 12 Lunar months (360 days) would "fall behind" a Solar Year (365.25 days) by about 11. 25 days every year. This means that in about 16 years, the Spring Feast of Passover on Nisan 14 (March/April) would be held in the middle of the Fall month of Tishri (September/ October). This could never be tolerated because God commanded them to be held *each at its appointed time*. In addition, the *Spring Feast of Firstfruits* is held with a Firstfruit offering of the Barley crops which emerge early in the Spring harvest season. This is why the Spring Feasts are all set from the 1st full moon of Nisan 1. The 6 Jewish Summer months (Nisan-Elul) *always* alternate between 30 days and 29 days. The 6 Fall months (Tishri to Adar) are adjusted each year to keep the basic Lunar Calendar in sync with a 365.25 solar Year. In addition, a 13th Month called Adar II is added 7 times over a 19-year period of time. A Hebrew 12-month Calendar with each month lasting 30 days (360 days), or a basic Jewish calendar of 12 months alternating between 29 and 30 days (354 days) simply does not exist. By construction, a Hebrew Calendar Year consists of 12 or 13 months. *Regular common* years have 12 months with a total of 353 days, 354 days, or 355 days. Leap years contain 13 months totaling 383 days, 384 days or 385 days. Those years which contain 13 months were called *leap years*. Over a perpetual 19-year cycle, an extra month is added 7 times... in the 3rd, 6th, 8th, 11th, 14th, 17th, and 19th years.

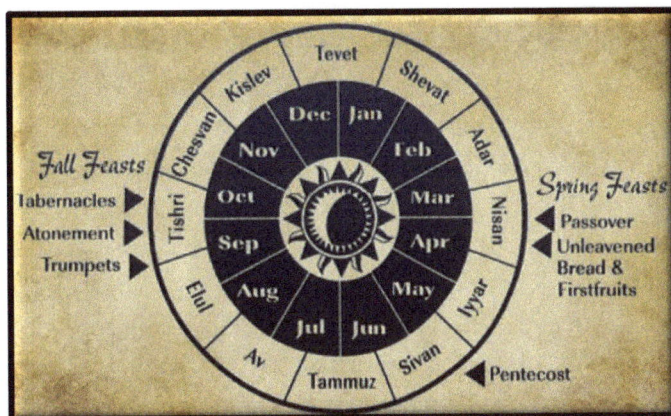

Before the Exodus, the calendar which was used in *Egypt* consisted of 12 months of 30 days (360 days per year). The most important time in Egypt each year was when the Nile River flooded in the Spring ... that would immediately precede planting season. The main purpose of the Egyptian calendar was to determine when crops should be planted and then harvested. It is obvious from our previous discussion, that the basic Egyptian 360-day calendar failed miserably. The cycle of yearly flooding, planting and harvesting must be determined by a solar year as the earth circled the sun in an elliptic orbit. That cycle takes 365.25 days. In order to keep the Egyptian lunar calendar in sync with the Solar year, periodically an extra month was added to the end of a year. This helped, but the Egyptian calendar year would still fall back from the Solar year about 1n day every 4 years. Eventually, about 4000 B.C. they added five extra days at the end of every year to bring it more into line with the solar year. These five days became an Egyptian holiday because it was thought to be unlucky to work during those 5 days.

To summarize, the Jewish calendar in use today is exactly the same as the calendar that was in use after the exodus. The 1st 6 months always alternate between 30 days and 29 days, but the last 6 months of the year are adjusted to keep the Lunar based calendar year in sync with the Solar based calendar year. It was discovered that by adding an extra month 7 times every 19 years, and adding a day periodically, the result is amazing...The (modified) Jewish calendar would cause the Jewish months to "drift" from year to year, but starting in year 1 the Solar date and the Jewish date on the same day 19 years later would exactly coincide! This cycle of 19 years was called the *Metonic Cycle*.

How many days are in a month? Ask anyone in the United States and they will tell you: *Thirty days have November... April, June, and November. There are 31 days in any other month but*

February… which has 28 days except in a leap year in which it has 29 years. Ask any Hebrew and they will reply: *Which month and which year?*

How many Days are there in a year? Ask anyone in the United States and they will tell you: *365 days usually, but a leap year has 366 days.* Ask any Hebrew and they will reply: *Which year in a Metonic Cycle?*

There is an old Hebrew story that starts with a man asking a Jewish Rabbi: *What day does Passover fall on this year?* The rabbi answered the man; Same as every other year… Nisan14.

This discussion will not further debate whether the Daniel 70-year prophecy and the Book of Revelation both use a Prophetic year of 360 days or a normal solar year of 365.2422 days. Evidence previously presented strongly indicates that the Hebrew Calendar used today by the Jews today was exactly the same as the one used by Daniel. It will be noted that since both the Book of Daniel and the Book of Revelation are linked to the Jews and the 70-week prophecy of Daniel, it would be natural to assume that the Jewish calendar that has been in constant use since the Exodus would be the correct calendar to use. The exact Gregorian or Julian calendar day is relatively unimportant, except Nisan 14 in 30 AD when Christ was crucified. That weekday must be a Wednesday, which is easily verified using modern computer date conversion programs. Rather than debate and discuss any system of measuring time, we suggest that the eternal plan of God and His Biblical truth be directly applied. The results which follow will be based upon two fundamental and invariant truths: (1) The 7 Feast Days were to be held on the same Hebrew calendar dates each year. Passover on Nisan 14, Feast of Trumpets on Tishri 1, Day of Atonement on Tishri 10, Etc. (2) God made the heavens and the earth, and when He completed His creative work, he spoke:

And God said: Let there be lights in the firmament of the heaven to divide the day from the night; and let them be for signs, and for seasons, and for days, and years   Genesis 1:14

Now, this is very specific…***God created day and night*** and ***they defined seasons, days and years***.

Since God spoke, modern computers, space exploration and NASA have accurately measured a Lunar month and a Solar year. They have also accurately determined when the Fall Equinox and the Spring Equinox will occur. These things have been the object of inquiry by practically all civilized societies… The Egyptians, the Maya and the Druids of England to name a few. The equinox(s) were used to determine seasons and days to determine years. Modern scientists and highly accurate digital computers fulfil an ancient prophecy given to Daniel:

*But thou, O Daniel, shut up the words, and seal the book, even to the time of the end: many shall run to and fro, and **knowledge shall be increased***   Daniel 12:4

We now know that a day consists of 24 hours of 60 minutes, a month is 29.53 days and a solar year is 365.2422 days. *Why would we need to look further?* In both the Book of Daniel and the Book of Revelation:

- A day was 24 hours long

- A year was 365.2422 days
- A month is 29.53 days
- The Hebrew Calendar has never changed since God revealed it to Moses after the Exodus from Egypt. Note that after 40 years of wandering in the wilderness:

And the people came up out of Jordan on the tenth day of the first month, and encamped in Gilgal, in the east border of Jericho   Joshua 4:19

And the children of Israel encamped in Gilgal, and kept the Passover on the fourteenth day of the month at even in the plains of Jericho   Joshua 5:10

The Children of Israel wandered in the wilderness for 40 years, and after crossing the River Jordan on Nisan 10, every male was circumcised and rested for 3 days. On Nisan 14 (Passover) they observed the end of their wandering *exactly* 40 years after they had left Egypt. This is a remarkable revelation which seems to prove that the Hebrew calendar had been in existence for the last 40 years before Joshua led them into the Land of Canaan.

Time, times and Half-a-time; 42 Months; and A Thousand, Two Hundred and Threescore Days

In Revelation 12 Chapter 12 we find the following two verses.

*And the woman fled into the wilderness, where she hath a place prepared of God, that they should feed her there a **thousand two hundred and threescore days***   Revelation 12:6

*And to the woman were given two wings of a great eagle, that she might fly into the wilderness, into her place, where she is nourished for a **time, and times, and half a time**, from the face of the serpent*   Revelation 12:14

In the same Chapter within 8 short verses, we see that there are two periods of time which reference the same event: (1) 1260 days in Revelation 12:6 and (2) a *time, and times, and half a time* in Revelation 12:14. Even more interesting is Revelation 11: 1-3.

[1] *And there was given me a reed like unto a rod: and the angel stood, saying, Rise, and measure the temple of God, and the altar, and them that worship therein.*
[2] *But the court which is without the temple leave out, and measure it not; for it is given unto the Gentiles: and the holy city shall they tread under foot **forty and two months**.*
[3] *And I will give power unto my two witnesses, and they shall prophesy a **thousand two hundred and threescore days**, clothed in sackcloth*   Revelation 11: 1-3

An angel commanded John to measure the newly rebuilt temple in Jerusalem (Revelation 11:1). He was told: "Do not measure the outer court because the Holy City (Jerusalem) would be taken over by the Gentiles (unbelievers) for *42 months*" (Revelation 11:2). Then John was told that there would be two witnesses that would prophesy for 1260 days (Revelation 11:3) …a very specific time period. Within the short space of 14 words there were two different time periods specified. This is highly illogical if two different names are sequentially used for the same period of time and all are assumed to be 1260 days. Further, these are two different events that are related but they are not necessarily the same time duration. It has always puzzled me that this would happen.

We have previously noted that almost prophecy scholars and teachers of which I am aware use 30-day months for the Daniel prophecy and to determine the duration of the *Great Tribulation*. All also then assume that 1260 days, 42 months and 3.5 years are each equal to 30 days. However, it has been shown that the Daniel 70 Week prophecy, which includes the 3.5-year Ministry of Christ and the *Great Tribulation*, has no direct reference to a 30-day, 12-month, 360-day year. Daniel never mentioned using a "prophetic year", and if this was the intent of the 490-year prophecy… why didn't the angel Gabriel say so?

> *Authors Comment:* Many biblical scholars and teachers have noted that in the Genesis flood account found in Genesis 7: 1-24 and Genesis 8: 1-18 it rained for 40 days and 40 nights. The rain began to fall on the 17th day of the 2nd month, and the ark floated in the flood waters until it came to rest on the 17th day of the 7th month. In Genesis 7:24, we are told that: *the waters prevailed for 150 days.* It is then assumed that each month in a 12-month year lasted exactly 30 days, and that each year was 12 months of 30 days, even though nothing is said in the biblical account which supports this assumption. There is also no indication that *every* month in a 12- month year was also 30 days. In fact, one can show the flood account spanned 365 days and possibly exactly 365.2425 days (Phillips, Noahs Ark: *Historical and Prophetic Truths*).

In the ancient Book of Enoch, a calendar is described which divides the year into four seasons of exactly 13 weeks each. Each season consisted of three 30-day months followed by one 31-day month, with the 31st day ending the season. Hence, the Enoch Calendar year was 364 days. Even the ancient calendar of Enoch did not use a 360-day year.

In spite of the obvious problems and no definitive biblical statement, this all led many scholars to an assumption that a *biblical prophetic year* is 12 months of 30 days or 360 days… and so the Daniel Prophecy was declared to be based upon a 360 day year and 490 years were 176,400 days . Where the term *prophetic year* came from cannot be found, but it is likely that it arose when Sir Robert Anderson used it to declare that every year in the Daniel 70-week prophecy was 360 days long. This then led to an assumption that 42 months. and Time, times and half-a-time in the Book of Revelation were all 1260 days long. Rather than enter into a debate of whether or not there is a prophetic month of 30 days and a prophetic year of 360 days in both the Daniel 70-Week prophecy and in the Book of Revelation, another argument will be presented which does not depend upon these assumptions.

There is almost universal agreement that it never rained before the Great Flood. This is supported by Genesis 1: 6-7 and Genesis 2:5. No rain is mentioned before the Great flood (Genesis 7: 4,12), and it is written in Genesis 2:6 that crops in the Garden of Eden were nourished by a mist which fell upon the earth. This is not *proof* that it did not rain before the flood of Noah, but the weight of written evidence indicates that it did not. If it did not rain before Noah's Flood, then a 30-day month and a 360-day year might be logical and believable. It was not until God established the 7 Feasts of Israel after the Exodus from Egypt that an accurate calendar was required which predicted the New Moon each month, the days upon which each Festival must be held, and the seasons of planting and reaping. That was when God gave the Hebrew calendar to Moses and Aaron. It was not until the Jewish patriarch Hillel II published the "secret operation" of the Hebrew Calendar in 358/359 AD were the details revealed. The operational rules of the Hebrew Calendar were guarded closely by the High Priest prior to that time. There is no Biblical or logical reason that the 70-Week Prophecy given to Daniel used a 360-day year of 12-months with 30 days in each month. Appealing to common sense… *Why would God hide this from both Jews and Christians if it was necessary to interpret the most important Old Testament prophecy that God revealed to man?*

Is there a place in God's Book of Truth that without controversy describes how days, months and years are defined? Yes, there is. God created the heavens and the earth in 6 days, and then he rested. In the creative process, he gave us the following information.

[4] *And God saw the light, that it was good: and God divided the light from the darkness.*
[5] *And God called the light Day, and the darkness he called Night. And the evening and the morning were the first day*   Genesis 1: 4-5

Since creation a day was defined as 24 hours, consisting of day and night. These periods of light and darkness are not equal except on two days: The Spring Equinox and the Fall Equinox. On any given day, these two periods equal 24 hours. Day and night are due to the Earth rotating on its axis, not its orbiting around the sun. The term 'one day' is determined by the time the Earth takes to rotate once on its axis and includes both day time and night time…24 hours.

[14] *And God said: Let there be lights in the firmament of the heaven to divide the day from the night; and let them be for signs, and for **seasons, and for days, and years***   Genesis 1:14

[16] *And God made two great lights; the greater light to rule the day, and the lesser light to rule the night: he made the stars also.*
[17] *And God set them in the firmament of the heaven to give **light upon the earth,***
[18] *And to rule over the day and over the night, and to divide the light from the darkness: and God saw that it was good*   Genesis 1: 17-18

When God in His infinite wisdom created the Heavens and the Earth, he did a remarkable thing.
The sun was created to provide light…the Earth rotates both around its axis and in an elliptical orbit around the sun to separate day from night and change the seasons. The moon orbits around the earth to create a new moon-full moon cycle.

- The time it takes the earth to rotate about its axis defines a day….24 hours

- The time it takes the earth to rotate about the sun defines a year…365.2422 days
- The time it takes the moon to complete a new moon-full moon-new moon cycle defines a month and is 29.53059 days (new moon to new moon)

If Daniel and John knew that 42 months and 3.5 years (time, times and half-a-time) were not identical…why would they use three different times in the Books of Daniel and Revelation? The answer is simple: No one on earth could comprehend these numbers nor even use them when these two books were written. These exact numbers were not meaningful in ancient times but they are now…particularly in space exploration (NASA). They were revealed in the fullness-of-time.

But thou, O Daniel, shut up the words, and seal the book, even to the time of the end: many shall run to and fro, and knowledge shall be increased   Daniel 12:4

Using these facts, we can now quantify the following measurements of time in the Book of Revelation.

- 42 Months= (42) * (29.53059) = 1240. 68 days or **1241** days
- 1260 days=**1260** days

The remaining time duration of *time, times and half-a-time* requires a deeper investigation.

We have proposed that the Hebrew Lunar/Solar Calendar was given to Moses at the Exodus from Egypt. Whether this is true or not, by the 1st century AD the Hebrew calendar was well established and used by all Jews. It has never been changed up to this day. Modern Computer Scientists have used several computational Programming Languages to reproduce the Hebrew calendar for any day, month and year from the Exodus to the current time. Of particular interest is the year 30 AD. Jesus Christ was crucified on the Feast of Passover in 30 AD (Phillips, The Birth of Christ: *A Forensic Analysis,* Phillips: *The Birth and Death of Jesus Christ*, Fred Coulter: *The Appointed Times of Jesus the Messiah*). In the 1st century there were two calendars being used in Jerusalem, the Roman Julian calendar and the Hebrew calendar. Using any validated and verified computer program, Nisan 1 in 30 AD was on Wednesday, April 5 on the Julian calendar, and April 3 on the modern (predated) Gregorian calendar. The Gregorian calendar replaced the Julian calendar in 1582 AD. It is very accurate. Thanks to the power and accuracy of modern digital computers, we know the Julian calendar day and the predated Gregorian calendar day when Christ was crucified: Nisan 14 in 30 AD was on a Wednesday. As previously noted, the 70-week prophecy given to Daniel was Jewish through and through. It was given to the Jews and faithfully written by Daniel while they were in Babylonian exile to assure them that God was not through with them. Although there is a raging and ongoing controversy of *when* the 70-week prophecy was issued (Daniel 9: 21-27) and *Who* issued the Decree, there is no controversy regarding *which calendar* was in use by both the Jews and the Babylonians during the Babylonian exile …Both used the same calendar. Almost all scholars and teachers agree that the Daniel prophecy spans time from the Babylonian exile to the Battle of Armageddon. No matter what assumptions are used, 490 years have long since passed since the decree was issued. This results in the 490-year Daniel prophecy being suspended/interrupted in the 1st Century AD.

A suspension or interruption of the Daniel 70-week prophecy creates the necessity for a *gap* to occur between when it was interrupted and *when it will resume* (the Gap theory). How many days remain in the Daniel Prophecy for the Great Tribulation is also hotly contested. There are only two legitimate possibilities....one will leave 7 years for the Great Tribulation and the other will leave 3.5 years. The last 7 years of the Daniel prophecy is called the 70th week of Daniel, and this last week will resume at some future point in time with either a full 7 years or only 3.5 years left for the Great Tribulation. We will now show that 3.5 years is the correct choice, and the exact time designated as time, times and half-a time will be determined.

There has always been tribulation and persecution of all Christians. It is prophesied in multiple places in the New Testament. However, the severe persecution and wrath of Satan in the *final days* will not begin until Satan is cast out of the heavenlies, and the Antichrist and False Prophet arise. As the 7 Trumpets sound, the *Wrath of Satan* will be unleashed upon this earth (Revelation 12:12). This period of time is the last half of the 490-year Daniel Prophecy (Daniel 12:7, Revelation 12:6 and Revelation 12:14). We have already shown that the tribulation period is not 1260 days but 1267 days. This is also the duration of a time, times and a half-a-time in both the Book of Daniel and the Book of Revelation. God told an angel (Possibly the archangel Gabriel or Michael) to give Daniel an incredible prophecy.

[24] *Seventy weeks are determined upon thy people and upon thy holy city, to finish the transgression, and to make an end of sins, and to make reconciliation for iniquity, and to bring in everlasting righteousness, and to seal up the vision and prophecy, and to anoint the most Holy.*
[25] *Know therefore and understand, that **from the going forth of the commandment to restore and to build Jerusalem unto the Messiah the Prince shall be seven weeks, and threescore and two weeks**: the street shall be built again, and the wall, even in troublous times.*
[26 a] *And **after threescore and two weeks shall Messiah be cut off**, but not for himself:*
Daniel 9: 24-26a

We have previously shown that 70 weeks (Daniel 9:24) is 490 days, and by the *one day equals one day principle* (Ezekiel 4:6) ... 70 Weeks is 490 years. All agree to this conclusion. All will also agree that the 490 years will start with a *decree* or commandment (Daniel 9:25) which authorizes the Jews to return to Jerusalem (Daniel 9:25a). From when this decree is issued, there will be two periods of time which will pass: (1) Seven weeks...*49 years* and (2) Threescore and two weeks ...*434 years*. Hence, a *total* of 486 years will pass **unto the Messiah the Prince**. *Unto Messiah the prince* refers to when Jesus Christ began His earthly ministry of about 3.5 years by being baptized in the Jordan River by John the Baptizer. His ministry of reconciliation ended on the *Feast of Passover*, Nisan 14 when He was crucified. Now the hard part: If one just knew the Hebrew calendar date that Jesus was baptized and began His ministry, the duration of his ministry could be determined by counting the days between when he was baptized by John and when He was crucified. *How could one possibly know The Hebrew date and year that Christ* *was baptized*? The answer lies in Daniel 9: 24-26a. From the *day* that the edict was issued which authorized the Jewish return to Jerusalem there will be 483 Hebrew years to Messiah the Prince. Two things must now merge into place. The Babylonian exile was over by the 6th century BC. The exact date when those who wished to return did so is not important, but it is important to note that the Hebrew calendar was well established and functioning between the 6th century BC and the 1st century AD.

Please understand that the entire 490 years of the Daniel prophecy is for the *Jews*. We have shown that it must be interrupted when God is *not dealing with the Jews*. That is why Daniel's 490-year prophecy was suspended after Christ was crucified on the Cross of Calvary. He had been speaking to the Jews exclusively during His 3.5 years ministry of reconciliation (Matthew 10:5). He was rejected and crucified by His own people... He would then turn to the Gentiles. The 490-year prophecy had to be interrupted at that time.

A short explanation of Daniel 9: 24-27 was given in Chapter 1. A detailed analysis of this prophecy is beyond the scope of this Chapter: The interested reader is referred to Phillips; The Daniel 70-week Prophecy: *Cornerstone of All Prophecy* or Phillips; The Book of Revelation: *Mysteries Revealed*. The important conclusions are as follows.

- The prophecy is for 70 weeks (490 years) ... Daniel 9:24
- The 70 years are divided into three parts: 7 weeks (49 years), threescore and two weeks (434 years) and 7 years (49+434+7) = 490 years ... Daniel 9: 25, 27
- After 483 years have expired, Messiah the Prince (Jesus Christ) will arise (Daniel 9:25). Sometime after 483 years have passed, Christ will be Crucified (Daniel 9:26). His death is specifically identified as *in the midst* of the last 7-year period. (Daniel 9:27)
- In Daniel 9:27 the *he* was Jesus Christ. Many teach that this *he* is the antichrist (Satan incarnate). Satan or the antichrist never confirmed any covenant...they made a covenant of death with Israel. There is a great deal of difference in *confirming* a covenant and *establishing* a covenant. The crucifixion of Christ was to redeem Jews and Gentiles alike from the curse of sin. This promise (covenant) which is recorded in the Old Testament by the prophets (Jeremiah 31:31, Malachi 3:1) was confirmed (Validated, proved, finished) by Christ.
- At His sacrificial death, Christ:
  - Caused Old Testament sacrifice and oblations to cease
  - He made the Temple *desolate*
  - Until *that determined* will be poured out (the 7 Bowls of God's Wrath) upon the *desolate* (Satan, the Antichrist and the False Prophet) ... Daniel 9:27

Jesus Christ was crucified on the Feast of Pentecost, Nisan 14 in 30 AD in the *midst of the week* (last 7 years, Daniel 9:27). It was at that point in time that God (temporarily) turned away from the Jews and replaced the Old Covenant with the New Covenant (Acts 18:6). Salvation and eternal life were then offered to Jews and Gentiles by faith and grace…not by works under the law. This is exactly where the New Covenant began, and God turned to the Gentiles (church) to proclaim salvation to all. It was *exactly* on Nisan 14 that the *gap* started in the Daniel prophecy. During this gap, God would have His Son build the church and the body of Christ. The last 3.5 years of the Daniel 490-year prophecy to the Jews would not begin until God once again began to deal with His chosen people… the Jews. this is the *Great Tribulation.*

With this extensive background, let us examine the nature of the unknown *Gap* in time. Suppose that there was no gap in the prophecy. In that case, the last 3.5 years of the Daniel Prophecy would expire in 33 AD. There *must* be a Gap, and it will not end until Satan and his fallen angels are cast down to earth in Revelation 12:9. It should now be understood that this will happen on some future Nisan 15. The time that will pass between Nisan 14 in 30 AD and some future Nisan 15 will be like a mere second to the Lord compared to eternity. It is not possible to predict a time, a day or a year for this to happen, but *if* the Great Tribulation (Matthew 24: 1-21) starts on some future Nisan 15, when will Satan's reign on earth end? It has already been established that Satan will be defeated with all of His followers on Tishri 10…*The Feast of Atonement.* It follows that the Great Tribulation which is composed of the *Wrath of Satan* (7 Trumpet Judgments) and the *Wrath of God* (7 Bowl Judgments) will last for a period of time that is identical to the number of days between the end of Nisan 14 and the end of Tishri 10 in 34 AD. This length of time can be determined from the Hebrew calendar using any one of a number of computer programs, the following data can be obtained. (The *Abdicate* computer program at https://abdicate.net/cal.aspx was used and validated).

Gregorian: **April 3, 30** (ante [1])	Gregorian: **September 21, 33** (ante [1])
Julian: **April 5, 30**	Julian: **September 23, 33**
Jewish: **Nisan 14, 3790**	Jewish: **Tishrei 10, 3794**
י"ד בניסן ג'תשצ"	י' בתשרי ג'תשצ"ד
SDN: **1732110.5** [2]	SDN: **1733377.5** [2]
Weekday: **Wednesday**	Weekday: **Wednesday**

This is a remarkable result. The Great Tribulation will begin and end on the end of Nisan 14 (Wednesday, April 3 on the pre-dated modern Gregorian calendar) and will end on Tishri 10 (Wednesday, September 21. The number of days during which the Wrath of Satan and the Wrath of God will be completed can be counted on the Hebrew Calendar and is *1267 days.* This same period of time is designated as a *Time, Times and Half-a-Time* in Revelation 12:14. To summarize, if the Daniel Prophecy was based upon the Hebrew Calendar… and the duration of a day, month and year is based upon God's creative process in Genesis 1.

- A day is 24 hours
- A year is 365.2422 days
- A month is 29.531 days
- *Time, times and half-a-time* (Revelation 12:14) The time that Satan will persecute Jews and Christians is *1267 days*

- The last 3.5 years of the Daniel Prophecy…the last half of Daniels 70th Week…the last 3.5 years of the Church age…and the Great Tribulation are all 1267 days (Daniel 7:25, Daniel 12:7)
- Jerusalem will be invaded and trod underfoot (Revelation 11:2) for 42 months or **1241 days**… (29.531*42) days
- Two Witnesses will prophesy for 1260 days (Revelation 11:3)
- The Woman in Revelation 12 will be nourished *in the wilderness* in a *place prepared for them* (Revelation 12:6) the for 1260 days (Revelation 12:6)
- The Woman will flee from the face of the serpent (Satan) *before Satan is cast down* (Compare Revelation 12:6 to Revelation 12:7), and will be protected (By God) for a *time, times and half-a-time* or the full *1267 days* (Revelation 12:14)
- The *Antichrist* and the *False Prophet* will arise *after* the war in heaven occurs and Satan is cast down (Revelation 13: 1-18).
- Satan will be furious (Revelation 12:12) and pursue the woman (Revelation 12:13) who is saved by God (Revelation 12: 15-16), and then Satan will return to *overrun Jerusalem* for 42 months or 1241 days (Revelation 11:3). During this invasion (the 1st Jerusalem campaign) the great world leader is slain (Revelation 13:3) and brought back to life as the Antichrist (Revelation 13:4). The Antichrist will then desecrate the temple (Matthew 24: 15-21),
- Jerusalem will be *trod underfoot* for 42 months or 1241 days (Revelation 11:2-3).

Revelation 11:2 reveals that the *Holy City* of Jerusalem will be trampled underfoot by the Gentiles (unbelievers) for *42 months*. There are two witnesses that will stand in the temple and prophesy for a *time, times and a half-a-time* (Revelation 11:3). The two witnesses will be sent by God to testify and witness during the entire tribulation period of 1267 days: *Do not yield to Satan or take the Mark of the Beast.* After they have finished their testimony, they will be killed and lay dead in the street for 3.5 days (Revelation 11: 7-10). After 3.5 days, God will command them to rise, saying: *Come up hither. And they ascended up to heaven in a cloud* (Revelation 11: 11-12). In these verses, 42 months and Time, times and half-a-time are clearly not the same period of time.

Revelation 12 is a remarkable and complex prophecy of how Satan will begin his 3.5-year reign of terror. The vision which was seen by John and recorded in Revelation 12: 1-17 is full of mystery. The mystery in Revelation 12 includes the description of a *sun-clothed woman* in Revelation 12: 1-6. The woman is Israel. There are two groups identified which come out of the Woman, but they are not the entire woman. One group is a Man-Child who is *caught up* to heaven (Revelation 12:5). The second group is a remnant who has turned to Jesus Christ as their Lord and Savior and is seen fleeing Jerusalem into the wilderness (Revelation 12:6 and Revelation 12:13-17). Both groups of redeemed Jews represent the *starry seed* of Abraham (Genesis 9:9, Genesis 15: 5). One group is a *Firstfruit Harvest*… the man-Child (Revelation 14: 1-4), and the other group will be part of the *main harvest* (the Rapture). These two groups which come out of the woman have been redeemed and saved in Jesus Christ (Revelation 12:11, Revelation 12:17). Those who will inherit and live in the promised land during the Millennial Kingdom (Revelation 7: 1-8) are the *earthly seed* (Genesis 13: 15-16, Genesis 15:18). The portion of the woman who is not caught up to the throne of God will flee into the Wilderness of Bozrah (Isaiah 63:1, Micah 2:12, Revelation 12:6, Revelation 12:14). It is proposed that Revelation 12:6 and Revelation 12: 13-16 are describing the same group. Revelation 12:6 is a broad statement concerning the protection of the woman, and Revelation 12: 13-16 provide details.

Reading Revelation 12 as it was revealed to John, the woman symbolically is seen in the heavens above the earth with Satan. She births a man-child who is *caught up* to God's throne room in the 3rd heaven. The Greek word translated as *caught up* is *Harpazo* which means to *seize* or *snatch away.* It is exactly the same Greek word used by Paul in describing the rapture.

*And she brought forth a man child, who was to rule all nations with a rod of iron: and her child was **caught** up unto God, and to his throne*   Revelation 12:5

*Then we which are alive and remain shall be **caught up** together with them in the clouds, to meet the Lord in the air: and so shall we ever be with the Lord*   I Thessalonians 4:17

This is not to imply that Revelation 12:5 is the rapture of all living believers revealed by Paul in I Thessalonians 4:17, but it is a rapture of some kind. This snatching away of the Man-child in Revelation 12:5 takes place *before* Satan is cast down to the earth (Revelation 12: 7-9). When the dragon (Satan) is cast down, he is full of *great wrath* because he only has a *short time* left Revelation 12:12).

*And when the dragon saw that **he was cast unto the earth**, he **persecuted the woman** which brought forth the man child*   Revelation 12:13

And to the woman were given two wings of a great eagle, that she might fly into the wilderness, into her place, where she is nourished for a time, and times, and half a time, from the face of the serpent   Revelation 12:14

> ***Authors Comment***: There are many who insist that the Man-child is Jesus and the woman is Mary. This would make the dragon King Herod in the 1st century. There are others who insist and teach that all of the Book of Revelation was fulfilled in 70 AD when Titus and his centurions destroyed the City of Jerusalem and Herod's Temple in 70 AD. What will they do with Revelation 12:12 and Revelation 12:17?

If the Woman which flees into the wilderness in Revelation 12:6 and the woman which flies into the wilderness in Revelation 12: 13-14 are the same woman, why are the times in Revelation 12:6 (1260 days) and in Revelation 12:16 (time, times and half-a-time) different? *How can this be explained?*

The following explanation will be proposed. Note that the force of Revelation 12:6 is simply that the woman will *flee to a place in the wilderness* prepared by God. This is a specific and real place and the wilderness is south of Jerusalem somewhere. Although the context of Revelation 12:6 seems to place this woman fleeing to the wilderness *before* Satan is cast down to the earth (compare Revelation 12:6, Revelation 12:7 and Revelation 11: 12-17). Revelation 12:6 clearly states that the woman will flee into the wilderness before Satan is cast down. *They* will feed her for 1260 days, but Revelation 12:14 states that she will be protected from Satan by God for a time, times and half-a-time which we have shown is 1267 days. *How can Revelation 12:6 and Revelation 12:14 both be true if they are both referring to the same woman?*

Careful exegesis will reveal that Revelation 12:14 is referring to the *total time* which will elapse from when the woman flees from Satan until Jesus Christ retrieves the remnant from where they are hiding in the wilderness (1267 days). Revelation 12:14 is only referring to the time which this same remnant is protected and fed in a wilderness sanctuary by the people who live there (1267 days). There is a strong indication that this place of sanctuary might be Petra. The 1267 days of Revelation 12:14 consists of two parts. The 1st part is the 7-day journey to the place of refuge which included the supernatural rescue of this remnant from Satan by Christ. The 2nd part is protection in the wilderness (Petra?) for 1260 days by a group of people called *they* who will nourish and feed the remnant (Revelation 12:6).

*Who are **they*** (plural)? We are not told but after the Great Tribulation has ended and the battle of Armageddon has been fought, Jesus Christ will go to Bozrah (possibly Petra) in blood-stained garments and retrieve a remnant who is there.

*Who is this that cometh from Edom, with dyed garments from **Bozrah**? this that is glorious in his apparel, travelling in the greatness of his strength? I that speak in righteousness, mighty to save.* Isaiah 63:1

Shortly after the battle of Armageddon and Jesus Christ gathers people from the nations (Matthew 25: 31-32), he will conduct the *Judgment of the Sheep and Goats* (Matthew 25: 33-46). Salvation will be granted to those who treated the Jews fairly and helped them.

[36] *Naked, and ye clothed me: I was sick, and ye visited me: I was in prison, and ye came unto me.*
[37] *Then shall the righteous answer him, saying, Lord, when did we see thee hungry, and fed you? or thirsty, and gave you drink?*   Matthew 25: 36-37

And *the King shall answer and say unto them, Verily I say unto you: Inasmuch as ye have done it*

unto one of the least of these my brethren, ye have done it unto me.   Matthew 25:40

We suggest that *they* who *fed her* in Revelation 12:6 are a part of the *sheep* in Revelation 25:33. *They* will feed and nourish her for 1260 days.

*And the woman fled into the wilderness, where she hath a place prepared of God, that **they should feed her*** *there a thousand two hundred and threescore days*   Revelation 12:6

In Revelation 12:14, John *sees* a *woman* that is fleeing into the wilderness (wings of eagles) to her *place* (same destination as the woman in Revelation 12:6, Same Greek word, *topos* (region or place). Revelation 12: 15-16 adds information to Revelation 14:6. When Satan saw that the woman was fleeing, he pursues her and evidently tries to drown her with a flood (Revelation 12:15). But God rescues the woman by opening up the earth and consumed the flood (Revelation 12:16). Satan is trying to drown the woman with water, just as God consumed the Egyptians with water at the Exodus. *If the woman in Revelation 12:6 and the woman in Revelation 12:14 are the same, why did John not see these two visions as one.*

The answer is both logical and relevant to this analysis. Revelation 12:6 only informs us that the woman will flee Satan and they will be supernaturally protected by God. They will flee to a specific *place prepared by God* and that *they* will feed her there for 1260 days. Revelation 12: 12-16 builds upon Revelation 12:6, revealing how Satan will pursue the woman, try to kill her with a great flood and how the woman will be saved by God (Revelation 12: 15-16). After the encounter, she will continue south to the wilderness of Bozrah. Bozrah and the natural fortress of Petra are about 100-125 miles south over treacherous terrain and the total journey will take about 7 days. The remnant which flees must not only be miraculously saved from Satan, but she will need to be nourished by God as she moves south. The *total* time that **God** will protect and nourish Israel is a *time, times and half-a-* time. (1267 days). The time, times and half-a time are *not* the same as 1260 days, but the 1260 days in Revelation 12:6 are contained in the 1267 days of Revelation 12:14. These times are imbedded in the time, times and half-a-time (1257 days) which define the Great Tribulation. ***They each describe different events, and they are not all 1260 days***. The Duration of each event has previously been calculated.

The Correct Timetable

There are five different time periods specifically mentioned in the Book of Revelation and one in the Book of Daniel.

- A day is 24 hours
- A year is 365.2422 days
- A month is 29.531 days
- 42 Months is 1241 Days
- Time, times and half-a-time is 1267 Days

Time Period	Start	Finish	Scriptural Reference
42 Months 1242 days	The Rebuilt Temple will be taken over by Antichrist	The Jewish Temple will be tread Underfoot by Gentiles for 42 Months	Revelation 11:2
42 Months 1242 days	From When the Beast (Antichrist) Arises	Antichrist is Destroyed at The Battle of Armageddon	Revelation 13:5
1260 Days 1260 Days	Two Witnesses will Start Prophesying	They will prophesy until the Saints (Jews and Gentiles) are Raptured. They will then be killed and lay in street 3.5 days. God will then say: "Come up Here"	Revelation 11:3
1260 Days 1260 Days	Woman is Nourised In wilderness by the people	Until Jesus Comes for Them After Battle of Armageddon	Revelation 12:6
Time, Times and Half a Time 1267 Days	The Woman (Israel) of Revelation 12 is protected by God from the Wrath of Satan and from the Wrath Of God	The Jews in the wilderness will be nourished to keep them alive so that they can enter the Millennial Kingdom and inherit the Promised land	Revelation 12:14
Time, Times and Half a Time 1267 Days	From the Time That the Rebuilt temple in Jerusalem is Desecrated	The Battle of Armageddon	Daniel 12: 1-7

The duration of Satan's reign and key events which take place over 1267 days are shown below.

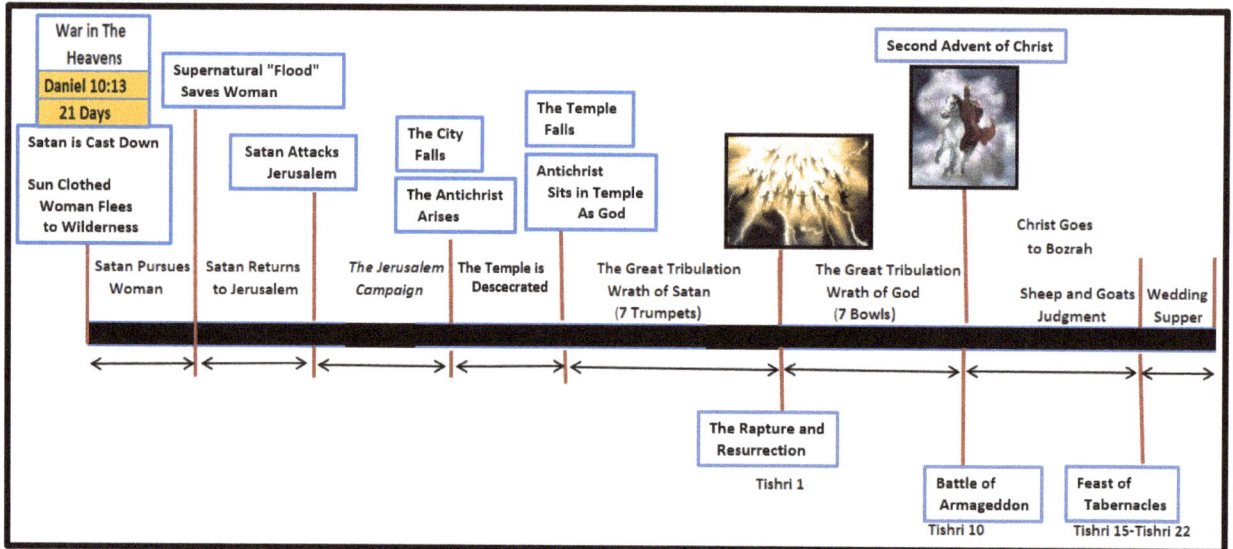

The 6 different time periods shown above (4 from the Book of Revelation and one from the Book of Daniel) have been placed on a timeline and are color coded to the previous Table.

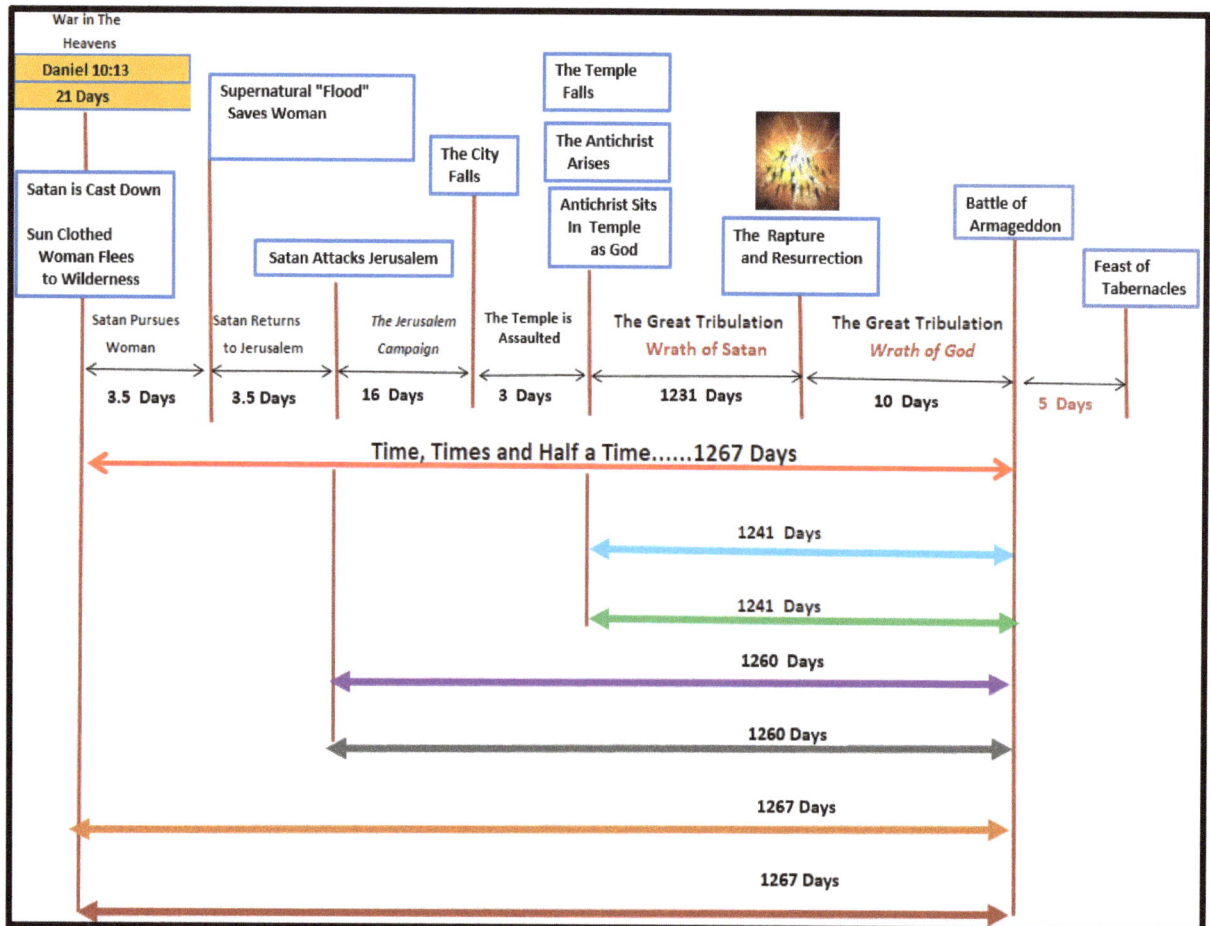

The first 7 days concern events which will initiate the Great Tribulation period. Those 7 days include the Woman fleeing from Jerusalem, being saved by God from Satan, and then arriving to a place prepared for them by God in the wilderness… possibly Petra in Bozrah. When God saves the woman, Satan is furious and turns back to Jerusalem (Revelation 12:17) where he will break the Peace Treaty with Israel (Isaiah 28:15), and invade the city. This is called the *Jerusalem Campaign*. When Satan invades the city, the European leader of a 10-nation confederacy will be killed with a sword or a knife (Revelation 13: 1-3) and he will become the *Antichrist* (Revelation 13: 4-10). The *False Prophet* will then arise (Revelation 13: 13-17), and the temple will be invaded by the Antichrist and the False Prophet. This will mark the beginning of great Wrath and Tribulation during which the 7 Trumpets (Wrath of Satan) will be sounded. The initial 23 days are not detailed in scripture and the times shown for these events are "best guesses". The important thing is the events which will take place immediately after Satan is cast out of heaven. When Satan falls along with his demonic angels, the Great tribulation will begin which will last *time, times and half-a-time* or 1267 days. The end of Satan's reign of terror will be when he is totally defeated and cast into the bottomless pit for 1000 years. This is the last day of this church age. The Millennial Kingdom will begin on Tishri 23 following the 8-day Feast of Tabernacles (Tishri 15-22). We will now show that this must be true.

The Last and Final Day of This Age

The previous results concerning the duration and sequence of events which will take place in the Tribulation Period have been based upon 3 fundamental assumptions. (1) The Daniel 70-Week Prophecy concerns only the Jew and the Nation of Israel (2) The prophecy spans the fate of the Jews from a Decree which was issued by King Nebuchadnezzar to Ezra the Scribe in 458 BC to the 2nd advent of Jesus Christ when he returns to fight the Battle of Armageddon (3) The 70th and last week (7 years) of Daniel's Prophecy (7 years) is composed of two parts: (a) The 3.5 years (1280 days) of Jesus Christ earthly ministry and (b) The 3.5 years (1267 days) of the Tribulation. (4) The 7 holy Feasts of Israel provide a *blueprint* of major events.

The Hebrew lunar/solar Calendar was in use by the Jews during the Babylonian captivity, it is in use today, and it will be in use during the (future) reign of Satan during the Great Tribulation. There is no reason to use either the Gregorian Calendar or the Roman calendar at all except to determine that Jesus Christ was Crucified on the Feast of Passover, Nisan 14 on a Wednesday in 30 AD. The 4 Spring Feasts of Israel (Feast of Passover, Feast of Unleavened Bread, Feast of Firstfruits and the Feast of Pentecost) were completely satisfied by Jesus Christ at His 1st coming, and the 3 Fall Feasts (Feast of Trumpets, Feast of Yom Kippur and the Feast of Tabernacles will be completely satisfied by Jesus Christ at His 2nd advent.

- Christ was crucified on the Feast of Passover (Nisan 14)
- His earthly ministry was 1280 days in duration
- The rapture of all saints will occur on the Feast of Trumpets (Tishri 1)
- The Battle of Armageddon will take place on the Feast of Yom Kippur (Tishri 10)
- The Feast of Tabernacles (Tishri 15- Tishri 22) will immediately precede the 1000-year Millennial Kingdom

- The three designations of time (Time, Times and half-a-time, 42 months and 1260 days are not identical). Time, Times and half-a time were found to be 1267 days and 42 months was found to equal 1241 days.
- The earthly ministry of Jesus Christ in His 1ˢᵗ coming was 1280 days and the duration of the Great Tribulation will be 1267 days.

This chapter has proposed that 42 months, 1260 days and a time, time and half-a-time are **not** all equal to 1260 days, and each month and year are not based upon 30-day prophetic months. Events described in the Book of Revelation may or may not start at the same time and end at the same time. The assumption that time, times and half-a-time and 42 months are both equal to 1260 days is both illogical and incorrect. The duration of 42 months and time, times and half-a-time were pre-ordained when God established months, days, years and seasons (Genesis 1:14). The entire Daniel 70-week prophecy (490) years is Jewish and concerns periods of time when God is dealing with the Jews… Exclusively during the 1ˢᵗ half of Daniel's 70ᵗʰ Week, and jointly with the Gentiles during the 2ⁿᵈ half of Daniel's 70ᵗʰ Week. A year is not 12 months of 30 days or 360 days. The duration of any one Hebrew year is determined by the Hebrew lunar/solar Calendar, and depends upon what adjustments are necessary to keep a Lunar year in sync with a Solar year. Any one year in the Hebrew calendar can be 353, 354, 355, 383, 384, or 385 days long. Years consist of either 12 months (normal year) or 13 months (leap year). The Spring months are always be 30 or 31 days long in any one year. The entire Daniel prophecy is not based upon a Prophetic year, but is based upon the Jewish Calendar which was in use during the Babylonian (70 year) exile. This was the same calendar that was in use in the 1ˢᵗ century AD and the same calendar that is in use today… and the same calendar that will be in use by the Jews when the Great Tribulation starts.

When Satan and his fallen angels are cast out of heaven, the Great tribulation will begin which will contain the 7 trumpet Judgments (Wrath of Satan…Revelation 12:12) and the 7 Bowl Judgments (Wrath of God…Revelation 15:1 and Revelation 16:1). The Great Tribulation will last a *times, time and half-a-time*…3.5 years (Daniel 7:25, Daniel 12:7, Revelation 12:14), or more accurately 1267 days.

It is interesting that the vast majority of prophecy teachers and students believe that the Tribulation will be 7 years in duration. We have shown that this is based upon non-biblical reasoning, but regardless of what anyone might choose to believe we have shown that the actual period of Wrath and Tribulation is only 3.5 years long or 1267 days…not a full 7 years… or 1260 days. If the notion that a prophetic month and a prophetic year is rejected, the timing shown in the previous charts will be true regardless of whether one believes in a 7-year tribulation or only a 3.5-year tribulation. The theology that determines that choice is based upon both when the Daniel prophecy starts, and whether or not *Prophetic* years and months are used.

Conclusions

As previously discussed, there are four things related to the correct interpretation of the Daniel 70-Week prophecy which is critical to reaching any sustainable decision: (1) *Who* issued the decree which allowed the Jews to return to Jerusalem? (2) *What year and date* was the decree issued? (3) *Was the prophecy based upon* a 360- day prophetic year or upon a standard 365.2422-day year? (4) Should the Julian Calendar, the Gregorian Calendar or the Hebrew Lunar/ Solar calendar be used to calculate relevant times and dates? We have challenged both the work of Sir Robert Anderson and Harold Hoehner and our conclusions have been supported by several other biblical scholars (Ice, Thomas; Harold Hoehner and Derek Walker to name a few) The body of Anderson's impressive work is found to be full of errors and his final conclusions cannot be sustained. Dr. Harold Hoehner launched an investigation of his own, and corrected the errors which had rendered the Anderson work unacceptable. Dr. Hoehner's work is to be commended but a Nisan 14, Friday crucifixion and the use of a 360-day prophetic year is questionable. It remains to be seen how the conclusions of this study can and will lead to a new Pre-Wrath Rapture. That will be dealt with in Chapter 7.

Chapter 7

Pre-Wrath Rapture and Resurrection

A Jewish and Christian Perspective

This Book has been written to introduce a new Rapture theory which is based upon two fundamental scriptural truths: (1) The 7 Seals, the 7 Trumpets and the 7 Bowls do not occur in lock-step sequence with one another. The 7 Seals are used to secure the contents of a Scroll or a Book which was kept by God until it was opened to reveal its contents to John. The scroll contains a written record of what will take place in the Great Tribulation, and John was told to write the Book of Revelation for us to study and understand. The contents of the scroll cannot be revealed until all of the 7 seals are removed. As the Seals are broken by Christ, John is shown general conditions which will exist when the tribulation period begins (Seals 1-4); and several specific events which will occur (Seals 5 and 6). When Seal 7 is removed, Heaven stands in silence because of the things which are about to take place (Revelation 8:1). (2) The 7 Trumpets represent and unleash the *Wrath of Satan* which is about to fall upon the earth, and the 7 Bowls represent *Wrath of God* which will fall upon all unbelievers. Every Christian who is secure in Jesus Christ has been promised that they will not experience the *Wrath of God* (Romans 1:18, Romans 5:1, Colossians 3:6, I Thessalonians 1:10, I Thessalonians 5:9) …which is without controversy or ambiguity the 7 Bowl Judgments (Revelation 15:1, Revelation 15:7, Revelation 16:1).

Why would any Christian expect or even want to be spared from the 7 Trumpet Judgments (Wrath of Satan)?

The Wrath of Satan will bring unprecedented tribulation and suffering upon Christians during the last half of Daniel's 70th and last week. It will also be a time during which many unbelievers… Jews and gentiles… will turn to Jesus Christ and be saved. *Who will preach the Gospel message and win these souls to Christ?* If all believers are raptured out before the great Tribulation begins: *Who will Witness to all unbelievers?*

And he said unto me, Son of man, I send thee to the children of Israel, to a rebellious nation that hath rebelled against me: they and their fathers have transgressed against me, even unto this very day Ezekiel 2:3

… I heard the voice of the Lord, saying: Whom shall I send, and who will go for us? Then said I: Here am I; send me Isaiah 6:8

It will be the privilege and destiny of the church to bring hope and eternal life to those who have no hope.

[19] *Repent ye therefore, and be converted, that your sins may be blotted out, when the times of refreshing shall come from the presence of the Lord;*
[20] *And he shall send Jesus Christ, which before was preached unto you:*
[21] *Whom the heaven must receive until the times of restitution of all things, which God hath*

spoken by the mouth of all his holy prophets since the world began
Acts 3: 19-21

[7] *Before she travailed, she brought forth; before her pain came, she was delivered of a man child.*
[8] *Who hath heard such a thing? who hath seen such things? Shall the earth be made to bring forth in one day? or shall a nation be born at once? for as soon as Zion travailed, she brought forth her children*   Isaiah 66: 7-8

[1] *And there appeared a great wonder in heaven; a woman clothed with the sun, and the moon under her feet, and upon her head a crown of twelve stars:*
[2] *And she being with child cried, travailing in birth, and pained to be* delivered
Revelation 12: 1-2

The last 3.5 years of Daniels 70th week and the last 3.5 years of the Church Age are composed of two parts: (1) The 7 trumpet Judgments which are the *Wrath of Satan* and the 7 Bowl/Vial Judgments which are the *Wrath of God*. The entire period of tribulation and Wrath is 367 days. The Wrath of Satan (7 Trumpet Judgments) will fall upon all those who dwell upon the earth (believers and unbelievers) over a 1257-day time period and (2) The Wrath of God (7 Bowl Judgments) will fall upon all unbelievers over a 10-day period of time. A fundamental truth that is contained throughout the entire New Testament is that Christians will face suffering and affliction in this world and will have trials and tribulations. Jesus told us so:

Blessed are you when others revile you and persecute you and utter all kinds of evil against you falsely on my account. Rejoice and be glad, for your reward is great in heaven, for so they persecuted the prophets who were before you   Matthew 5: 11-12

John told us so:

In the world you will have tribulation. But take heart; I have overcome the world   John 16:33

Paul told us also:

Indeed, all who desire to live a godly life in Christ Jesus will be persecuted   II Timothy 3:12

We should not fear suffering and tribulation. While we may desire to be spared from suffering and tribulation in this life, we need to recognize that suffering is not antithetical to the Christian life but rather part of it as we follow Christ in this world. All who have followed Christ will not be alive during the 3.5 years of great tribulation, but all will experience tribulation while on this earth. So, let us heed the call to the church in the Book of Revelation to hold fast to our faith in all circumstances. Jesus continually tells us that we should be ready because he will come at an hour we do not know and do not expect. Our lives could end at any time or he could return at any time, so let us remain faithful and remind others of this important truth. As repeatedly stated, and revealed in the scriptures, those who believe upon Jesus Christ as the Son of God (Christians… Jew or Gentiles) will experience tribulation but will never experience the Wrath of God (Revelation 15:1, Revelation 15:7 and Revelation 16:1).

Those who accept and believe that Christ is the Son of God and become *Christians* will be rewarded with eternal life through Him. This is a free gift based upon faith and grace…but there was a great price that was paid for redemption from sin. Many might reject this higher calling to the Church, saying: *But I might be Martyred.* Do you mean: Just as Christ was for you and I?

Anyone who accepts Christ as their Lord and savior is called a *Christian*, and becomes part of the body of Christ. The collective body of both Old Testament believers and New Testament Christians is called the *ecclesia*. Christ has risen, but we are here on earth to proclaim his victory over death and win souls to Christ. Every Christian is expected to proclaim the Gospel Message to unbelievers. This is part of becoming a *new creature in Christ*. A fundamental and integral part of this mission is to convert the Jews to a blood-bought believer. *This is what is expected of any individual who has accepted Jesus Christ as their Lord and Savior.*

All Christians are saved by faith and grace. When a Christian accept Jesus Christ as the Son of God and as their Lord and Savior, they become part of the *Body of Christ*. This is not just symbolic: Each blood-bought Christian represents Christ here on this earth: preaching the Gospel of salvation and winning Souls to Christ. There are no exceptions...Jews and Gentiles alike. The Jews are God's chosen people, but they have been *blinded in part* until God removes the scales from their spiritual eyes. It is our responsibility and calling to win Jews to Christ. Make no mistake about it ...An Orthodox Jew does not believe in Jesus Christ as their Savior and Redeemer, and if anyone (Jew or Gentile) dies in a state of disbelief they will be tortured forever in the Lake of Burning Fire. I did not say this...Jesus did.

Jesus saith unto him, I am the way, the truth, and the life: no man cometh unto the Father, but by me   John 14:6

Neither is there salvation in any other: for there is none other name under heaven given among men, whereby we must be saved   Acts 4:12

A Pre-Tribulation Rapture in which all Christians are removed from earth is one of the worst lies ever placed by Satan upon theologians. The general belief and attitude of all Pre-Tribulation believers is that Christ will return some day (soon) and remove all Christians from the earth: *Just hang on...the Wrath of Satan or the Wrath of God will never be experienced by any Christian.* If this is true: *Who is left to preach the everlasting gospel, save souls, and transform unbelievers into true believers*? Many who would not be raptured out before the Tribulation begins might turn to Christ when they realize what has happened. But, who will save them and tell them about Jesus Christ if every believer is gone? Those who would remain after a Pre-Tribulation rapture and turn to Christ as their Lord and Savior would have to go through the Wrath of Satan... and possibly be Martyred for their faith...but they will *never* experience the Wrath of God. Every born-again Christian has been justified, sanctified and will be glorified. This division of Saints over whether we serve our Lord Jesus Christ or do not serve is not taught anywhere in scripture. *Is this really the plan of God?* God has promised that *anyone* who accepts His Son as Lord and Savior and receives the free gift of eternal life is expected to pick up the cross and serve Him. It is God's eternal plan that not only the Gentiles, but His chosen people...Israel...will turn from their current disbelief and be saved, but not until the fullness of the Gentiles has come to pass. This will happen.

Brethren, my heart's desire and prayer to God for Israel is, that they might be saved.
Romans 10:1

[25] *For I would not, brethren, that ye should be ignorant of this mystery, lest ye should be wise in your own conceits; that blindness in part is happened to Israel, until the fulness of the Gentiles be come in.*
[26] *And so all Israel shall be saved: as it is written: There shall come out of Sion the Deliverer,*

and shall turn away ungodliness from Jacob:
[27] *For this is my covenant unto them, when I shall take away their sins*   Romans 11: 25-27

And the Redeemer shall come to Zion, and unto them that turn from transgression in Jacob, saith the LORD. And the Redeemer shall come to Zion, and unto them that turn from transgression in Jacob, saith the LORD   Isaiah 59:20

Who would not want to be a part of this glorious transformation of Israel? If all of Israel (those who remain alive) will be saved, the church will play a major role. Oh, what a glorious time… thousands and perhaps millions of Jews will finally realize that their only hope of salvation is Jesus Christ. This is a time when Christians will preach the gospel and save many souls from eternal damnation. *Who would not want to be there?* If Christians are not raptured out before the Great Tribulation, then *when will the rapture take place?*

The Rapture Revelation

The Apostle Paul is our main source of information concerning the Rapture of all living saints, and the resurrection of those who have died in faith and accepted Jesus Christ as their Lord and savior. (1) All who died in the Old Testament with the faith of Abraham that a redeemer would be sent by God to permanently forgive their sins. They did not know his name, but they died in faith that (Jesus Christ) would come and: (2) All who will accept Jesus Christ as their Lord and savior under the New Covenant.

And the Redeemer shall come to Zion, and unto them that turn from transgression in Jacob, saith the LORD   Isaiah 59:20

Paul wrote that this would happen, but did not say when.

[13] *But I would not have you to be ignorant, brethren, concerning them which are asleep, that ye sorrow not, even as others which have no hope.*
[14] *For if we believe that Jesus died and rose again, even so them also which sleep in Jesus will God bring with him.*
[15] *For this we say unto you by the word of the Lord, that we which are alive and remain unto the coming of the Lord shall not prevent them which are asleep.*
[16] *For the Lord himself shall descend from heaven with a shout, with the voice of the archangel, and with the trump of God: and the dead in Christ shall rise first:*
[17] *Then we which are alive and remain shall be caught up together with them in the clouds, to meet the Lord in the air: and so shall we ever be with the Lord.*
[18] *Wherefore comfort one another with these words*   I Thessalonians 4: 13-18

The word *rapture* does not appear anywhere in the scriptures. In I Thessalonians 4:17 we are told that those saints which have died in faith would rise to meet Christ… and then those who are alive and remain will be *caught up* to meet Christ in the air. The phrase *caught up* is translated from the Latin word *Raptura*, from which we derive the word *rapture*. Jesus Christ told us *when* the Rapture would occur.

[29] *Immediately **after the tribulation of those days** shall the sun be darkened, and the moon shall not give her light, and the stars shall fall from heaven, and the powers of the heavens shall be shaken:*
[30] ***And then*** *shall appear the sign of the Son of man in heaven: and then shall all the tribes of*

the earth mourn, and **they shall see the Son of man coming in the clouds** *of heaven with power and great glory.*

[31] *And he shall send his angels with a great sound of a trumpet, and* **they shall gather together his elect** *from the four winds, from one end of heaven to the other* Matthew 24: 29-31

This hardly sounds like a Pre-Tribulation Rapture. Matthew 24:29 was predicted to happen when the 6th seal is removed by Christ.

And I beheld when he had opened the sixth seal, and, lo, there was a great earthquake; and the sun became black as sackcloth of hair, and the moon became as blood Revelation 6:12

Matthew 24:29 was predicted as the 6th Seal was removed, and in context it should take place late in the Tribulation period of time...and it does....as the 7th Trumpet sounds just before the Wrath of God (7 Bowl judgments) fall upon all unbelievers (Revelation 10: 6-7). Every Christian will be gone before the Wrath of God falls upon all unbelievers. They will be Raptured out as the 7th and last trump sounds. This is what is called a **Pre- Wrath Rapture.** Everything falls into place if a Pre-Wrath rapture takes place as the 7th Trumpet sounds. This has been analyzed and shown to be true in Chapters 2-6. The rapture will now be discussed in some detail.

Resurrection and Rapture Theology

In Chapters 2-6, we have presented overwhelming evidence that the Seals only predict *conditions* (Seals 1-4) and selected events (Seals 6-7) which are about to take place as the 7 Trumpets are sounded and the 7 Bowls are poured out. When Seal 7 is removed the scroll can be unrolled and the contents revealed. The scroll will contain a description of the 7 bowls and the 7 trumpets, The 7 Trumpets are called the *Wrath of Satan* (Revelation 12:12) and the 7 Bowls are called the *Wrath of God* (Revelation 15:1, Revelation 15:7, Revelation 16:1). The *Day of God's Wrath* is the Battle of Armageddon (Isaiah 13:9, Isaiah 13:13, Zepeniah 1:15, Ezekiel 39:22, Zachariah 12:8).

There are 4 main Rapture positions that are held by an overwhelming number of all theologians and Christians: (1) Pre-Tribulation Rapture (2) Mid-Tribulation Rapture (3) Post-Tribulation Rapture and (4) Classic Pre-Wrath Rapture.

1.0   Pre-Tribulation Rapture

A Pre–Tribulation rapture is held by most dispensationalists today, and is the most popular theology among prophecy teachers. It is a relatively new view that seems to have been popularized by a British pastor named John Nelson Darby around 1827 and by a Scottish girl named *Margaret McDonald* in the early 1830's. She had a *vision* and an *utterance* in a Presbyterian church pastored by Edward Irvin (1792-1834). John Darby, pastor of the *Church of Ireland*, accepted the vision as a divine prophecy from God and began to preach its acceptance. The fact John Darby first popularized the pre-tribulation rapture doctrine around 1832 AD is unquestionably true. However, much credit must be given to C. I. Scofield. When Scofield wrote his popular *Scofield Reference Bible* in 1909, he was greatly influenced by Darby and adopted the belief of a Pre-Tribulation rapture. This concept never existed in the ancient church fathers and I can find no reference to a Pre-tribulation Rapture before 1800 AD. So, there you have it.... The *pre-tribulation Rapture* theory is only about 200 years old and places the rapture of the church *before* a commonly taught seven-year period of tribulation.

Authors Comment: Another interesting observation concerning the pre-tribulation rapture position is that scriptural justification is largely based upon Revelation 4:1

After this I looked, and, behold, a door was opened in heaven: and the first voice which I heard was as it were of a trumpet talking with me; which said, come up hither, and I will show thee things which must be hereafter   Revelation 4:1

All Pre-Tribulation believers considerably stretch the imagination in asserting that when John was taken from the Island of Patmos in the spirit (Revelation 4:2) and transported to heaven that this represents the rapture of all saints. *First*, when the rapture of all living Christians takes place, they will be taken to heaven by Jesus Christ Himself (I Corinthians 4:16), who will meet them in the air. There is no hint that this took place in Revelation 4:1 *Second*, at the Rapture the dead will be raised first. There is not even an indication that John was preceded by anyone dead. *Third*, those who are raptured out will be given a new, indestructible and non-corruptible body. There is not even a clue that John went through this type of transformation. *Fourth*, flesh and blood cannot enter into the kingdom of heaven (I Corinthians 15:50), so John was taken to heaven in the *spirit*. *Fifth*, when the rapture does take place *all* of the saints will meet Christ in the air, and then they will forever be with the Lord. John returned to earth and lived several years after he penned the Book of Revelation. *Sixth*, When the saints are raptured, they will all be called forth by the sound of a *trumpet*. In Revelation 4:1 John was told to *come up here* by a *voice* which *sounded like a trumpet* (Revelation 1:10). *Seventh*, the only reason that John was taken to heaven was to see what *must take place hereafter* (Revelation 4:1). The idea that John 4:1 types and represents the rapture is so far-fetched that it hardly deserves consideration, yet a pre-tribulation rapture is widely believed and taught in seminaries.

2.0 Post-Tribulation Rapture
A Pre-Tribulation rapture was not taught or held by the ancient church fathers. The predominant position was that of a Post-Tribulation Rapture. This belief places the rapture of the church immediately *following* a 7-year period of tribulation, and after the 7 bowls have been poured out. The Rapture occurs just before the final Battle of Armageddon. The raptured saints then immediately return with Christ to join Him in the Battle of Armageddon. The post–tribulation belief has largely disappeared among modern prophecy teachers because of multiple scriptural problems which we will not address. A *Post-Tribulation* rapture position assumes that the church is not promised any protection from either the Wrath of Satan or the Wrath of God. In fact, there is no distinction between the two at all. The Post-Tribulation proponents teach that God's elect will have a full and clear understanding of the timing of the second coming of Christ, and Christ's coming will not catch believers by surprise, but only those who are spiritually misinformed regarding the truth. Almost no modern prophecy teacher will propose a post-Tribulation rapture.

3.0 Mid-Tribulation Rapture
The mid-tribulation rapture theory is exactly as the name indicates; it assumes that the rapture will occur just before Satan is cast down to earth in a great celestial battle, and the ecclesia who are raptured out are usually associated with the *Man-Child* in Revelation 12:5. The belief was spawned by (properly) recognizing that the man-child of Revelation 12 is not Christ, but they are believers who will be raptured out at that time. One of the problems with this position is that the

Man-Child would need to be composed of only living believers (Revelation 12: 1-4). Paul revealed that when the rapture will occur, those taken up to meet Christ in the air will be both living and dead and there is not one hint that this is true in Revelation 12. The Man-Child is immediately caught up to the throne as it is birthed. Another major problem is that if all believers are raptured out, how can Revelation 12:17 be explained? Almost all prophecy teachers assume that the Man-Child is Jesus Christ, which will destroy any Mid-Tribulation rapture belief. The mid-tribulation position has only a few supporters.

4.0   Classical Pre-Wrath Rapture

The most recent rapture theory to surface is called a *Pre- Wrath* rapture. It was popularized by Robert Van Kampen (*The Sign*) and Matthew Rosenthal (*The Pre-Wrath Rapture of the Church*). Rosenthal was a Jew who converted to Christianity. The Pre-Wrath rapture position fails to distinguish between the Wrath of Satan and the Wrath of God. In a classical Pre-Wrath theology, the rapture takes place when the 6th seal is broken (Revelation 6:12). Like a Pre-Tribulation rapture, the Pre-wrath Rapture does not deny a 7-year tribulation period. *Exactly* when the Rapture occurs in the 7-year tribulation is a matter of choice, but it must take place as the 6th seal is removed. Van Kampen and Rosenthal both placed their entire belief in a pre-wrath rapture on the premise that Christians (the church) would be spared from *all* wrath (Revelation 6:17). This belief led him to believe that wrath would commence as the 6th seal is removed, since Revelation 6:17, clearly states that the *Day of His Wrath* has come. *First*, this would demand that *His Wrath* must mean the Wrath of Satan and the Wrath of God, since the 7 Trumpet judgments and the 7 Bowl Judgments are yet to come. This also demands that both the tribulation and wrath that will span the entire tribulation period must be executed by God; which is simply untenable. It is true that the 7 Trumpet Judgments of Satan's Wrath are allowed by God, but this is hardly the same as being executed by God. *Second*, this demands that the *Day of Wrath* which is mentioned in many Old and New Testament scriptures cannot be a single day as we have shown, but spans the 7 trumpet Judgments and the 7 Bowl Judgments. The basic premise of both Van Kampen and Matthew Rosenthal is, we believe, correct. Where both meet an impasse in scriptural harmonization was/is a failure to recognize what we have presented as scriptural truth... that the seals simply provide an overview of the tribulation period and that all Christians are not spared from the Wrath of Satan but from the Wrath of God.   Realizing this, all scriptural conflicts disappear between Revelation 6:17 and Revelation 16:1.

The 7 Feasts of Israel

To understand Jewish, Messianic expectations, one must recognize and understand the meaning of the 7 Feasts of Israel. They were ordained and established by God after the Exodus from Egypt (Leviticus 23).

The 7 Feasts of Israel are historical in that they were to be observed forever as a memorial and remembrance of how God rescued Israel from Egyptian slavery, and then formed a New Nation which would by divine appointment serve the Lord and be the *apple of His eye* (Deuteronomy 32:10). The 7 Festivals were called *moeds* which mean *ordained* and *appointed* times, and each were to occur at a specific time each year. If the 7 festivals are to be held at specific time(s) during each year to recall and celebrate something which happened to Israel (Exodus), why would Christians be interested? It is because that each feast is not only a *moed* but a *rehearsal*.

The Seven Feasts of the Lord

'These are a shadow of the things that were to come; the reality, however, is found in Christ.' Col 2:17

The Spring Feasts (fulfilled @ Jesus' first coming)				Feast Gap Period (fulfilled by Church Age)	The Autumn (Fall) Feasts (fulfilled @ Jesus' second coming)		
Passover	**Unleavened Bread**	**FirstFruits**	**Pentecost**		**Trumpets**	**Atonement**	**Tabernacles**
Crucifixion Of Jesus	Burial Of Jesus	Resurrection Of Jesus	Coming of the Holy Spirit		Rapture & Resurrection Of Believers	Second Coming Of Jesus	Messianic Kingdom Age
Nisan 14	Nisan 15-21	Nisan 18	Sivan 7		Tishri 1	Tishri 10	Tishri 15-22
Exodus 12 Matt 26:17-27	Lev 23:6-8 I Cor 5:7-8	Lev 23:9-14 I Cor 15:20-23	Lev 23:15-22 Acts 1 & 2		Lev 23:23-25 1 Cor 15:51-52	Lev 23:26-32 Matt 24:29-30	Lev 23:33-44 Rev 20:1-6

——— 'The Days of Awe' ———
Time of Jacob's trouble

A rehearsal of what? The 7 Feasts of Israel are not only *historical* but *prophetic* of things to come. They prophesy of the 1st and 2nd coming of their savior and redeemer…*Jesus Christ* (Colossians 2:17).

The first 4 Spring Feasts are (1) *The Feast of Pentecost* on Nisan 14 (2) The *Feast of Unleavened Bread* on Nisan 15-Tishri 21 (3) The *Feast of Firstfruits*, which is to be observed on the only Sunday that falls during the 7-day Feast of Unleavened Bread and the (4) *Feast of Pentecost*, which is held on the 50th day from the Feast of Firstfruits. Christ died on the Feast of Passover. He lay in the grave during the Feast of Unleavened Bread and satisfied the Feast of Firstfruits when he arose from the grave and ascended to His Father in Heaven. Fifty days after the Feast of Firstfruits (inclusive count), the Holy Spirit fell upon all of the people who were in Jerusalem on the Feast of Pentecost, just as Christ had promised and to satisfy parts of Joel 2.

[28] *And it shall come to pass afterward, that I will pour out my spirit upon all flesh; and your sons and your daughters shall prophesy, your old men shall dream dreams, your young men shall see visions:*
[29] *And also upon the servants and upon the handmaids in those days will I pour out my* spirit
Joel 2: 28-29

When Christ was crucified, ascended from the grave, rose to heaven, and sent the Holy Spirit on the Day of Pentecost…. he completely and totally fulfilled the first 4 (Spring) Feasts of Israel. Christians who have studied the 7 Feasts of Israel realize that if the 1st four (Spring) Feasts of Israel spoke of the first advent of Christ, and that the last three (Fall) Feasts of Israel prophesy and speak of the second coming of Christ. The second advent of Christ will fulfill Joel 2: 30-32.

[30] *And I will shew wonders in the heavens and in the earth, blood, and fire, and pillars of smoke.*
[31] *The sun shall be turned into darkness, and the moon into blood, before the great and the terrible day of the LORD come.*
[32] *And it shall come to pass, that whosoever shall call on the name of the LORD shall be*

delivered: for in mount Zion and in Jerusalem shall be deliverance, as the LORD hath said, and in the remnant whom the LORD shall call Joel 2: 30-32

We will see that the Feast of Rosh Hashana (Feast of Trumpets) is when the resurrection and rapture of all true believers will take place; The Feast of Yom Kippur (Day of Atonement) is when each person is to confess their sins to God and seek to make right those sins that they have committed against God. There are 10 days between the last Feast of Trumpets (Tishri 1) and the last Feast of Atonement (Tishri 10) which will be the last chance to accept Christ as their Lord and Savior. Jews call this period of time the Days of Awe. It is during this period of time that God will pour out His wrath upon all who were not raptured out on the Feast of Trumpets. The Feast of Tabernacles (Tishri 15-22)) is an 8-day feast that commemorates how the Children of Israel spent 40 years in the wilderness. It also celebrates the end of harvest season. The victory of Jesus Christ at the Battle of Armageddon will be celebrated on the last Feast of Tabernacles, the Wedding Supper of the Lamb will be held, the Promised Land will be allocated to 10 tribes of Israel, and the 1000-year Millennial will begin.

The 2nd return of Jesus Christ to fight the Battle of Armageddon will be *preceded* by what we call the *Resurrection* and *Rapture* of the *ecclesia*. It is widely believed that what we call the Rapture will occur on the Feast of Trumpets. The 2nd advent of Christ is not the rapture. The rapture will take place before the Bowl Judgments (Wrath of God) fall upon all living unbelievers. Christ will suddenly appear in the air, and with the sound of a Trumpet call all true believers to be with Him forever. The dead in Christ will rise 1st, followed by all who remain and are still alive. The Battle of Armageddon will take place on Yom Kippur when He physically returns. This is the second coming or the second advent of Jesus Christ.

The *Feast of Trumpets* or Rosh Hashanah celebrates the beginning of a new year on the Jewish social calendar and ushers in what is called the *Ten Days of Awe*, culminating in a major fast on *Yom Kippur* or the Day of Atonement. **This period is considered to be the holiest time of the Jewish year.** The Jews believe that the world was created on Tishri 1. The Jewish 10 days of awe will correspond to the Wrath of God, and it is the last chance for any unbelievers to accept Jesus Christ as their Lord and savior. On Tishri 1, Christ will descend from Heaven to the Mount of Olives from which He ascended. His feet will stand on the Mt. of Olives and it will split into two parts…one part to the East and one part to the West. He will then march to a place called Megiddo where He will fight the Battle of Armageddon (Revelation 19). After Satan and his army are defeated, it is believed that Christ will then go to the Wilderness south of Jerusalem in blood-stained garments where He will retrieve a believing remnant (Isaiah 63:1, Micah 3:12) which has been there since they fled Jerusalem in Revelation 12: 6. Christ will then judge the *nations of the world* in the Judgment of the Sheep and Goats (Matthew 25: 31-46). The 7th and last Feast of Israel is the *Feast of Tabernacles* (Tishri 15-21). This is a joyous occasion at which He will hold the Wedding Supper of the Lamb with His bride the church. After the glorious Feast of Tabernacles, the 1000 Year Millennial Kingdom will begin…. and Israel will finally inherit the promised land.

> **Authors Comment**: The sequence of events which we propose will happen in the final days includes the final offer of eternal life and salvation by faith and grace to the Jews and to the Gentiles. After the Rapture of all true believers, there will be no one left on

earth who has accepted Jesus Christ as the Son of God and as their Lord and Savior. However, there is a mystery which was revealed to us by Christ in Matthew 25: 31-46. This is a part of the Olivet Discourse at which He spoke of what would happen at the end of the Age when He will return. This discourse is not discussed very often. Christ reveals that there will be one final judgment called the *Judgment of the Nations* or the *Judgment of the Sheep and Goats*. After the Battle of Armageddon has taken place, He will evidently assemble people from all *nations* (Matthew 25:32). *Who are these people?* We can only know what little is revealed to us in this mysterious account. They are evidently people from all over the world (nations of the world) who have not taken the Mark of the Beast (Revelation 19:20) and have not been raptured out. They are identified by Christ as people who have fed the poor... clothed those who were cold... gave water and food to the poor and starving... were sick or in prison, etc. This is very mysterious, Jesus Christ offered forgiveness of sins and eternal life by grace to all who would believe in faith. The theme of the Judgment of the Sheep and Goats are *works*... not faith. Jesus further stated that by doing these things, those humanitarians were doing it to HIM (Matthew 25:40). This reminds us of when Saul of Tarsus was converted on the road to Damascus by Christ after he had been dead for some time: He said: *Saul, Saul...Why do you persecute ME.*

This is a significantly different type of judgment. Christ separated everyone into two groups: One were called *Sheep* and the other *Goats*. Those who had helped His people and were compassionate, merciful and kind were called *His Sheep*...Those who did not care were called *Goats*. The Sheep inherited eternal life and lived in His kingdom...The Goats were cast into everlasting punishment. *How can we explain this*? First, we cannot explain this strange salvation by works under the New Covenant, but Jesus Christ is the Son of God and He can do anything that His father tells him he can do. Consider the following: The Age of Grace...The Church Age... and the dispensation of the New Covenant has ended at the Battle of Armageddon. The Bema Seat Judgment has already taken place. Hence, salvation, forgiveness of sins on the Cross of Calvary and the free gift of eternal life was over. Jesus Christ can do anything He chooses to do without compromising or violating the Old Testament law or the New Covenant....both have passed away. This explanation is offered in all humility and human understanding of what the Holy Scriptures reveal. This is one of those things that we will ask Jesus Christ to explain when we sit with Him.

When God says *Go*...Jesus Christ will return to earth to receive those who believe upon Him (the *ecclesia*) at the sound of a trumpet...the last trumpet... and *meet them in the air* at what we call the *Rapture*. The second advent of Christ is when he will physically return to Earth to fight the Battle of Armageddon. We are now further concerned with the Rapture and the Second Advent of Christ

Paul's Revelation Knowledge

The Apostle Paul provides the foundation of all scriptural truth concerning what we call the *Rapture*. The word *rapture* does not appear in the bible anywhere. It is taken from the Latin word *Raptura* which means to be *caught up* or *snatched away*. When the Latin Vulgate and the original Hebrew and Greek manuscripts were translated into Greek, the Greek word *Harpazo* was used which means to be *caught up* or *taken away*. When the KJV was translated from

Greek... *Harpazo* was consistently translated as *caught up* (II Corinthians 12: 2-4, I Thessalonians 4:17, Revelation 12:5).

Authors Note: In Revelation 12:5, the Man-child is said to be *caught up* to God's throne.

In I Thessalonians 4: 14-17, Paul revealed:

[15] *For this we say unto you by the word of the Lord, that we which are alive and remain unto the coming of the Lord shall not prevent them which are asleep.*
[16] *For the Lord himself shall descend from heaven with a shout, with the voice of the archangel, and **with the trump of God**: and the dead in Christ shall rise first:*
[17] *Then we which are alive and remain shall be **caught up** together with them in the clouds, to meet the Lord in the air: and so shall we ever be with the Lord*   I Thessalonians 4: 15-17

Jesus also referred to the *rapture* in Matthew 24:31 as being launched by a *sound of a trumpet*. Paul later added that the rapture will be preceded by a *trumpet call of God* (I Thessalonians 4:16). In I Corinthians, he is specific about which trump.

[51] *Behold, I shew you a mystery; We shall not all sleep, but we shall all be changed,*
[52] *In a moment, in the twinkling of an eye, at the **last trump**: for the trumpet shall sound, and the dead shall be raised incorruptible, and we shall be* changed   I Corinthians 15: 51-52

Paul tells the saints to whom he is speaking (and us) that ***we will all be changed***, whether we are alive or dead, at the ***last trump***. Now that is fairly specific, but: *When would the **last trump** be sounded*? Those who casually read I Corinthians 15:52 are tempted to assume that since there are 7 trumpets which will be blown by 7 angels in the Book of Revelation; that the 7th trumpet is the last. Hence, one might conclude that the rapture will occur as the 7th trumpet sounds. This is certainly true, but it is not the real reason.

The Last Trump: *Jewish Perspectives*

The term ***last trump*** is a Jewish eschatological term always connected to the *Feast of Rosh Hashanah* or the *Feast of Trumpets*...which occurs on the 1st day of the 7th Jewish fall month, Tishri 1. Jewish people see Rosh Hashanah or the Feast of Trumpets as the beginning of a 10-day period of introspection, confession of sins and a time of repentance leading up to the *Feast of Yom Kippur* or the *Day of Atonement* on Tishri 10. There are also 30 days of blowing the trumpet on each day *preceding* Tishri 1. A ***last trump*** is blown on the Feast of Trumpets. But there is also a trumpet blown on Tishri 10, so again.... *When is the last trumpet*? Here we must dig deeper into Jewish Rabbinical teachings. According to the ancient Jewish rabbis and teachers, the ***last trump*** is specifically related to the ***binding of Isaac***. Recall that Abraham was called by God to sacrifice his only natural son Isaac, and he went up onto the mountain to do so. Ancient Hebrew teachings say that Abraham went to where the ***Dome of the Rock*** now stands. He built an altar of sacrifice, and just as he was about to kill his son, God stayed his hand and produced a ***ram*** for a suitable sacrifice. This ram was offered as a ***burnt offering*** to the Lord and totally consumed by fire. The only thing that survived were the two ram's horns. Tradition holds that the *first horn* was blown by God himself when the Law was given to all the people at Mt. Sinai. The *second horn*.... the ***last horn***.... is to be blown at a future ***Feast of Rosh Hashanah*** (Feast of

Trumpets). The Feast of Trumpets is also called *Yom Teruah* or the *Day of Awakening Blast*. The *awakening blast* on some future Feast of Rosh Hashanah refers to a belief that the dead will be raised on this day. The resurrection of all Jews on Rosh Hashanah was widely taught and believed by the Jewish Rabbis of old, and by the Jewish prophets.

On the Feast of Trumpets (Tishri 1), there are actually 100 trumpet blasts. The final, long, and most significant trumpet blast using the 2nd ram's horn is called the **last trump** and will be sounded by God using the 2nd ram's horn. The fact that the last trump in the Book of Revelation is the last in a series of 7 does not fully justify that the Rapture of all living saints and the resurrection of all dead saints will occur when the 7th trumpet sounds, but once it is supported by Jewish beliefs it is a distinct and logical possibility. *Jewish* beliefs concerning the *last trump* are largely unknown to Western prophecy scholars who have not studied the *7 Feasts of Israel*.

Thy dead men shall live, together with my dead body shall they arise. Awake and sing, ye that dwell in dust: for thy dew is as the dew of herbs, and the earth shall cast out the dead
                                        Isaiah 26:19

For in the time of trouble he shall hide me in his pavilion: in the secret of his tabernacle shall he hide me; he shall set me up upon a rock   Psalms 27:5

Jewish belief is also that on the last Feast of Trumpets two *Books* will be opened (Daniel 7:10). These two books will be: (1) The *Book of Life* which contain the names of the righteous and (2) The *Book of Death* which contains the names of the wicked. It is also taught that there will be people who will not have their name inscribed in either book. Those people will be given 10 days to repent until their fate is sealed. These 10 days are between the Feast of Trumpets on Tishri 1 and the Feast of Yom Kippur on Tishri 10. This belief has been taught by Jewish Rabbis for thousands of years. The 10 days between the Feast of Trumpets (Tishri 1) and the Feast of Yom Kippur (Tishri 10) are called the *Days of Awe*. In the Old Testament if a person turned to God, confessed his sins and offered a *Sin Offering* to God upon the *Altar of Sacrifice*...and then if God accepted their offering for sins......they could be given another year to live. This was called *atonement* in the Old Testament *which* was only a *temporary covering* for sin (Hebrews 10:4). On the Feast of Yom Kippur (*Day of Atonement*), the High Priest would cleanse himself, make a sin offering to God for himself and all of the people, walk behind the veil which separated the Ark of the Covenant from the Holy of Holies and the Holy Place, and plead with God to forgive the sins of the people. These rituals which were performed by the Jewish high priest have not been practiced since Herod's Temple fell in 70 AD. When Christ died on the Cross of Calvary, He became the final and acceptable sacrifice for the sins of the world...He was the perfect sacrificial Lamb of God. Christ ended the rituals of the Tabernacle and Herod's Temple in 30 AD when He died on the Cross of Calvary. However, personal atonement for sin on Yom Kippur is still *Jewish tradition* and is still taught and practiced today by all Jews.

If this scenario causes one to reflect on the things which are written in this book...it should. This is the *Church age* or the *Times of the Gentiles*. In 30 AD Jesus Christ...who is our eternal high priest.... died on the Cross of Calvary and offered himself as the permanent, final and perfect sacrifice for all sins (past and present). Since that point in time, the rituals and atonement (temporary covering) for sins that were practiced in the Old Testament are meaningless. The entire sacrificial system and the rituals which took place year after year on the 7 Holy Feasts of Israel are finished. However, there will be a future *Day of Yom Kippur* in which all of Israel will turn to Jesus Christ and be saved. This is the eternal plan of God that Israel will be blinded in part (there will be a believing remnant of Jews during the Church age), and there will be a future 10-day period of repentance (Tishri 1 - Tishri 10) during which all of Israel will be saved...those who are alive and remain. It should now be clear that the end-times theology proposed in this book are perfectly in line with Jewish expectations...Which they must be.

> **Authors Comment:** I have a dear friend of mine who is a fine student of the Book of Revelation and a wonderful preacher. He adamantly states that the Temple will not be rebuilt because animal sacrifice and temple rituals were ended by Christ at His sacrificial death. Such things are now an insult and an abomination to God. He is correct. However, in all love and respect he is right but he is wrong. Jesus did replace the Old Covenant based upon works with a New Covenant based upon faith and grace when he died on the Cross of Calvary. However, the Jewish temple *will* be rebuilt (Matthew 24:15, I Thessalonians 2:4, Revelation 11:1). However, God will have nothing to do with this. It will be rebuilt by a great European world leader who will be slain and then inhabited by Satan...he is called the Antichrist. There is a Jewish belief that if anyone can reclaim the Temple mount from the Muslims and restore/rebuild the Temple of Herod... that person would be the conquering King for which they still await. This is not an act of God, but an act of Satan. The temple will be rebuilt to deceive the Jews. Satan as the Antichrist will sit in the Temple, declare himself to be God, and force all who hear his voice to take the mark of the Beast, which will condemn them forever (Revelation 19:20).

The average Christian does not take the time to research biblical principles and try to resolve scriptural difficulties by studying Jewish beliefs. Remember that each of the 4 Spring Feasts of Israel is a *moed* or *remembrance* of what God did when He rescued them from Egyptian slavery, but they also prophesy of the death, resurrection and ascension to heaven following His crucifixion on the Cross of Calvary. The last 3 Fall Feasts of Israel prophesy and point to His second advent. There was a trumpet blown on each of the 7 Feasts of Israel, and there will be a Jewish *last trump* blown on the *last Feast of Trumpets*. Paul clearly taught that there would be a trumpet that would be blown to initiate the rapture, and that it would be the *last trump*.

There are several different types of trumpets that are sounded in the biblical records. There are silver trumpets, gold trumpets and trumpets that inaugurate a King, call the people to battle and initiate Holy Days ...But the **trumpet blast** that was sounded when the law was given (*first trump*), and the one that will be sounded at the last Feast of Trumpets (*second trump*), are uniquely reserved for those two special occasions They are very special trumpets, and represent when the Jewish nation received God's law at Mt. Sinai and when they will finally accept Christ as the Son of God and as their promised Messiah at the end of the age. This is all very persuasive and interesting, but *is it substantiated anywhere in God's word?* Once again, notice again what Christ says in the **Olivet Discourse.**

[29] *Immediately **after** the tribulation of those days shall the sun be darkened, and the moon shall not give her light, and the stars shall fall from heaven, and the powers of the heavens shall* *be shaken:*

*[30] And **then** shall appear the sign of the Son of man in heaven: and then shall all the tribes of the earth mourn, and **they shall see the Son of man coming in the clouds** of heaven with power and great glory.*

*[31] And he shall send his angels with a great **sound of a trumpet**, and they shall **gather together his elect** from the four winds, from one end of heaven to the other*
                    Matthew 24: 29-31

Notice several extremely important *clues* in this discourse.

- This is clearly the rapture of the church
- It occurs *after* the tribulation of those days (not before, not in the middle).
- The sun is darkened, moon loses her light, and the havens are disturbed. These are events which occur *after the 7th trumpet is sounded* (Joel 3: 15-16)
- Everyone will see this happening… and it will be a *sign*
- He (Christ) will send his angels to *gather the elect to him* in the air

The conclusion is that the rapture occurs immediately after what Christ called a great tribulation period at the *sound of a trumpet*. This perfectly aligns with Revelation 11: 15-18, ancient Jewish beliefs, and the prophetic meaning of the 7 Feasts of Israel. The 7 bowl judgments will be poured out quickly between the Feast of Trumpets and the Feast of Yom Kippur. This is the *Wrath of God* upon a non-believing world. *Why does the rapture occur before the 1st bowl is poured out*? Listen carefully, understand and open your mind…Christ answered this question also.

A Pre-Wrath Rapture

*[21] For then shall be great tribulation, **such as was not since the beginning of the world** to this time, no, nor ever shall be.*

*[22] And **except those days should be shortened**, there should no flesh be saved: but for the elect's sake those days shall be shortened*   Matthew 24: 21-22

Christ warned us that we would need to experience great tribulation in the end-times, but we are assured that no one who has believed upon His holy name before the rapture occurs at the 7th Trumpet will ever experience the *Wrath of God.* The following evidence demands a verdict.

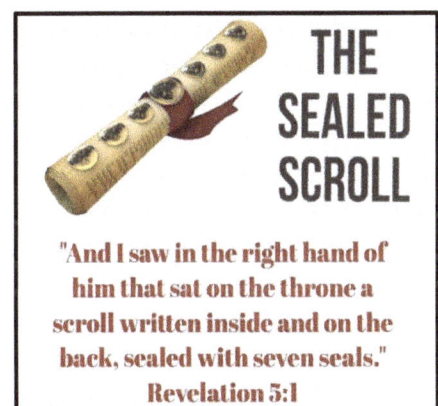

THE SEALED SCROLL

"And I saw in the right hand of him that sat on the throne a scroll written inside and on the back, sealed with seven seals."
Revelation 5:1

- The scroll (Revelation 5 :1-14) which God holds in His right hand contains the Revelation Record which was shown to John by Jesus Christ to be passed on to us as the Book of Revelation.
- The Scroll is sealed with 7 seals with writing on the front and back
- The 7 seals are removed by Jesus Christ one by one.
- The contents of the scroll cannot be revealed until all 7 Seals are removed

- As each of the 7 seals are removed, there are conditions (Seals 1-4) and specific events (Seals 5 and 6) which are about to occur which are shown to John
- The Conditions and events shown to John will occur during the Great Tribulation
- The Great Tribulation is the last-half of Daniels 70th Week (3.5 years)
- The Great Tribulation will begin when Satan is cast down to Earth with His fallen angels by Michael and his Holy Angels
- Satan will then turn upon all who inhabit the earth and attempt to kill all who will not worship Him as God
- This period of great persecution and Tribulation is called the Wrath of Satan.
- The Wrath of Satan against all Christians and Jews is the duration of the 7 trumpet Judgments
- The Wrath of Satan is the 7 Trumpet Judgments and the Wrath of God is the 7 Bowl Judgments
- No blood- bought Christian who has accepted Christ as their Lord and Savior will ever experience the Wrath of God.
- All true believers (alive) will be Raptured out as the 7th trump sounds to escape the Wrath of God.

The conclusion is that the Rapture of all saints will occur as the 7th Trumpet sounds, and it will occur *after* Satan unleashes Great Tribulation (Wrath of Satan) upon all who refuse to worship him as God and *before* the Wrath of God falls upon all unbelievers. Christ himself revealed this to his apostles in the Olivet Discourse (Matthew 24-25). It was also prophesied by Joel over 2000 years earlier.

[29] *Immediately **after the tribulation of those days** shall the sun be darkened, and the moon shall not give her light, and the stars shall fall from heaven, and the powers of the heavens shall be shaken:*
[30] *And **then shall appear the sign of the Son of man in heaven**: and then shall all the tribes of the earth mourn, and **they shall see the Son of man coming** in the clouds of heaven with power and great glory.*
[31] *And he shall send his angels with a great sound of a trumpet, and they shall gather together his elect from the four winds, from one end of heaven to the other* Matthew 24: 29-31

[30] *And I will shew wonders in the heavens and in the earth, blood, and fire, and pillars of smoke.*
[31] *The sun shall be turned into darkness, and the moon into blood, before the great and the terrible day of the LORD come.*
[32] *And it shall come to pass, that **whosoever shall call on the name of the LORD shall be delivered**: for in mount Zion and in Jerusalem shall be deliverance, as the LORD hath said, and in the remnant whom the LORD shall call* Joel 2: 28-32

 Paul provided to us a 3rd witness to this great event.

[16] *For the **Lord himself shall descend from heaven with a shout**, with the voice of the archangel, and **with the trump of God**: and the dead in Christ shall rise first:*
[17] *Then we which are alive and remain shall be **caught up** together with them in the clouds, to meet the Lord in the air: and so shall we ever be with the Lord.*
[18] *Wherefore comfort one another with these words* I Thessalonians 4: 13-18

Paul revealed that Christ would *descend from heaven*… and with the *sound of a trumpet* all believers… living or dead…will be called to meet him in the air where they will be with Him forever. In his first letter to the Church at Corinth, Paul revealed more about the sound of a trumpet.

[51] *Behold, I shew you a* **mystery***; We shall not all sleep, but* **we shall all be changed,**
[52] *In a moment, in the twinkling of an eye,* **at the last trump***: for the trumpet shall sound, and the dead shall be raised incorruptible, and we shall be changed*   I Corinthians 15:52

Christ will call forth His ecclesia… living and dead… to join Him in the air at the sound of a trumpet…the *Last Trumpet*. Many have misunderstood the phrase *at the last trumpet*, and have assumed that since there is a series of 7 trumpets blown during the Tribulation period the 7th trumpet is the last in a series of 7 and that is when the Rapture will occur. That is true, but that is not what Paul meant when he said at the *last trump*. Paul was a Jew who by his own admission was a Pharisee, the son of a Pharisee (Acts 23:26). The last trump is an eschatological term derived from the Jewish understanding of death and resurrection. It should be understood that the tribulation period of time is when God will remove the scales from the eyes of Israel (Acts 9:18).

What then? Israel hath not obtained that which he seeks; but the elect hath obtained it, and the rest were blinded   Romans 11:12

They will recognize that Jesus Christ is their long-awaited redeemer and Messiah, and so:

All Israel shall be saved*: as it is written: There shall come out of Sion the Deliverer, and shall turn away ungodliness from Jacob*   Romans 11:26

A primary purpose of the Tribulation is to redeem and save God's chosen people to God through His Son Jesus Christ. There are Jewish traditions, Messianic Expectations and Rabbinical writings which reveal such an event.

Surely the Lord GOD will do nothing, but he reveals his secret unto his servants the prophets
Amos 3:7

Can Jewish teachings and Old Testament scriptures tell us more about the rapture?

Jewish Messianic Expectations

Jews believe in both the resurrection of the dead and rewards in the afterlife. The *Torah* promises worldly rewards for faithfulness, and punishment to those who fail to obey the law. Given the ancient world's belief in immortality and afterlife, the lack of direct and complete teaching on these subjects is hard to understand. Daniel promised that there would be a resurrection of the dead to eternal life or to eternal punishment (Daniel 12: 2-3). Traditional Jews believe that Herod's Temple will one day be rebuilt in Jerusalem, the Jewish people will eventually be gathered from the far corners of the earth, and the bodies of the dead will be brought back to life and reunited with their souls. The *Mishnah* states that those who don't believe in resurrection: *Have no share in the world to come* (Mishnah, Sanhedrin 10:1). Among Orthodox Jews, belief in the resurrection is generally understood as a literal prophecy that will come to fruition when the Messiah comes (Internet; My Jewish Learning).

While the doctrine of the resurrection of the dead was taught by the Rabbi's during the second temple period, it was not universally accepted. According to that great Jewish historian,

Josephus, the questions of resurrection and how the afterlife would be spent was a major point of contention for Jewish theologians of the period. Mainstream Judaism does not decisively teach about Heaven or Hell, but many Jews believe that upon death all people will descend to a dark place called Gehenna or Sheol to await the resurrection. Later teachings about life after death include the idea that a judgement would take place after the coming of a Messiah. Some teach that the soul and body would be reunited, while others believed that it would only be the soul that would be eternal. The Rabbi's teach there will be punishment or reward for the way that an individual had lived, but there was no clear teaching on the exact nature of Heaven or Hell.

The Mystery of the Feast of Trumpets

It should be noted that the Feast of Trumpets is the only feast of 7 ordained by God which is not fully explained in Leviticus 23. This may be because the Feast is a *moed* or a *rehearsal* of the *Rapture of the saints*, which was completely hidden from the Old Testament prophets and from the Church until it was revealed by the Apostle Paul. Even Christ did not know when that day might arrive. The Jewish Rabbis offered various attempts to explain the festival. A respected and well-known Rabbi, Rav Saadiah Gaon, listed 10 reasons why the shofar is blown on Rosh Hashanah. These 10 reasons are listed below and are applied to Christian belief.

(1) *Coronation of a King*
A trumpet is sounded on Rosh Hashanah to remember or celebrate the coronation of a King. A trumpet will be sounded at the Rapture of the saints to acknowledge that God has appointed Jesus Christ his son as King of Kings that will reign during the 1000-year Millennial Kingdom.
> *And the seventh angel sounded; and there were great voices in heaven, saying: The kingdoms of this world are become the kingdoms of our Lord, and of his Christ; and he shall reign for ever and ever*   Revelation 11:15

(2) *Repentance*
Rosh Hashanah marks the beginning of a ten-day countdown to the Feast of Yom Kippur (The Day of Atonement). Yom Kippur will be the Battle of Armageddon. judgment day, the shofar is sounded as a reminder that judgment is very near and the time for repentance is short. Every Christian (Jew or Gentile) will be raptured out when the 7th trumpet (the 2nd ram's horn sounds. Those who have not accepted Jesus Christ as their Lord and Savior will be given 10 days to repent and be saved. This is not a 2nd chance…it is the last chance. The time of the Gentiles has ended at the Rapture and the fullness of the Gentiles has come. Israel will finally recognize Jesus Christ as their long-awaited redeemer:

> [25] *For I would not, brethren, that ye should be ignorant of this mystery, lest ye should be wise in your own conceits; that blindness in part is happened to Israel, until the fulness of the Gentiles be come in.*
> [26] *And so all Israel shall be saved, as it is written: There shall come out of Sion the Deliverer, and shall turn away ungodliness from Jacob*   Romans 11: 25-26

> *And the Redeemer shall come to Zion, and unto them that turn from transgression in Jacob, saith the LORD*   Isaiah 59:20

(3) *Giving of the Law at Mt Sinai*

Jewish tradition is that the law was given to Israel at Mt. Sinai. As the *voice of a trumpet sounded* (Exodus 19:19) God gave the law to Moses and the people of Israel. When all of Israel finally turns to Jesus Christ as their savior and redeemer, the law will be written on their hearts and not on two tablets of stone (Hebrews 8:10).

(4) *A Warning of Impending Danger or a Call to War*

The shofar is sounded to: (1) Announce a new year or a full moon (2) Coronate a King or (3) Call the people to a military engagement. It is a call to assemble and make ready for war, or to assemble and make ready for impending danger such as an enemy surprise attack (Ezekiel 33: 4-5, Jeremiah 4:19). There are two New Year days in the Jewish calendar. One was when it was taught that God created the Earth on Tishri 1, and the other was on Nisan 1 when God declared after the Exodus from Egypt that Nisan 1 would be Month number 1 and Tishri 1 would be month number 7. This did not change God's Calendar it only renumbered the months. When the last trump (shofar) is sounded it will precede the Battle of Armageddon by 10 days. These 10 days are between the Feast of Trumpets on Tishri 1 and the Feast of Yom Kippur on Tishri 10. They are *Days of Awe* by the Jews. It is time for Christ to come out of His chambers with His Bride to engage Satan and his demonic forces.

(5) *Remembrance of the Temple Destruction*

The Temple in Jerusalem was destroyed twice. The first Temple was built by King Solomon, and was destroyed by the Babylonians, in 586 BCE. (There are historians who claim it was in 483 BC). The Second Holy Temple was built 70 years later, and was destroyed by the Romans in 70 AD. Regardless of any controversy about the actual date(s) of the events, the fact is there were two Holy Temples on the same site, the first being destroyed by the Babylonians and the second by the Romans. In both cases, the temple was under siege until it fell, and then completely destroyed. The Holy scriptures are silent regarding exactly when the rebuilt temple will be destroyed, but there is no doubt that it will be…probably after they are called to Christ after witnessing for 3.5 years. The millennial temple of Jesus Christ will be rebuilt just north of the old site.

(6) *The Binding of Isaac*

In Genesis 22: 1-14 we are told the story of how God tested the faith of Abraham. God called to Abraham and instructed him to take his only son Isaac up on a mountain in the land of Moriah, where he was to sacrifice his only son as a burnt offering to the Lord. Abraham did as he was commanded. He laid bound his son Isaac, laid wood on top of him for the sacrificial fire and raised his knife to kill his son. Just as he was about to slay his son, an angel of the Lord stopped him. As Abraham looked up, he saw a ram caught in a thicket by his horns. And: *Abraham went and took the ram, and offered him up for a burnt offering in the stead of his son.* According to Jewish tradition, the ram was offered as a burnt offering to the Lord and was totally consumed in the fire. The only thing that remained was the two ram's horns (Shofars). The Rabbi taught that one of these horns was used on a feast of trumpets when God spoke the law to Israel from Mt. Sinai. The second horn will be blown at the last feast of Trumpets when Israel is redeemed...this blowing of the shofar is said to be the *Last Trump*. Isaac was saved by God by the *faith* of Abraham.

Paul revealed that one day on a future Feast of Trumpets that those who have accepted Christ as their Lord and Savior will be raptured to meet him in the air, following the resurrection of the righteous dead. How were the redeemed in Christ caught up to be with the Lord forever? It was by *faith*...the faith of Abraham.

(7) *To Calm Fear*

When the shofar is blown for a battle, the people prepared themselves in fear and trembling. The Prophet Amos wrote: *Shall a trumpet be blown in the city, and the people not be afraid?* (Amos 3:6). Luke spoke of the day that the Lord would come.

> [25] *And there shall be signs in the sun, and in the moon, and in the stars; and upon the earth distress of nations, with perplexity; the sea and the waves roaring;*
> [26] *Men's hearts failing them for fear, and for looking after those things which are coming on the earth: for the powers of heaven shall be shaken.*
> [27] *And then shall they see the Son of man coming in a cloud with power and great glory.*
> [28] *And when these things begin to come to pass, then look up, and lift up your heads; for your redemption draws nigh.*   Luke 21: 25-28

(8) *To Remind Sinful Israel that Judgment was Coming*

Zephaniah warned apostate Israel that on a future Feast of tabernacles that:

> *The day of the shofar is a day of wrath, darkness, gloom and alarm. Indeed, it is the Day of the LORD*   Zephaniah 1:14-16

The Feast of Trumpets is the Torah New Year's Day (the anniversary of creation). On the Feast of Trumpets, the Books of Judgment are opened and all the deeds of each person are reviewed by the Heavenly Court. Ten days later, on Yom Kippur, everyone's name will be written and sealed for final judgment in either the Book of Life or the Book of Death.

This imagery is reflected in Revelation 20:12-15 where John sees the ultimate and final Day of Judgment. On the Day of Judgment, Yom Kippur, the righteous are written in the Book of Life. The wicked are written in the Book of Death. The intervening days between Rosh Hashanah and Yom Kippur are traditionally regarded as the final time to be written in the Book of Life through serious prayer, repentance and acts of charity.

(9) *The Return of Israel to the Lord*

On the Last Feast of Trumpets, it is believed that all f Israel will repent of their sins and   be redeemed. This belief is based upon a prophecy written by Isaiah.

> [12] *And it shall come to pass in that day, that the LORD shall beat off from the channel of the river unto the stream of Egypt, and ye shall be gathered one by one, O ye children of Israel.*
> [13] *And it shall come to pass in that day, that the great trumpet shall be blown, and they shall come which were ready to perish in the land of Assyria, and the outcasts in*

the land of Egypt, and shall worship the LORD in the holy mount at Jerusalem
Isaiah 27:3

(10) *Resurrection*

In the 1st Century AD there was a disagreement between the Sadducees and the Pharisees concerning the resurrection of the dead. The Sadducees did not believe in either spirits or the resurrection. The Pharisees believed in both. After the 1st Century AD, The Pharisees became highly influential and their views of death and the afterlife were institutionalized.

And how does the Holy One, blessed be He, resuscitate the dead in the world to come? We are taught that the Holy One, blessed be He, takes in His hand a Great Shofar... and blows it, and its sound goes from one end of the world to the other. At the first blow the whole world shakes. At the second blow the dust breaks up. At the third blow their bones gather. At the fourth blow their members become warm. At the fifth blow their skins are stretched over them. At the sixth blow they become alive and stand up on their feet in their clothes. (Patai, 1988) The Apostle Paul concurs in 1 Corinthians 15:52. In that passage he explicitly states: **The shofar will sound, the dead will be raised.** *Therefore, the sound of the shofar on Rosh Hashanah is a remembrance of the future resurrection of the dead.* Sar Shalom…a Messianic Jewish Synagogue in the Twin Cities located at 2734 Rhode Island Ave S in St. Louis Park

The Classic Pre-Wrath Rapture

A great deal of gratitude and recognition should be attributed to Matthew Rosenthal and Van Kampen for investigating and proposing the Pre-Wrath Rapture theology that has now been widely accepted and taught. The ideology of a classic Pre-Wrath Rapture is fundamentally correct, but there are conclusions associated with this teaching that are hard to accept and believe. The basic premise of the Rosenthal/ Van-Kampen Pre-wrath Rapture is based upon six key beliefs.

- The great tribulation is a 7-year period of time which is identical to the 70th Week of Daniel's 70-Week Prophecy
- The final 7-year period of time is characterized by the sequential execution of 7 Seals as Jesus Christ removes them one by one, the 7 Trumpet judgments and the 7 Bowl judgments.
- The period of time between the 6th seal and the 7th bowl constitutes what Kampen and Rosenthal call the Wrath of God. Note that the Book of Revelation calls the 7 Bowl Judgments the *Wrath of God* (Revelation 15:1, Revelation 16:1).
- The Church Age will end after the 7th Bowl is poured out and will precede the 1000-year Millennial Kingdom
- The rapture and resurrection of all true believers will occur between the 6th and 7th Seal. This is by definition a *Pre-Wrath Rapture.*

The fundamental premise is that all Christians who have joined the Body of Christ are promised that they will never experience the *Wrath of God*. As Rosenthal and Van-Kampen studied the scriptures, they read Revelation 6: 12-17.

[12] *And I beheld when he had opened the sixth seal, and, lo, there was a great earthquake; and the sun became black as sackcloth of hair, and the moon became as blood;*
[13] *And the stars of heaven fell unto the earth, even as a fig tree casts her untimely figs, when she is shaken of a mighty wind.*
[14] *And the heaven departed as a scroll when it is rolled together; and every mountain and island were moved out of their places.*
[15] *And the kings of the earth, and the great men, and the rich men, and the chief captains, and the mighty men, and every bondman, and every free man, hid themselves in the dens and in the rocks of the mountains;*
[16] *And said to the mountains and rocks, Fall on us, and hide us from the face of him that sits on the throne, and from the wrath of the Lamb:*
[17] **For the great day of his wrath is come; and who shall be able to stand?**
Revelation 6: 1-17

In their mind, Revelation 6:17 was clear… When the 6th Seal was opened the Wrath of God had come

> **Authors Comment:** Note that Revelation 6:16 does not say this at all, it says that the *Wrath of the Lamb* had come, and it was a *great day*.

Rosenthal and van Kampen believed that two key concepts emerged from Revelation 6:17: (1) The Wrath of God had come, which would constitute both the 7 Trumpet judgments and the 7 Bowl judgments. (2) Since the Trumpets and bowls obviously spanned more than one day, they were forced to declare that the *great day* was at least 3.5 years long. *According to the classic pre-wrath rapture theory, the church will be present to experience the first six seals, and the rapture will occur as the 6th Seal is broken.* Those Raptured out will escape the Wrath of God.

There are several assumptions that need to be examined in this rapture theology. The *First* is that the text does not say that the Wrath of God has come, but that the Wrath of the Lamb has come. The Wrath of God is without question the 7 Bowl Judgments (Revelation 15:1, Revelation 16:1). The 1st six trumpet judgments parallel and launch acts of persecution by Satan. The Trumpet judgments are called the Wrath of Satan based upon Revelation 12:12 and the 7 bowl judgments are clearly identified as the Wrath of God. (2) The designation of over 3.5 years as the *day* of His (Gods) Wrath cannot withstand scriptural investigation. We have shown elsewhere from multiple Old Testament and New Testament scriptures that: (a) *His Wrath* (Revelation 6:17) is exactly *one day* and that day is the great Battle of Armageddon. what the text implies: a single day that is the Battle of Armageddon. *Second*, the Battle of Armageddon is that glorious and long-awaited day when Jesus Christ will defeat Satan and cast him into the Bottomless Pit. This one day and this final battle is not fought by God but by Jesus Christ. This is why it is called the *Wrath of the Lamb* in Revelation 6:16 and not the Wrath of God which corresponds to the Bowl Judgments. *Third*, Rosenthal and Van Kampen must believe that the sun will go dark and stars will fall from heaven throughout the rest of the tribulation period (Revelation 6:12-13 precedes Revelation

6:17). This cannot be true. *Fourth*, the most damaging objection to a Pre-Wrath rapture as the 6th Seal is opened concerns Revelation 6:14

*And the heaven departed as a scroll when it is rolled together; and **every mountain and island were moved out of their places.***   Revelation 6:14

This is incredible! *Every* mountain and island will be moved from their place. This would destroy any city or homes in those places. Now the most important observation:

 And every island fled away, and the mountains were not found   Revelation 16:20

Revelation 16:20 is placed just after the 7th Bowl Judgment is poured out within hours of the Battle of Armageddon at the 2nd advent of Christ. Are we to believe that every island and every mountain and every city in these places will be destroyed twice within 3-4 years? This thought is illogical and inconceivable.

Can these problems and clear violation of scriptural truth be resolved? The answer is YES and that is the purpose of this book.

A Pre-Wrath Rapture *After* The 7 Trumpets but *Before* The 7 Bowls

One must recognize a critical biblical distinction between *Tribulation* and *Wrath*. Specifically, Tribulation and the *Wrath of Satan* (7 Trumpet Judgments) and the wrath which is the *Wrath of God* (7 Bowl Judgments). The Wrath of God is reserved for all unbelievers, but no true believer has ever been promised that they were exempt from the Tribulation and Wrath of Satan... now or during the Great Tribulation period.

*Therefore rejoice, ye heavens, and ye that dwell in them. Woe to the inhabiters of the earth and of the sea! For Satan is come down unto you, having **great wrath**, because he knoweth that he hath but a short time*   Revelation 12:12

*And I heard a great voice out of the temple saying to the seven angels: Go your ways, and pour out the vials of the **Wrath of God** upon the earth*   Revelation 16:1

This new Pre-Wrath Resurrection and Rapture resolves all of the difficulties associated with either a Pre-Tribulation or a Classic Pre-Wrath Rapture.

- The first 6 seals must be broken and removed before the scroll can be read to reveal what will happen as the 7 Trumpets are blown and the 7 bowls are poured out.
- The Tribulation (last half of Daniel's 70th week) will not begin when the 1st Seal is broken. It will not begin until the 7th Seal is removed by Christ. No one knows when Christ will begin to remove the Seals.
- Removal of the 7 Seals is a prerequisite to the Great tribulation, but they only describe things which will take place during the Great Tribulation.

- The Great tribulation will be initiated by a Great Heavenly conflict between good (Michael and his angels) and evil (Satan and his fallen angels). When Satan is cast down and confined to this earth, the Great Tribulation will begin
- The 7 Trumpet Judgements and the 7 Bowl Judgments are not both the Wrath of God. He Wrath of Satan are the 7 Trumpet Judgments and the Wrath of God are the 7 Bowl judgments.
- The Rapture of all living Saints and the Resurrection of all dead Saints will take place after the Wrath of Satan but Before the Wrath of God.
- The current Age of Grace (the Church age) will end after the Battle of Armageddon.

The Three-Day Prophecy

There are two prophecies in the Word of Truth that state:

*After **two days** will he revive us: **in the third day** he will raise us up, and we shall live in his sight* Hosea 6:2

[8] *But, beloved, be not ignorant of this one thing, that **one day is** with the Lord as a thousand years, and a thousand years as one day.*
[9] *The Lord is not slack concerning his promise, as some men count slackness; but is longsuffering to us-ward, not willing that any should perish, but that **all should come to repentance*** II Peter 3: 8-9

God made the Heavens and the Earth as we know them today in 6 days, and then rested on the 7th day. There is a popular "theory" that this was a shadow and type of when this world will come to an end. The world that God created would last for 4000 years until Christ appeared to redeem all men from sin and salvation. Then there would be another 2000 years that would pass until the 2nd advent of Christ. Finally, the last 1000 years will be a Day of Rest (The Millennial Kingdom). II Peter 3:8 might now make sense. The theory is that this world between the fall of Adam and Eve and the Millennial kingdom will last 6000 years, and that after this period of time Christ will return a 2nd time to rule and reign over a 1000-year Millennial Kingdom. *Could this be true?* Only time will tell.

Summary and Conclusions

This chapter has examined the fundamental conclusion of this study. The rapture of all living believers and the resurrection of all the righteous dead is not a Pre-Tribulation Rapture, but a Pre-Wrath Rapture. It is not the traditional Pre-Wrath Rapture popularized by Rosenthal, Van Kampen, and a host of other Pre-wrath believers… It is a Pre-Wrath Rapture which recognizes three fundamental truths. *First*, the breaking and opening of the first 6 seals only reveals conditions and events which are about to occur. Second, that no Christian will ever be exempted from tribulation but not one Christian will experience the Wrath of God (Revelation 15:1, Revelation 16:1). *Third*, the Resurrection and the rapture of all saints will take place *after* the

Wrath of Satan occurs (the 7 trumpet judgments but before the Wrath of God falls upon all the earth.

As Jesus Christ breaks and removes each of the 7 seals from the Scroll which was kept by God, John is shown a vision of what is about to take place over the last 3.5 years of the Church Age. This is the last half of Daniel's 70th Week and is the Great Period of Tribulation and Wrath which will end at the Battle of Armageddon. The removal of Seals 1-4 reveals general conditions that will exist during this period of time.

- Seal 1: A world leader with deception and power will arise
- Seal 2: Conflicts and Wars
- Seal 3: Famine
- Seal 4: Death and Hell
- Seal 5: The 5th Seal reveals to John that many Jews and Christians will be Martyre
- Seal 6: As the 6th Seal is removed, there are unprecedented and unique events revealed to John which will take place during the Tribulation (Revelation 6: 12-17).

  - The Sun turns dark
  - The moon has no light
  - Star in the heaven fall to earth
  - The heavens are disrupted and roll up like a scroll
  - Kings and rulers hide in fear
  - Every Island and Mountain are moved out of their place

- Seal 7: There is stunned silence in heaven. The Wrath of Satan and the Wrath of God are about to begin.

The events described to John as Jesus Christ breaks the 6th Seal are those that cause concern… Not concern for *if* they will take place, but **when**. All prophecy teachers of which I am aware…Pretribulation or classical Pre-Wrath… teach that: (1) The first 6 seals must be broken and removed before the scroll can be read to reveal what will happen as the 7 Trumpets are blown and the 7 bowls are poured out. This is correct (2) When the first Seals is broken, the Tribulation will begin… This is incorrect (3) The events described as the 6th Seal is removed will initiate the Great Tribulation and will consume some amount of time… This is incorrect (4) breaking the 7th Seal will initiate or start the 7 Trumpet judgments. This is correct (5) The 7 Trumpet Judgements and the 7 Bowl Judgments are both the Wrath of God. This is incorrect (6) The Rapture of all living Christians and the resurrection of the dead will precede opening the 7 seals (Pre-Tribulation Rapturists) **or** the Rapture and resurrection will take place between when the 6th and 7th Seals are broken (Classic Pre-Wrath Rapturists) …These are both incorrect. (7) Blowing the 7th Trumpet will initiate the 7 Bowl Judgments and pouring out the 7th Bowl will herald the 2nd coming of Jesus Christ and the Battle of Armageddon…This is correct (8) No Christian will experience the persecution and wrath which correspond to both the 7 Trumpet judgments and the 7 Bowl Judgments… This is incorrect. The Trumpet

The Four Horsemen of the Apocalypse

Art used by permission by Pat Marvenko Smith, copyright 1992.

judgments are Satan against mankind and the Bowl judgments are God against Satan. No Christian has ever been promised that they would be exempt from the tribulation of Satan.

> **Authors Comment**: The martyrs slain as revealed in Seal 5 cannot be confined to before the Great Tribulation begins but there is no doubt that many Christians will be martyred by Satan during this period of time. In contrast, most of the devastating and monumental events which are described as Seal 6 is removed will take place late in the Tribulation. For example. All of the mountains and Islands are predicted to move out of their place in Revelation 6:14 but this does not take place until after the Rapture has occurred and the 7th Bowl is poured out just before the Battle of Armageddon (Revelation 16:20).

A great deal of evidence has been presented to support that the Rapture will occur as the 7th trumpet (shofar) is blown. Is has also been discussed and shown that the expectations of traditional Jews and their core beliefs concerning the resurrection of righteous Jews support both the beliefs and conclusions of this book…... Actually, it could be no other way.

For by one Spirit are we all baptized into one body, whether we be Jews or Gentiles, whether we be bond or free; and have been all made to drink into one Spirit   I Corinthians 12:13

Rapture

Resurrection

Jesus said to her,
"I am the resurrection and the life.
The one who believes in me will live,
even though they die; and whoever lives by
believing in me will never die. Do you believe this?"
John 11:25-26

Bibliography

Coulter, Fred R., The Appointed Times of Jesus the Messiah, York Publishing Company, PO Box 1038, Hollister, California, 95024-1038

Dake, Finis J., Dake's Annotated Reference Bible, Dake Bible Sales, P.O. Box 1050, Lawrenceville, Ga., 30246

Finegan, Jack, Handbook of Biblical Chronology, Hendrickson Publishing Company, Peabody, Ma.

Good, Joseph, Rosh HaShanah and the Messianic Kingdom to Come, Hatikva Ministries, PO Box 3125, Port Arthur, Texas 77643-0703

Horn H. S. and L. H. Wood, The Chronology of Ezra, TEACH Services, Inc., www.teachservices.com

Larkin, Clarence, Dispensational Truth, P.O. Box 334, Glenside, Pa., 1920

Logos apostolic Church of God and Bible College, Interlinear Greek and Hebrew Translation, Logos apostolic.org, United Kingdom, Logos apostolic.org

Nee, Watchman, Come Lord Jesus, Christian Fellowship Publishers, Inc., 11515 Allecingie Parkway, Richmond, Virginia 23235

Phillips, Don T., The Book of Revelation: *Mysteries Revealed*, 2nd Edition, Virtual Bookworm. com, PO Box 9949, College Station, Texas 7784.

Phillips, Don T., The Book of Ruth: *Historical and Prophetic Truths*, Virtual Bookworm. com, PO Box 9949, College Station, Texas 7784.

Phillips, Don T., Life After Death: *Mysteries Revealed*, Virtual Bookworm. com, PO Box 9949, College Station, Texas 7784.

Phillips, Don T., The Eternal Plan of God: *Dispensations, Covenant Promises, Salvation*, Virtual Bookworm. com, PO Box 9949, College Station, Texas 7784.

Phillips, Don T., The Birth and Death of Christ, Virtual Bookworm. com, PO Box 9949, College Station, Texas 7784.

Phillips, Don T., The Book of Exodus: *Historical and Prophetic Truths*

Virtual Bookworm. com, PO Box 9949, College Station, Texas 7784.

Phillips, Don T., A Biblical Chronology from Adam to Christ,
Virtual Bookworm. com, PO Box 9949, College Station, Texas 7784.

Phillips, Don T., Life After the Great Tribulation: *The Millennial Kingdom*
Virtual Bookworm. com, PO Box 9949, College Station, Texas 7784.

Phillips, Don T., The Last 50 Days of Jesus Christ
Virtual Bookworm. com, PO Box 9949, College Station, Texas 7784.

Phillips, Don T., The Daniel 70 Week Prophecy
Virtual Bookworm. com, PO Box 9949, College Station, Texas 7784.

Phillips, Don T., The Birth of Christ: A Forensic Analysis
Virtual Bookworm. com, PO Box 9949, College Station, Texas 7784.

Rosenthal, Matthew, The Pre-Wrath Rapture of the Church, Thomas Nelson Publishers,
Nashville, Tennessee

Ryrie, Charles C., The Ryrie Study Bible, King James Version, Moody Press, Chicago

Salerno, Donald A., Revelation Unsealed, Virtual Bookworm.Com, P.O. Box 9949, College
Station, Texas, 77842

Thiele, Edwin R., The Mysterious Numbers of the Hebrew Kings: Revised Edition, Kregel, Grand
Rapids, Michigan

Thomas, Robert L., Revelation 1-7, An Exegetical Commentary, Moody Press, Chicago, Illinois

Thomas, Robert L., Revelation 8-22, An Exegetical Commentary, Moody Press, Chicago, Illinois

Van Kampen, Robert, The Sign, Crossway Books, 1300 Crescent Street, Wheaton, Illinois 60187

Walvoord, John F., The Millennial Kingdom, Academic Books, Zondervan Publishing Company,
1415 Lake Drive S.E., Grand Rapids, Michigan 49506

Footnote: This manuscript has drawn upon several excellent websites found by GOOGLE search. It is my intention to recognize every biblical scholar and source of information from those *giants that walked before me*. This information was sometimes not made available. In other cases, information was marked open source or not marked at all. If any author(s) sees any material that they want referenced, please contact me and will acknowledge their previous research and scholarly work. In any case, I am extremely grateful for previous investigations o or conclusions that may (or may not) support this work. God will know them and He will know the source.

Don T. Phillips
Senior Author
phillipsdon60@gmail.com

Spring, 2022

www.ingramcontent.com/pod-product-compliance
Lightning Source LLC
Chambersburg PA
CBHW060946100426

42813CB00016B/2877